D1381508

THE A - Z OF
BRITISH MOTORCYCLES
FROM THE
1930S, 1940S, 1950S

———————◆———————

The A - Z of
British Motorcycles
From The
1930s, 1940s, 1950s

———————————◆———————————

Roy Bacon

First published as two separate volumes:-
British Motorcycles of the 30's © Roy Bacon 1986
British Motorcycles of the 40's and 50's © Roy Bacon 1989

This edition published 1996 by The Promotional Reprint
Company Limited exclusively for Bookmart Limited,
Desford Road, Enderby, Leicester LE9 5AD and
Chris Beckett Limited in New Zealand.

ISBN 1 85648 300 2

Printed in China

CONTENTS

CONTENTS

Contents

BETWEEN WARS

From 1919 to 1939 motorcycling underwent great changes. The period began with machines of near veteran style, went through the flat-tank era of the 1920s, turned to saddle tanks and chromium plate for the depressed 1930s and ended with a call-up for machines and men. In that time design changed the appearance and many features, with the greater effects occurring in the 1920s, a decade often termed the Golden Age of Motorcycling.

The start of that decade saw many machines still with belt final drive, although most had a gearbox. Handchange was to start to give way to the foot pedal from late in the decade, but was still to be seen into the fifties. Engines were singles or V-twins in the main with few exceptions and four-strokes outnumbered two-strokes. Valves moved from the side to overhead on many machines in the 1920s, which also saw the advent of the overhead camshaft (ohc) in some numbers.

Motorcycle electrics progressed to replace acetylene gas lights, but ignition remained the province of the magneto for most models. Lighting was fitted as standard to many, but was often listed as an extra to hold the quoted price to a low level. Engine lubrication, tyres, brakes and steering all improved as engineers applied the lessons of metallurgy to the motorcycle, so that by the end of the 1920s and the close of the vintage period (1 January 1915 to 31 December 1930) machines were good and reliable.

This was as well, for in October 1929 came the Wall Street crash and this ushered in the Depression of the thirties. Money was short and trade poor so firms kept a staple diet of low-priced economy models with few frills but plenty of options to entice every possible customer to buy. The exotic did not vanish, but few were to survive more than a season or two and there were far fewer odd but interesting vari-

A pair of Triumph Speed Twins from 1939 or 1940 on official duties and complete with wartime headlamp masks

Very nice period picture showing a lady rider on a 1932 Royal Enfield Cycar being assisted by the RAC. Little protective gear at that time but handy for the shopping

ations on the scene.

Typically, machines became four-stroke overhead-valve (ohv) singles with a separate gearbox in a rigid frame with girder forks and saddle. Lubrication was dry sump and the electrics a mag-dyno, with the third brush giving way to the regulator box around 1937. A saddle tank was often the only painted part not in black, but the brightwork had its chrome veneer, which was much less trouble to keep nice than the nickel that preceded it.

There were trends and fancies then as now with twin-port engines popular for many years despite the extra cost of the second pipe and silencer. A fancy that

failed was enclosure - which the makers liked as it was cheaper than polishing the parts it hid - but it did not catch on, although it continued to appear sporadically over the years.

So the British motorcycle progressed through the 1930s, reacting to the influences of trade and politics, laws and taxes, and what technical developments the public could afford. Those still in business then went to war and after that many carried on for some years, with the change to telescopic forks the only significant improvement - which went to show how tough and endearing the designs were in the first place.

Most models were built to a very conventional

English design, but there were some less so, such as the Ariel Square Four, the OEC, the AJS and Matchless fours and, of course, the Scott. Sadly many of the more interesting and progressive designs were not to survive in those hard commercial years, for, as ever, press and public acclaimed innovations but bought the tried and tested model. Always there was the feeling that it was best for someone else to spring their cash the first year while you waited for any problems to surface and be dealt with. 'Maybe next year if work holds out' was so often the word, but for some manufacturers next year was not to come.

So the bulk of the industry built singles up to 500cc and V-twins to around twice that size. The latter were mainly side-valve (sv) plodders made to haul a big sidecar along at 40mph, but among them were some real gems that could perform well with a chair and were really fast used solo – a true 100mph on the road at a time when much of the Great North Road was two lanes, narrow and bumpy. The conventional English machine had an engine with a vertically-split crankcase

in which a built-up crankshaft with roller big-end ran on ball or roller mains. The timing chest went on the right, the magneto aft of the cylinder and a dynamo was strapped to its back. Lubrication was dry sump with the oil tank under the saddle, and side valves were as common as overhead. Head and barrel were in iron with the valve gear often exposed. Carburation was usually looked after by an Amal and the exhaust pipe went on the right for most by the middle of the decade.

The transmission went on the left, with chain drive back to a separate gearbox with outboard clutch, except on Velocette, of course. The box had the output sprocket concentric with the input and over the decade changed from three speeds and handchange to four speeds and footchange. Final drive was by chain on the left and this dictated that the oil tank went on the right with the battery on the left of it. A toolbox went in the rear quarter of the frame and a saddle and pillion seat carried the riders.

The frame was built up from tubes brazed into forged lugs and was rigid at the rear. At the front went girder forks with friction damping. Braking was by drum brakes front and rear with single leading shoes controlled by hand and foot. In time the brake pedal finished up on the left, once footchange was adopted, but for much of the decade it could be found on either side where hand gearbox control remained.

V-twins were much the same but bigger, longer and heavier, while the bottom end of the market was looked after in the main by machines powered by Villiers two-strokes. These were also constructed on the same lines but to a lighter scale.

The lightweights went through some legislation problems at the start of the decade, with the first change coming during 1929. In the Budget the weight limit for the lightweight taxation class was raised from 200 to 224lb and a number of firms quickly took advantage of this, especially on their 250s and light 350s. The difference was important at the time, for below the limit the tax dropped from £3 to £1 10s. 0d., which was a significant sum in those days.

Then, in the middle of 1929, there was an election and a change of government and the weight change was cancelled, too late for some firms to backtrack. There were protests, but such is government inertia that it was not until April 1930 that the limit was raised to ease the problems of a hard-pressed industry a little. It must also have improved safety, for firms were often listing models with acetylene lighting to drag the weight down below the 200lb mark and capture customers. The same machines would also be sold with electric lights, and the change meant that the owner was not penalised for selecting the better system.

In August that year a Road Traffic Act was passed which raised the minimum age for a licence from 14 to 16 and compulsory insurance became mandatory, but the old general speed limit went. This meant that it was as fast as you liked, but at the same time the offence of careless driving was introduced, so the speed had to be safe in the eyes of the police. Other changes called for proper pillion seats, so a tied-on cushion was no longer acceptable, and a statement as to physical fitness when applying for a driver licence was no longer required.

Near the end of 1931 the industry coaxed a further concession out of the government with a reduction of tax to 15s. for machines below 150cc. This brought a rash of Villiers-powered models in 1932 along with one or two rather nice ohv singles. In recognition of the Chancellor of the Exchequer concerned, these machines were often called Snowden models.

This move introduced the concept of taxation by capacity, still in use half a century later, and it was fully adopted by the 1932 Budget. With this, from 1 January 1933, up to 150cc paid 15s., 150 to 250cc paid 30s. and over 250cc paid £3. Machines under 224lb registered by 31 December 1932 qualified and remained at 30s., hence the run-on by such models that season.

The happy days of no speed limit did not last for long, and in March 1935 the 30mph town limit appeared along with driving tests and moves to improve safety on the roads. The limit was a real problem in some regions as it was applied to lighted roads and in the industrial North large areas ran into each other with little break. In time came by-passes, but these were few in the 1930s and congestion in towns due to through-traffic caused many hold-ups as the volume of vehicles built up.

And build up it did as the economy gradually improved. More people bought cars and motorcycles as the years rolled by and the machines themselves became brighter and were better equipped. Autocycles appeared to draw customers on to the bottom rung of powered transport and the industry provided plenty of rungs from then on up the ladder.

The British motorcycle dominated road racing for most of the decade before having to give best to the supercharged multis from Europe. Off-road, in the ISDT, the country was equally successful, and in the lonely world of record-breaking British men and machines produced many fine performances on the slenderest of resources. Perhaps the finest were the capture of the very tough one-hour record and the outright world speed title.

So the decade came to a noisy end and the motorcycles put on their khaki paint and went to war. The 1930s came to a close having placed their mark on the motorcycle as surely as the 1920s had. In those years it matured and settled down. Postwar it was to have twins!

A 1930 Radco with 247cc Villers engine in a typical street scene of the time when a rider wore a hat rather than a helmet

WARTIME

War broke out on 1st September 1939 and for six long, hard years the motorcycle was called upon to do its duty along with everything else. In Britain, this meant a call up of a rag-bag of civilian machines and any new stock at the factories in the early days, but then a concentration on basic single-cylinder models from a handful of firms. Most were four-strokes but there were a few lightweight two-strokes. All played their part with little or no change, other than to service finish, and this proved a sound policy.

The Wartime Matchless G3L, on which the postwar range was based and which was sold off with many others to provide early postwar transport

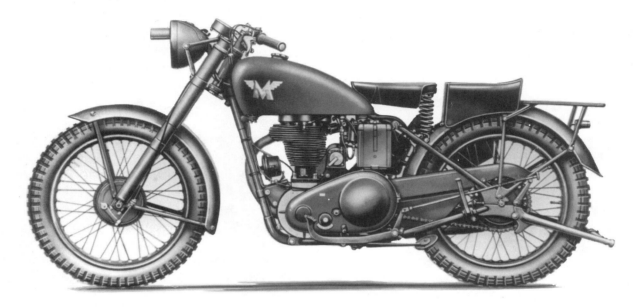

AUSTERITY TO BOOM

Peace came to Europe in May 1945, and by June there was a modest ration of two or three gallons of petrol per month for motorcyclists. Modest indeed, but after years without any private motoring, it was better than nothing, and in those days a restrained throttle hand could easily wring over 100 miles from a gallon of fuel.

Before then, in March, there had been news of the new Triumph range, hints as to the form of the big Vincent-HRD, and a patent for BSA relating to an ohv twin and its valve gear. Later came articles in the magazines on how to get the most from your fuel ration, and on how to persuade reluctant machinery back into life after the long period off the road.

The results of some backroom work appeared with a preview of the Wooler and its flat-four beam engine, but of rather more practical interest was the announcement, in June, that AJS were about to return

to civilian production. A week later the equivalent Matchless models were unveiled and, as the months rolled by, more and more firms introduced their wares.

Some machines were really new, such as the Vincent and Douglas twins, while others simply picked up the reins again after the six long years of war. The latter were either exactly the same as those from the 1939, or the aborted 1940, range, or were the same with the exception of a fresh coat of paint and the addition of the new telescopic front-fork design. Rear suspension remained virtually unknown. For most of the industry, it was a case of restarting with black paint in the spray-guns instead of khaki.

Machine prices were high thanks, in part, to the imposition of purchase tax at 33⅓ per cent. This was to prove the bane of the car and motorcycle industry, until it was replaced by VAT, as its rate was varied by the government to either stimulate or retard the economy as it thought fit. Early postwar writers thought that this tax was temporary, for it had been introduced in April

1940 as a wartime measure. On some goods it had risen to as much as 100 per cent in the darker days of war, and although, in time, it was reduced, it was never to drop to zero.

The early post-war years were a period of continued hardship in Britain; the people had been drained by their six-year struggle for existence, but faced a battle for economic survival. Rationing of many items continued for some years, and everything was in short supply. All manufacturers, regardless of product, were exhorted to produce more and more, the phrase 'export or die' being frequently quoted by politicians. The task was not made easy by the acute shortages of many materials and a plethora of wartime controls, which the bureaucrats were reluctant to relinquish.

For all these reasons, it was a time to concentrate on producing the goods, and most firms did this with as few changes as possible. In general, the new designs

Above: Typical prosaic model and background of a road test of those times. The 1956 Panther 10/4 was powered by a 9E Villiers engine.

came from the smaller firms, many of which had been shifted from motorcycles to other work during the war. A considerable number of them never produced complete machines again, for they found that they had viable businesses which could switch to peacetime parts production with little trouble and minimal investment.

The major firms, which had been kept in production, were better placed to continue much as before but, under these conditions, kept innovation to a minimum. Most of their production went for export, and this was to continue for some years. Even in the early 1950s, certain new models were restricted to export markets when first introduced, and later only released at home in a trickle. In 1945 supply was even more restricted, and before being able to buy a new machine, the purchaser had to obtain a 'licence to acquire', which was only issued where an essential need could be shown.

This situation altered only gradually during the 1940s. World-wide there were many changes as the old British Empire broke up, new nations were formed, and East-West attitudes hardened. Times were austere for

most, and rationing and controls remained in Britain as a new socialist government sought to give fair shares to all, nationalise major industries, and to introduce substantial social reforms.

Motorcycling played its traditional role in that period as a means of getting to work, plus giving an occasional outing at the weekend. Despite the bombing, many workers, both office and manual, still lived close to where they worked, often only a few streets away. New towns, high-rise blocks, and longer journeys to work were still a decade away, so for many the daily round included a bus, tram, train or bicycle ride. Few aspired to cars, and anyway these were restricted in their supply which, for a period, was hedged with covenants on resale.

The motorcycle became a means of easing longer journeys for many. Some had little option if their route did not coincide with public services, while others found it less costly and gradually came to prefer the freedom of their own road. Despite the rationing, which continued until 1950, and the shortages, it always seemed better to ride past the bus queue than stand in it, even in the rain.

Many machines were pre-war types, often repaired with guile and whatever came to hand, for there were few spares available. Exceptions soon became the ex-WD models, for many of these were auctioned off to the trade for resale. Most were given a quick, all-over respray in black, although a few of the avant-garde used maroon, but more likely because it was to hand than for aesthetic reasons.

It was a time for making do, and the reliance of the services on a few models, nearly all fitted with an

Amal carburettor and Lucas electrics, was a great help. The same parts could be used on many pre-war models, and were just as effective for those riders lucky enough to obtain a new machine.

The magazines were full of hints and tips on how to repair, renovate, modify and make good, while, in the main, the machines would run with minimal service. Tyres were a major problem, as they were hard to find and none too good when obtained. Most riders learnt to ride on bald ones and to deal with the inevitable punctures.

In time, the situation improved, but the prewar machine remained a common sight well into the 1950s, as did the ex-WD one. Before then, there were additions to the manufacturers' ranges, most major firms fielding a vertical twin before the end of the 1940s. These differed in many details, but all followed the same outline and all used many parts from the singles of the same marque.

So, whether with one or two cylinders, many models continued in much the same form as they had in the 1930s. The engine remained separate from the gearbox and had a vertically-split crankcase. The barrel was invariably iron, but a few of the more adventurous did turn to light-alloy cylinder heads. Valve gear was generally simple, but over the years the side-valve models were dropped, until only the services, and the AA and RAC road patrols were using this type.

The electrics featured a magneto and dynamo, with a change to the alternator during the 1950s, but this was by no means universal. Lubrication was normally dry sump, with the oil tank under the saddle and twin pumps in the engine. The carburettor of larger

Postwar racing at Scarborough in late 1946, with Allan Jeffries on his Triumph ahead of Denis Parkinson and Roy Evans on Nortons.

machines was invariably an Amal, and most singles carried their exhaust system on the right.

The chassis was much the same as it was in 1939, with the addition of telescopic forks. Frames were still brazed, using forged lugs and pinned tubes, while rear suspension was slow to catch on. Where offered, it was often in plunger form, with little or no damping, other than that provided by the inherent friction of the system.

Larger machines had a four-speed gearbox, and virtually all used a positive-stop change mechanism. The gear pedal gave an up-for-down movement, in most cases, and it was on the right of the machine, together with the kickstarter. The primary and secondary drives were both on the left, as was the rear brake pedal; the first had a pressed-steel or cast-alloy case while rear chain enclosure was rare.

Wheels had steel rims with wire spokes, and the 19in. size was by far the most common, except for competition use, where a 21in. front rim was fitted. A few models did use 20in. wheels, but none 18in. Tyres tended to be studded front and rear, except for sports models, which would have a ribbed front. Sections were invariably 3.25in. front and the same, or 3.50in., rear on the larger models, and 2.75 or 3.00in. on the smaller ones. Brakes were offset, single-leading-shoe drum types in most cases.

Supporting the traditional 350 and 500cc singles, together with the newer 500cc twins, were a line of similar, lighter 250cc singles and many small two-strokes. The former were built on the same lines as the

larger models, and some used common parts, but usually they were lighter and cheaper. The two-stroke models were nearly all powered by Villiers engine and gearbox units, as they had been in prewar times. The cycle parts were often minimal, but these models fulfilled their role of basic transport and, while the detail parts often gave trouble and caused annoyance, the machines normally completed their journeys.

By the beginning of the 1950s matters began to improve, with better petrol, fewer restrictions and more machines on the market. Many of the scars of war began to disappear as new buildings rose on bomb sites in the cities, and air-raid shelters in parks and suburbs were filled in or demolished.

Styles began to brighten, and the motorcycle followed suit with such models as the Golden Flash and Thunderbird, which broke away from the traditional black finish. Other colours were less successful, such as the blue used by Tandon but, in time, Francis-Barnetts became a pleasant green, James maroon and, of course, the Speed Twin was always in its Amaranth red.

Part of the reason for this was to suit the export market, and it was the American sector that sparked off the gradual increase in vertical-twin capacity. With vast stretches of straight roads, plus a performance and sports market on both coasts, the Americans needed more power, and the easy way to get it was with more 'cubes'. The big Vincent shone in this respect, as did the bigger twins from the major firms.

This process continued through the decade, together with a gradual refining process which, too

Preparing Bob Ray's Ariel twin with puncture sealant for the 1951 ISDT, in which it was a member of the winning Trophy team.

George Buck and Bob Ray about to set off on an ACU observed test through seven countries in seven days, late in 1953, to launch the new Huntmaster.

often, was too slow. Detail changes only became the norm for each year's models, showing the complacency that lay behind the facade of prosperity.

There were new designs, but too few came from the home industry, while those that did were usually under-funded and never really got off the ground. Often, as with the Wooler, the designer tried to do too much at once, combining a new engine, transmission and cycle parts, so was unable to develop any one area completely.

The conservative nature of the buyer was no help, but too many had seen friends burn their fingers on the radical for them to risk their own money. Too often, final development was left to the riders of the initial production machines, and the word soon went round to let someone else buy the new design. Thus, too many would put off purchase for a year or two until

the model was sorted out, and the resultant low level of sales would hold the price too high.

While there may have been little that was innovative and which reached volume production, there were exceptions, such as the LE Velocette and Ariel Leader. Neither was fully sorted when launched, but both were closer than most and near enough to be successful. Thus, they ran on from slightly shaky starts to a reasonable life span.

The one really good feature the traditional singles and twins had going for them was that the steady improvements made them reliable. At the same time, the parts that wore out tended to remain the same, so spares were easy to stock and obtain, while problem areas became well known. At club and dealer level, the solutions to problems were passed around, and any modified detail parts could usually be bought or

Far away in Japan, this Meguuro twin followed the copy route, with its BSA lines, and remained in the Kawasaki list into the late 1970s

machined by a friend in industry.

Meanwhile, the world moved on, and other events affected motorcycling. The Korean war, early in the 1950s, caused a world-wide shortage of nickel, so chrome plating was restricted by government decree. Petrol-tank styles changed to suit, and some never went back to the older arrangement of chrome, painted panels and lining, for the new designs were often cheaper.

Later came the Suez crisis and, once more, there was petrol rationing, although it did not last for long and time spent building up stocks in advance proved to be wasted. Prior to the appearance of the coupons, there were queues at the pumps, which were repeated in the 1973 oil crisis, but the affair came and went with little long-term effect, except that petrol never cost under five shillings a gallon again.

At various times during the 1950s, there were booms in clip-on attachments, scooters, mopeds, and bubblecars, but few British firms had any significant investment in these. In the main, the industry kept to its solid, worthy models, which it produced in ever-increasing numbers up to 1959, after which the numbers began to fall away. Total sales were to rise again in the 1970s, but these were nearly all imports, and sales figures fell again in the following decade.

That final year of the 1950s was a great one for

motorcycling, as the sun shone, the economy was buoyant and even motorcycle dealers smiled. Motorcycles and scooters were in demand to beat the traffic jams and parking problems, while the appearance of the Mini and the Japanese had not yet made any impact. The former was to kill off the bubblecar and sidecar market, virtually at a stroke, while the latter were looking for expansion outside their home market to accommodate their enormous production rate.

Soon learners would be restricted to 250cc machines, and later other measures would further limit the appeal of motorcycling, but that fine summer of 1959 was a good way to end the decade. John Surtees won every 350 and 500 classic, albeit on the Italian MV Agusta, the M1 opened, and the industry thought that good times had come to stay.

It was downhill from then on, but the legacy remained and was resurrected 30 years later with the classic revival.

Top right
Typical 1959 scene at the dealers on a Saturday morning with decisions and deals to be made

Bottom right
The ACU National Rally finished at Weymouth in 1958, where this mass of machines is parked

ABERDALE

The Aberdale firm was located in Edmonton, London, but the machines were built at the Bown factory in Wales. They offered just one model, an autocycle which was typical of the type with a 98cc Villiers JDL engine, simple tubular frame and blade girder forks.

It was a smart example of the type, capable of 30mph and 150mpg and was built from 1947 to 1949. After then it was sold as the Bown.

ABJ

Company chairman, A.B. Jackson had this firm located in Pope Street, Birmingham, and was no stranger to two wheels, having built the Raynal prewar and also bicycles. Their postwar range was based on the Villiers engine and comprised two 98cc models.

The first was the Autocycle, powered by a 2F engine, and the second, the Motorcycle, with the 1F, both with more of a motorcycle than autocycle look, a simple frame and telescopic forks. The electrics of both models were powered by the flywheel magneto, but the Motorcycle had a battery and an electric horn. Both machines were finished in black with gold lining and

the two models continued to be offered up to 1952.

In July of that year they were joined by the Auto Minor cyclemotor whose 49.9cc two-stroke engine went above the front wheel which it drove by roller. The bicycle that ABJ supplied with this engine had hub brakes, heavy-gauge spokes and oversize tyres, which made it more suitable for its intended use. The range went forward for 1953 but only the Auto Minor was sold and only for part of the year, after which the firm reverted to bicycles.

Top
ABJ Autocycle of 1950 with 2F engine and pedals, but very similar to the two-speed Motorcycle from the same firm

The ABJ Minor cyclemotor introduced in 1952 with friction drive to the bicycle front tyre

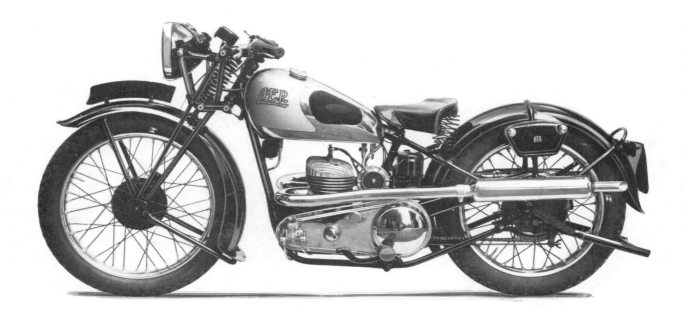

The 1938 AER with twin cylinder 340cc engine and dynamo mounted in front where it drove the oil pump

AER

A.E. Reynolds was first a Scott dealer and then built some special, de luxe Scotts under his own name. Later, he progressed to the AER, using his initials, and the prototype was first seen in 1937. Like the Scott it had a twin-cylinder, two-stroke engine, but was of 340cc and air-cooled. It was an all-alloy unit with the centre section of the crankcase split horizontally on the centre line, a feature not usually seen until the postwar days, but was otherwise conventional and drove a four-speed Burman gearbox.

The production model came in 1938, and had a flywheel magneto and a dynamo fitted to the front of the crankcase. On the chassis side there were duplex downtubes in place of the simple loop of the prototype and Webb forks. The finish was silver, blue and chrome plate for the tank and polished aluminium for the primary chaincase. For 1939 the 350 twin continued and was joined by a second model with a 249cc Villiers engine which went into the same cycle parts.

The war brought production to a halt, and long after it the last half-dozen were still sitting on the top floor of the shop, dusty but mainly complete.

AJS & MATCHLESS

These two firms appear under this single heading as they became so closely linked over the years. Matchless bought AJS in 1931 and in 1935 introduced a model style which quickly became common to both marques. Postwar, this continued to become pure badge engineering, so that era is treated under the above heading while the prewar years have a section for each marque.

AJS

The old-established firm of A. J. Stevens made the mistake of diversifying in 1930. As producers of a fine and successful range of motorcycles during the 1920s they chose the wrong time to take their existing skills of building sidecar and car bodies to establish themselves not only as car makers but also to offer lorries and single-decker buses. A further offshoot was to use the wood-working equipment of the body shops to make radio and radiogram cabinets, then massive pieces of furniture, and AJS found themselves in that business also.

Sadly the Depression finished this and in 1931 the bank foreclosed, the Stevens family settled their debts to the full 20s. in the pound and the AJS name

*The 1931 transverse twin AJS model S3 with 498cc engine,
outboard camshafts and the distributor driven from the left one*

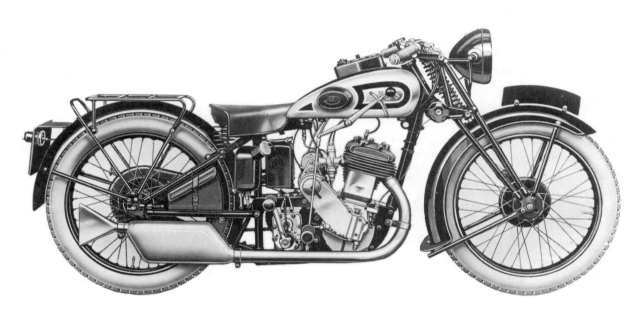

*AJS model S4 from 1931 with inclined 400cc side-valve engine
and nice tank-top instrument panel*

was bought by Matchless. The tools were moved from
Wolverhampton to Woolwich and little by little the
two marques became closer and closer in parts and
design. Late in 1937 the group became AMC, although
both marque names were to continue for many years.
The Stevens brothers retained some equipment and
continued to build machines under their own name.

This commercial hiatus had less effect on the AJS
machines than expected, for the models ran on without
much alteration in the range or its contents. At the

start of the decade the firm had nine models in the list,
some with the fashionable inclined engine, others with
it upright, but all four-strokes. Smallest was a 249cc
ohv, next came both sv and ohv machines of 348 and
499cc and largest of these types was the 998cc sv V-
twin. All these were conventional in layout with three
speeds, rigid frame and girder forks but there were two
other models of greater interest to the enthusiast.

These had overhead camshaft engines, of 346 and
495cc, the camshaft driven by a chain housed on the

*The 1932 Big Port AJS 498cc model TB8
with inclined engine and typical of the marque
in the early thirties*

right with the housing extended forward to the magneto and were much as the factory machines of the previous year. The rest of the machine was along standard lines with the oil tank under the saddle, but it was built for racing rather than the road, so came without lights and with long exhaust pipes with a minute muffler on the end.

The range continued for 1931 with few changes other than the smallest side-valve which grew to 400cc although the 348cc engine remained available. Few camshaft machines were built and they were to drop out of sight for a year or two. New models were simply variations of the established theme, but two did have the Big Port name first used in the 1920s.

The one completely new model came in April 1931 and had a transversely mounted 498cc sv, V-twin engine driving a three-speed gearbox but with chain final drive. Unusually, the engine had the valves located on the outer sides of the barrels so there had to be two camshafts. The gearbox sat aft of the engine and was driven by a shaft which had universal joints to deal with any misalignment, then came the clutch, and then a bevel gear so that the box itself could be a stock three-speed type. The remainder of the machine was conventional with full electric equipment and a tank-top instrument panel that looked an afterthought.

It was a pleasant machine, although the clutch action prevented good gear changes, but otherwise it

*The 998cc V-twin AJS on the firm's stand at the show of
1931 models. Note footboards and Klaxon horn*

Top
*1934 346cc ohc AJS model 34/7 Trophy built
for road use rather than racing, hence the raised
exhaust*

Below
*By 1935, and this model 14 AJS of 497cc, the
side-valve engine was upright and the magneto in
its front mounting position*

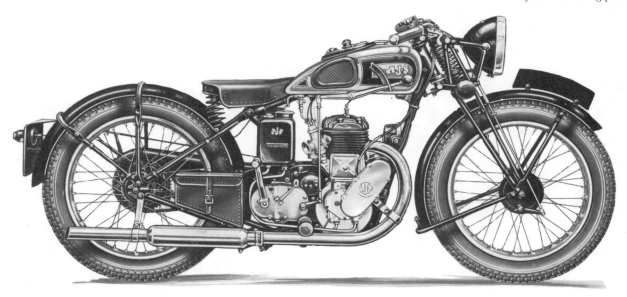

was smooth and quiet, and maybe it was these features that stopped it selling too well. The price cannot have included any profit for AJS and the sale of the firm prevented many being made.

For 1932 the new owners of the name were sensible enough to realise that moving the production centre was enough trauma for one year so they kept the machines unchanged but dropped the 400cc single and V-twin side-valve models along with the camshaft models, although the V-twin returned in July, but with a 982cc Matchless engine.

The camshaft models returned in 1933 in a revised form with the magneto moved to behind the cylinder and in racing form with long, open exhaust

pipe and no lights, or in competition form as the Trophy model in recognition of some success in the ISDT. In either case there was dry sump lubrication, a four-speed gearbox and a new frame.

All except the side-valve singles had four speeds for 1934 and most had the option of hand or footchange but otherwise it was a period of consolidation. While that year was near static, 1935 brought many changes and the start of the use of the ohv Matchless single engine for both marques. This was installed vertically, had dry sump lubrication, dynamo behind the crankcase and the magneto usually driven from the exhaust camshaft, although coil ignition was used that first year. Capacities were 245, 348 and 497cc with single or two-

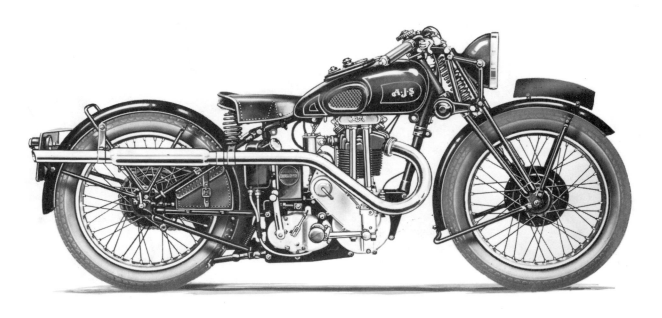

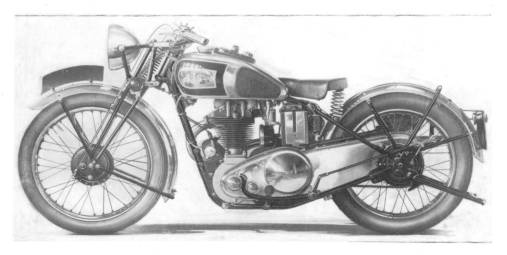

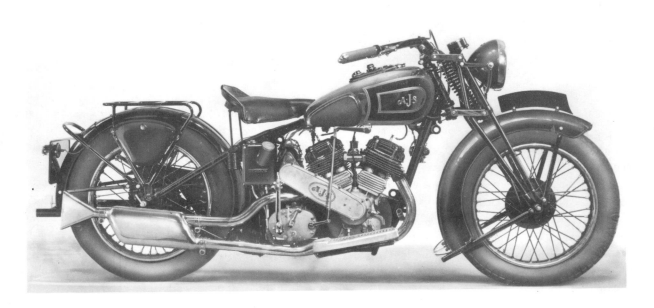

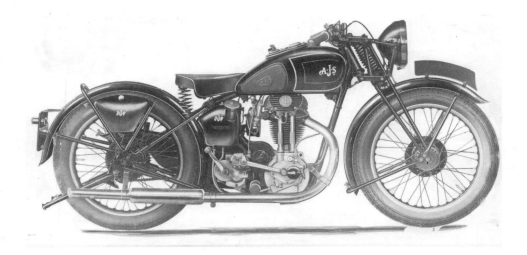

port heads. The side-valve models continued, as did the camshaft ones but usually in racing form, and with hairpin valve springs and bronze cylinder heads.

In March 1935 the two-port versions of the new design appeared in the three capacities and all had magneto ignition. This essentially completed the pre-war AJS model list for it then concentrated on this style although a 497cc side-valve did remain after the 348cc one was dropped. The three ohv models were all built with the choice of single or twin ports and later in a competition format for trials and a Silver Streak super sports form with tuned engines, plenty of chrome-plating and a special tank finish.

The 346cc camshaft model remained listed right up to 1939 but the 495cc one was dropped after 1936 by when the smaller was built purely for racing. At the other end of the scale the 982cc V-twin soldiered on with limited changes and was to remain listed to 1940, built in two forms, one traditional English and the other to suit the American market.

Aside from these stock models, the firm created a sensation for 1936 when they showed a 495cc V-four at the Olympia show. Their aim was to race the machine as well as to sell it as a road model and it had its two pairs of air-cooled cylinders set at 50 degrees. All had a single overhead camshaft and these were driven by a chain which ran up and down between each cylinder pair. Four exhaust pipes and two carburettors were fitted, while ignition was by twin magnetos, bevel driven, and mounted on the right side of the crankcase. The cycle parts were essentially as any other model and a dynamo could be fitted in front of the engine. Rumour had it that a supercharger could go in its place.

The works raced the four in 1936 and again in 1938, by when it was supercharged but this caused

overheating. For 1939 it was water-cooled, ran in the TT and later had its moment of glory at the Ulster, where it led for three laps before a fork link broke, thought to be due to the strains put on it by Walter Rusk keeping it on the road and between the hedges. Post-war it did run again and won a race before blowers were banned. Of the road models, only the prototype is believed to have been built and run.

By 1940 the model list was much shortened and the supply of civilian machines gradually dried up as the AMC plant concentrated on their war work.

Top left
Rear magneto on this model 18 AJS of 1936, this being the single-port engine. Footchange Burman and nice raised pipe

Middle
1938 Silver Streak AJS model 26SS of 348cc. Very extensively chrome-plated which reflects the improved times as the decade progressed

Bottom
1940 export version of the 982cc V-twin model 2 AJS had footboards, special saddle, swept-back bars and left-side handchange

Top right
245cc model 12 AJS from 1938 with coil ignition and rather small front brake

*1930 Matchless Silver Arrow model A of 394cc
with its narrow V-twin engine*

MATCHLESS

For a time Matchless were the largest British motorcycle maker and from the turn of the century the Collier brothers, Harry and Charlie, were involved in powered two-wheelers. Both won TTs and had success on the board tracks of the Edwardian period and at Brooklands, so that well before World War 1 the marque was well established in premises at Plumstead, to the south-east of London. They might have been well removed from the Midlands centre of the industry, but this seemed to have little effect on their prosperity.

At the start of the 1930s Matchless had a range of singles much as others, plus a big V-twin for sidecar work. The singles were 245, 348, 497 and 583cc, most in side and overhead valve form, while the twin was a typical sv of 982cc. They also had their all-new Silver Arrow which was an attempt to provide the touring rider with the fully equipped, sophisticated machine it was said he wanted. A common trap.

The machine had a sv, 394cc, narrow angle, V-twin, the cylinders set at 26 degrees and cast as a single block with just one exhaust pipe emerging from the front. The result looked odd, rather like a single that was too long for its width. The skew gear-driven camshaft lay along the machine in the right crankcase and extended to the rear to drive the mag-dyno which suggested shaft drive, but this was an illusion, for chains conveyed the power to the three-speed gearbox and then on to the rear wheel. The oil tank bolted to the

*1930 Matchless T/5 with 497cc engine set
vertically in the frame*

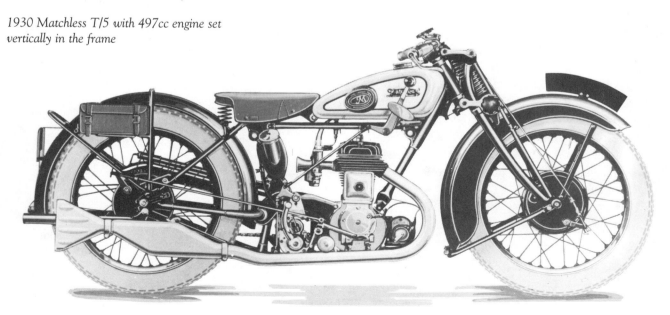

front of the crankcase, so there were no external oil pipes.

The engine and gearbox went into a frame with pivoted-fork rear suspension but at the front went girders. The drum brakes were interconnected and an instrument panel was mounted above the bars to carry both dials and switches. This was to provide the final touch to a machine sold to the discerning as quiet, smooth running and as comfortable as a car. In truth it was quiet but this was to be expected from a low output side-valve twin. This also meant a restricted performance which spelt death to sales.

The Silver Arrow might have been too small and placid to excite but 12 months later this changed when the firm unveiled their Silver Hawk at Olympia, for this had a four-cylinder, overhead-camshaft engine. Close by stood the Ariel Square Four and either model would have been a show-stopper, but for two such machines, with dissimilar engine layouts, to appear during the Depression was remarkable.

The 592cc Hawk engine was in essence two Silver Arrows placed side by side so the 26-degree vee angle remained while the single camshaft was driven by

Above
Engine of the Matchless Silver Hawk from 1934. Listed as the ohc 34/B with 592cc in its V-four cylinders
Below left
The 1934 Matchless 982cc 34/X2 V-twin
Below right
Inclined 245cc engine for the 1934 Matchless model 34/F

shaft and bevels on the right and from that side the engine looked like a massively finned ohc single although from the left it was much less impressive with just the carburettor. There was a duplex primary chain and four-speed, handchange gearbox, all installed in a frame with rear suspension, coupled brakes and an instrument panel. It had no more success than the twin for it was expensive when the world was hard-up. It also ran into head joint problems and the bevels were noisy which was not acceptable for a de luxe machine.

So the customers stuck with the singles and for them there were new models with inclined cylinders in the trend for the time and most of the range was revised in some way. In May 1931 a Light 500 was added and took its name from its low weight, which

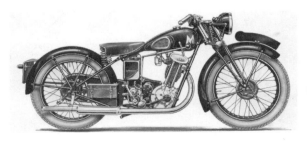

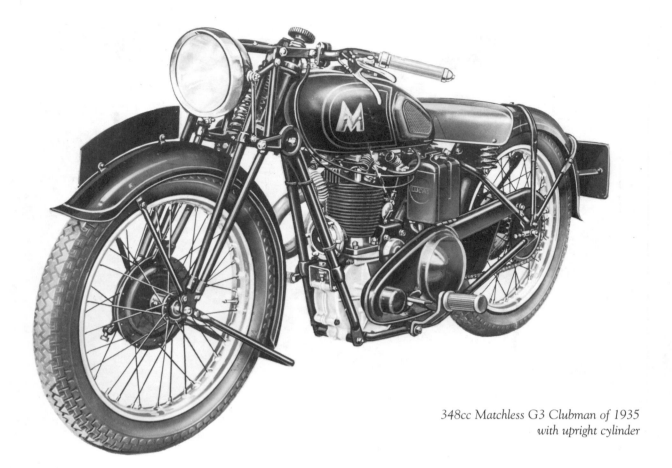

348cc Matchless G3 Clubman of 1935
with upright cylinder

just came under the tax barrier. This was quite an achievement, for the machine was equipped with electric lighting powered by a Maglita unit. It was much the same for 1932 and 1933 with detail changes and additional models derived from those listed.

The 1934 range was thinned down a little, and among the casualties was the Silver Arrow and some of the older models, but the Silver Hawk remained and a pair of 245cc machines with inclined engines were then added. In this way the range ran into 1935 with more improvements which reflected the improved times and brought a super sports 497cc model.

In April 1935 a most important new model was announced by Matchless which was to set the style and format for the range from then on. All the existing models had inclined engines, which was a style that had come in fashion in the late 1920s but was no longer what the buyers wanted.

The new machine was the G3 and was known as the Clubman. It had a 348cc, ohv engine with vertical cylinder, a magneto tucked in behind the engine and a dynamo beneath that, where it was chain driven from the crankshaft. The engine design was similar to the existing ohv models, but there were hairpin valve springs and dry sump lubrication. It drove a four-speed

footchange Burman gearbox and it and the engine went into a cradle frame while the remainder of the machine followed company lines and a single high-level exhaust system was fitted. A Clubman Special was also listed, this being a trials version with suitable tyres, gear ratios and fitments and typed the G3C.

The range had a major revision for 1936 when only a couple of side-valve models and the old V-twin were kept. In came singles based on the G3 in 245 and 497cc capacities and in touring, sports and competition forms, all very similar in design. The Silver Hawk was dropped and in 1937 so were the inclined engines which were replaced by upright ones in the style of the G3. The V-twin alone from the past remained to haul sidecars along, but it too had some changes and improvements.

During 1937 Matchless decided to stop supplying machines to the technical press for road tests and this action was maintained for many years. The company also bought the rights to the Sunbeam motorcycle and this led to the formation of the Associated Motor Cycles, or AMC, group, although the Sunbeam name was sold on to BSA in 1943.

For 1938 the range ran on in its stabilised form and the sports models had their finish brightened by

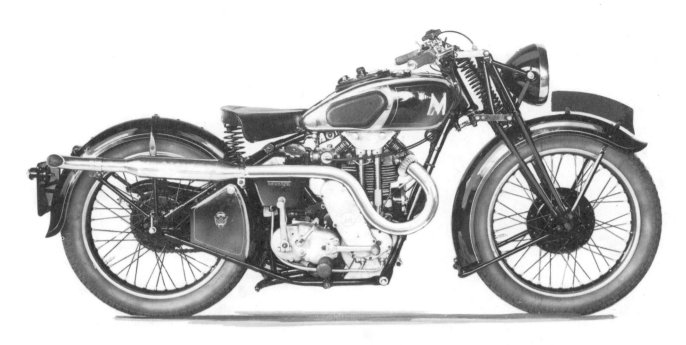

Top
1937 Matchless 497cc G80 Clubman with the magneto
tucked in behind the engine

Engine of the 1940 497cc Matchless G5 with coil ignition.
Note flying M on tank

chrome-plated petrol tanks with red panels. 1939 was much the same with the concentration on ohv models and only two side-valve singles left. During this late-1930s period Matchless supplied engines to other firms, including Brough Superior, Calthorpe, Coventry Eagle, OEC and OK Supreme. The V-twins also went into the Morgan three-wheeler, so to an extent AMC began to take over the mantle worn by JAP and Blackburne in earlier years.

Most of the range was still listed for 1940 and except for the side-valve singles had the tank finished

First post-war G3L Matchless of 1946, which was based heavily on the wartime model

in red and chrome. The competition models were dropped but not the sports ones from the ohv range. During the war AMC built some 80,000 motorcycles for the services, nearly all as a Matchless. At first this was the G3 in its 1940 form with a new frame which had a single downtube, a type adopted for all the singles that year, and a service finish. In 1941 the model changed to the G3L which was lighter and had telescopic front forks which made it a service favourite

AJS & MATCHLESS

Postwar, the firm continued with the two marques, although it was well known that the machines were built on the same production line, largely with the same parts but, for all that, each kept its adherents. The firm fostered this attitude with competition riders on both makes and separate advertising in the press, but at club level we all knew that only the badges and, up to 1951, the magneto position distinguished one

from the other.

AJS announced their two models a week before the Matchless pair and all were based on the wartime G3L but in both 348 and 497cc sizes. All had a single-cylinder, ohv engine, four-speed gearbox, rigid frame and the front forks known as Teledraulics. Other than badges and finish they differed only in the magneto position. Competition versions were added in March 1946 in small numbers, but the changes were minimal and affected wheels, tyres and mudguards in the main.

With production the key issue, there were few changes until 1949 but before then there was one new model, built as an AJS only and as a pure road racing machine. This was the 348cc 7R whose all-alloy engine kept the chain-driven, overhead camshaft of prewar days with magnesium crankcase halves which were finished in a gold paint to protect them from corrosion. The engine had fully-enclosed valve gear and the gear-

driven magneto went behind the cylinder, the whole well made and oil-tight. It drove a close-ratio, four-speed Burman gearbox and they went into an all-welded duplex frame with pivoted-fork rear and Teledraulic front suspension, the rear controlled by AMC-designed units. Both wheels had conical hubs with massive brakes and the result was a competitive machine for the class. The megaphone fitted at the end of the exhaust pipe was enormous and became a sore point for riders who tried to slipstream the AJS which was soon know as the Boy Racer, a name which stuck.

The range expanded a good deal for 1949, with both spring frames and twin-cylinder engines making their debut on the road models, while the rigid models ran on in standard and competition forms. Unlike many, AMC went straight to the pivoted rear fork, using their own rear units which became known as 'candlesticks'.

The new 1949 models were the ohv 498cc twins, which were in the British mould except for a third, central, main bearing. The camshafts, dynamo and magneto were gear driven and went fore and aft while

Top
Similar 1947 AJS ohv single with conventional construction and fine finish

Right
A 1951 348cc Matchless competition springer in action at a Normandy scramble

Left
Despite the packing, there is a Matchless G45 under there en route to Venezuela

Below
Fine, traditional Matchless springer in the form of a 1953 G80S with jampots at the rear and the comfortable dualseat

Top right
A 1957 AJS model 16MC built for trials use only, hence the small saddle and raised silencer

Bottom right
The Matchless G9 twin in 1958 when it still had the lovely mega-phone silencers, which set it off so well

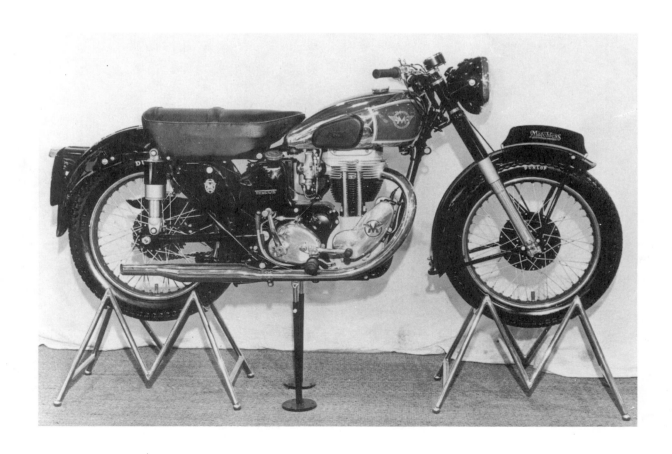

the iron barrels and alloy heads were separate. Internally, there was a one-piece crankshaft, while twin-gear pumps in the timing case looked after the dry-sump lubrication system. The timing covers bore the marque logo and differed a little in shape, but otherwise the engines were identical.

The rest of the twin was based on the sprung single, so the gearbox, frame and forks were common, as were a large number of the detail fittings. There were minor differences between the two marques, and the most obvious were the seats and silencers. The Matchless had a dualseat and very neat megaphone-shaped silencers, but the AJS stuck to the saddle, pillion pad and tubular silencers, as on the other models.

In 1950 the competition engines changed to all-alloy and the next year were also listed in spring frames as well as rigid. For all the sprung models the rear units were enlarged and immediately named as 'jampots'. From then to 1955 the road range changed little, although the Matchless moved its magneto to the front of the engine for 1952 and twin pilot lamps, one on each side of the headlamp shell, came for 1954. Full-width hubs were adopted and most models changed to the Monobloc carburettor for 1955. The 7R

was developed through these years and for 1953 was joined by the Matchless G45 which was based on a tuned version of the 498cc twin engine fitted into the 7R cycle parts.

There were major changes to the range for 1956, when all the rigid models were dropped and the road models had a new frame. On the competition side, the trials machines were given a new frame with pivoted-fork rear suspension, and the scrambles ones were given short-stroke, all-alloy engines. The twin was joined by a larger version of 593cc, which gave it more power to meet the demands both at home and abroad. The scrambles machines had new engines with shorter strokes than before and integral push rod tunnels, while the frame had extra bracing and stiffer suspension. All road and competition models were fitted with the AMC gearbox from the middle of 1956, and this was based heavily on the pre-war Norton design, which had its roots in the Sturmey-Archer box of the early 1930s.

The whole range went over to Girling rear units

for 1957, the last year for the G45. Otherwise, the range ran on as it was, but there were plenty of changes for 1958. The most obvious went on the road singles which adopted alternator electrics as did the twins, although they kept to magneto ignition. All road-equipped machines lost the twin pilot lights, which had never been too successful.

Two new sporting 593cc twins joined the range using the scrambles frame and tuned engines. The first was the CS or street scrambler model with siamesed pipes, small tank, fat tyres, alloy mudguards and quickly detachable lights. The second was the CSR which was quickly dubbed 'Coffee Shop Racer'. It used the CS engine, frame and exhaust with the standard tank, but kept the shorter competition dualseat and special lights. There was also a new road racing machine to replace the G45; the 496cc G50. It was simply a bored-out 7R, and no one could understand why it had not been built back in 1948, for AJS had produced both 350 and 500cc ohc singles in prewar days.

During 1958 one more road single appeared to create the beginning of a lighter line. The 248cc ohv engine followed AMC practice in many respects, but differed in having the oil for the dry-sump lubrication system carried in a chamber within the vertically-split crankcase, and the four-speed gearbox strapped to the rear of the case. This gave the appearance of unit construction and the primary drive was enclosed by an alloy case, which also held the alternator. The engine unit went in a built-up cradle frame with telescopic front and pivoted-fork rear suspension, and the 17in. wheels had full-width hubs with drum brakes. The mudguards, seat and side panels reflected a touring image or a machine for learners and riding to work.

The trials models had a new frame and small off-set hubs to reduce weight, but there were few other changes for 1959. The 593cc twins were enlarged to 646cc and both these and the 498cc ones were listed in standard, de luxe, CS and CSR forms. The 248cc single ran on as it was for 1959 and was joined by a scrambles version which had a tuned engine, heavier frame and forks, 19in. wheels, and suitable fittings. However, it was not successful, as it was too heavy and too expensive.

That brought the decade to a close, with AMC ready to move to a duplex frame for 1960 and, later still, to an even closer amalgamation with the Norton name and component parts.

Top left
A special press test on a Matchless 248cc G2 at Silverstone in 1958, when the model was set the task of covering 250 miles in the same number of minutes, but it took just five more

Bottom left
Late AMC single in the form of the 1959 AJS, which used the same cycle parts for both models 16 and 18

Above
The 1959 Matchless G50, which was derived from the AJS 7R, and a model much to the fore in today's classic racing

A 1934 AJW Red Fox fitted with a 499cc Rudge engine made and supplied by Rudge with four valves in pent-roof form

AJW

AJW were a firm on the edge of the industry who bought in engines, gearboxes and most else to assemble their own package. Very grey porridge one might think, but they were astute enough to keep going right through the 1930s and postwar when many others floundered. Production was, however, always on a small scale.

The firm's initials came from Arthur John Wheaton, whose background was publishing, and for his 1930 range he built lightweights to supplement a big V-twin programme, these with special frames based in part on a triangular principle. Into the smaller went Villiers engines to provide the 172cc and 196cc Black Foxes, the 247cc and 343cc Silver Foxes and a 196cc

Utility model. The bigger models began with the 500 Double Port, which had a 498cc JAP engine, conventional cycle parts and a tank with a bulbous nose.

The other models had JAP V-twin engines in the same style and used the 677cc ohv, 982cc 8/30 side-valve or the 995cc 8/55 ohv to power them. Top of the list was the four-port special with a 994cc ohv British Anzani engine, inter-connected brakes and a four-speed Jardine gearbox.

Most of these models continued for 1931, but the Anzani-powered twin was listed for racing only and there were two new models powered by the 348 and 499cc Rudge engines. The frames of these models had a total of six tubes either bolted or brazed to the headstock, which could thus be said to be well supported.

January 1931 brought a further model to the range as a Silver Fox with the long-stroke 346cc

Nice 1935 AJW Red Fox now fitted with a 488cc JAP engine

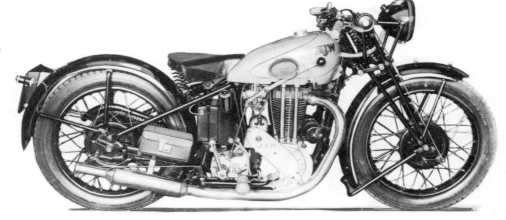

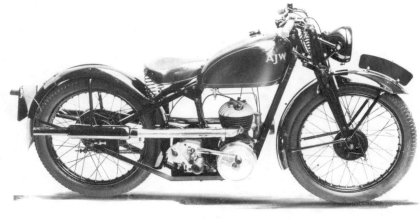

AJW two-stroke from 1939 fitted with 249cc Villiers engine and sold as the Lynx

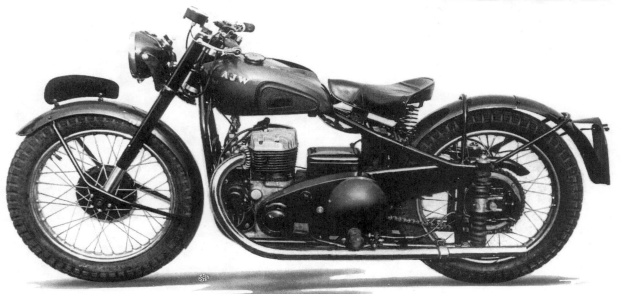

The 1949 AJW Grey Fox with its 494cc JAP vertical twin, side-valve engine

Villiers engine. Most of the smaller machines remained for 1932 but only the 680 from the big V-twins. The Rudge-powered models took the name Flying Fox and the larger had the option of the Ulster engine. A special feature for the firm was a rain deflector fitted to the top of the petrol tank with a pipe near the saddle peak to lead the water away. This gutter was to remain on many of the larger AJWs for the rest of the decade.

There were only the Rudge-powered models for 1933, as Flying Foxes with 348, 499 and 499cc Ulster engines. The same trio of motors also propelled the Vixenette, Vixen and Flying Vixen, which were models with some degree of enclosure. There were just three models of 499cc for 1934, still with the Rudge engine and the base was the Red Fox, which had the distinction of being the lowest priced 500 on the market at £42. The next year saw JAP engines being used while for 1936 there were two with JAP power and a third using a 495cc Stevens engine as the Silver Vixen but

this was dropped for 1937. Just the Flying Fox was listed for 1938 but it was joined for 1939 by a pair of two-strokes using 249cc Villiers engines and named the Lynx.

All three models were listed for 1940 but after the war the firm changed hands, and it was late in 1948 before any more AJW motorcycles appeared. When they did, there were two models. One, the Speed Fox, was a speedway machine fitted with the usual 498cc JAP engine and built in very small numbers indeed, some being produced in a grass-track form.

The other 1949 model was the Grey Fox which used the 494cc JAP vertical twin, side-valve engine which had its single carburettor fitted between its two exhaust pipes. It was a rather basic design and AJW fitted it plus a four-speed gearbox, into a cradle frame with plunger rear suspension and Dowty Oleomatic telescopic forks, which relied on air as the suspension medium, backed up by oil to provide hydraulic damp-

ing. They worked well but depended on fine-tolerance parts so wear could have a dramatic effect and repairs were difficult. Virtually all the initial production went for export, but the numbers were limited by the availability of the JAP twin engines. Manufacture continued into 1950, when the engine supply dried up, so there were no more Grey Foxes on the road.

The firm continued with the Speed Fox and a speedway sidecar outfit, but around 1952 built two prototypes with horizontal, single-cylinder engines fitted into spine frames with pivoted-fork rear and telescopic front suspension. The larger used a 500cc JAP ohv engine with an Albion gearbox mounted above it which forced the rear fork pivot to be higher than normal, and it had a bell-crank lever to connect to the suspension springs in monoshock style. The rear of the machine was enclosed by a tail-unit. The second machine used a 125cc JAP two-stroke engine, which was built in unit with its three-speed gearbox and this was positioned in the same manner.

The 125 was listed as the Fox Cub for 1953, but the other models were to special order only and included the Flying Fox. which had a sports 500cc JAP engine coupled to a four-speed Albion gearbox in a frame with pivoted-fork rear and telescopic front suspension. Unfortunately for AJW, the supply of JAP engines, except for speedway, dried up, so their production of road models ceased. They left the market for a while, but returned in 1958 with another Fox Cub; this time a 48cc light motorcycle but in truth, it was an import with a FBM engine and three-speed gearbox hung from a pressed-steel spine frame with front and rear suspension. However, they continued to produce it into the next decade, when it was joined by others. The company remained in the motorcycle business until 1964.

Top left
AJW Fox Cub with 49cc FBM engine unit, as imported and sold at the end of the decade

Bottom left
AJW prototype built in 1952 with JAP 500cc ohv engine. This was laid down with the gearbox above and mounted in a spine frame

Below
One of the AKD models from 1930, possible of 248cc capacity and rather basic. Note the stand under the engine pointing forward and ready to cause an accident if the spring fails

AKD

From 1925 these machines took their name from the combination of Abingdon tools and King Dick spanners. By 1930 they offered eight models, all with their own ohv engine of vintage looks, three-speed gearbox and conventional cycle parts. There were three of 172cc, the models 10, 70 and 80, the 196cc 20 and 60, the 248cc 90 and 100, plus the sv 296cc model 40.

For 1931 it was names in place of numbers plus the 148cc ohv Comet and 349cc sv Polar. The 172cc machines became Orion or Mercury, the 196cc the Jupiter and the 248cc Neptune. The whole range went forward as it was for 1932, but during that year the firm stopped building motorcycles and concentrated on hand tools.

AMBASSADOR

Founded by Kaye Don, an ex-Brooklands rider and driver, after the war, this company produced well-finished lightweights with Villiers engines and, from around 1954, also imported Zundapp mopeds, motorcycles and scooters. One early prototype, built in 1946, differed and used the 494cc vertical-twin JAP engine fitted into a cradle frame with girder forks and typical cycle parts were of the period, but no more was heard of this machine.

The first production model appeared in 1947 and used the Villiers 5E 197cc engine unit with three-speed gearbox in a simple frame with girder forks. The finish was silver with black and red lining and the lighting was direct. It was listed as the Series I, became II for 1948 and III for 1949 with a change to a 6E engine. It continued for 1950 with battery lighting, joined by two more models with 6E engines. First was the Series IV, better known as the Popular, while the Series V, was fitted with MP telescopic front forks. Its name was Embassy in 1951, when the Series II was Courier. Together with the Popular, they ran on. They were joined by the Supreme with plunger rear suspension and finished in grey.

The range was down to three for 1952 but grew the next year with changes for the Supreme. New was the Self Starter version which was a Supreme with a Lucas starter motor, and the Sidecar machine which comprised an Embassy fitted with a single-seat sidecar and Webb girder forks. During 1953 the 6E engine was replaced by the 8E and in 1954 the Supreme changed to the 224cc 1H engine with its four-speed gearbox which went into a new frame with pivoted-fork rear suspension and dualseat. The Embassy went to the plunger frame, and the Popular was fitted with telescopic forks.

All the models continued for 1955, the Embassy being given the option of a four-speed gearbox, and there was one new machine. This was the Envoy with the 8E engine, but in the pivoted-fork frame. The range was reduced to three models for 1956, the Envoy and Supreme being joined by a new version of the Popular. This used the 147cc Villiers 30C engine with three-speed gearbox, which was fitted into the pivoted-fork frame. It was finished in a rather more basic manner than the other models, so some parts did not blend together very well, but it offered basic transport.

Effectively, there was a fourth model for 1956, as the Envoy was also offered with the 9E engine and four-speed gearbox instead of the 8E. Of the range, it

42

continued alone into 1957, when it was listed with only the 9E engine, but with a choice of three or four speeds. At the same time, the Popular switched to the 148cc 31C engine, again with a choice as to the number of gears, and the Supreme to the 246cc 2H engine. This had the word 'Single' added to its name.

The 1957 range was completed with the Supreme Twin model, which was fitted with the 249cc Villiers 2T twin engine unit in place of the 2H. All the models had full-width, light-alloy hubs which contained 6in. drum brakes for all models, except the Popular, which

had to manage with 5in. The entire range ran on for 1958 with little change, the Popular and Envoy continuing to be offered with a choice of gearbox. The Supreme remained on offer as a Single or a Twin, but to this selection could be added the Statesman model. This used the 174cc Villiers 2L engine, again with a choice of three or four speeds, so it slotted in between the other two singles.

This did not last for long as, for 1959, the 148cc model was dropped and the 174cc one took its name to become the Popular. The Envoy continued, but only for

Far left
Ambassador prototype of 1946, with the 494cc JAP vertical twin side-valve engine in rather dated cycle parts

Top
A batch of early Ambassador models in 1947, when they still used the prewar style 5E Villiers engine

Left
The Ambassador Sidecar model, with its girder forks, was only sold as a complete outfit and gave the 8E engine a hard time

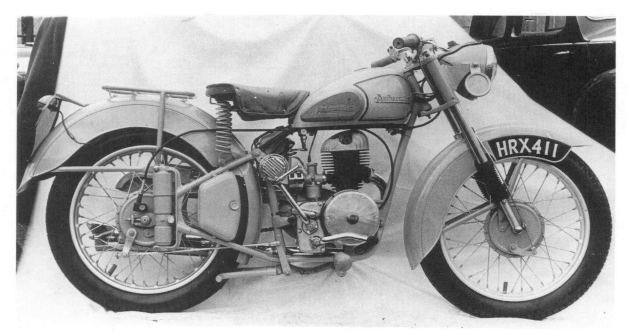

Above
Ambassador Supreme of 1953 with plunger frame and Villiers 8E engine

Below
*The Super S Ambassador of 1959 with its Villiers 2T twin engine,
some rear enclosure and full-width hub*

the first few months of the year, and the two Supreme models were also dropped. In their place came the Super S, which had the 249cc 2T engine and a new, more enclosed, style. This was all the rage towards the end of the decade, and Ambassador followed the trend with a rear enclosure that ran from the seat nose to the rear number plate, but which kept the wheel in view. To go with it, there was a well-valanced front mudguard and 17in. wheels with 7in., full-width hubs.

In April 1959 the Envoy was replaced by the Three Star Special, which was similar to the Super S, but fitted with the 9E engine offering a choice of three or four speeds. The rear panels had a trio of stars to decorate each side, while the front mudguard enclosed even more of the wheel. The style was enhanced by a pressing over the bars and controls to conceal the cables, and there was a grab handle to the rear of the dualseat. An option of a rear chaincase was listed and the finish was in Tartan red and black.

All three models ran on for 1960, when the Super S was fitted with the front mudguard from the Three Star. However, in 1962, Kaye Don retired and the make was taken over by DMW, who continued to produce the marque for a few years only.

ARIEL

Three decades of Ariel singles had their basic design laid down by Val Page late in 1925, when he first joined the firm. For the 1927 models he moved the magneto behind the engine with chain drive from the camshaft and so set the pattern. Cylinders may have been inclined for some years, but the essence was untouched.

In the redesign for 1926 most of the cycle side had remained unchanged and veteran, but Page did deal with the poor stopping power of the old models by fitting 7in. brakes to both wheels. For 1927 there was a new frame, which gave problems, plus a new gearbox and saddle tank. The frame was redesigned for 1928, when the Ariel horse trademark first appeared, and dry sump lubrication adopted in 1929 with the twin-plunger pump bolted to the inner timing case and driven by the camshaft. Thus, by the end of the vintage period the design was well established and in little need of radical alteration. So the 1930 range was much as the one for the previous year and comprised three each of 249 and 499cc plus two of 557cc. These last had side-valve engines, as did one 249, the rest were ohv, the smaller known as Colts.

There was a considerable change for 1931, for the trend was to inclined engines, and Ariel backed their horse both ways by following the new style and keeping some of the old. They also notched up a sensation at the show where the Square Four made its debut. Both 249cc models had the engines inclined by 30 degrees as did the sole 346cc ohv model but two of 499cc and one 557cc had vertical engines and the same sizes were also built with them inclined by 60 degrees. In either case, one of the ohv engines had four valves.

Inclined 346cc 1932 engine of the MH32 Red Hunter

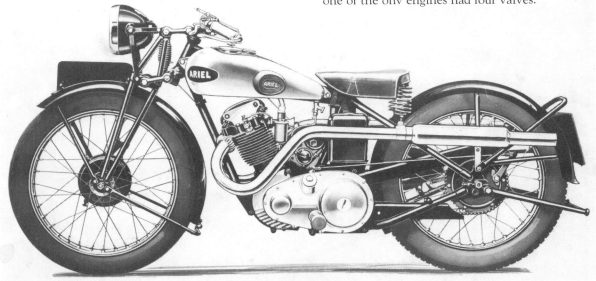

Top left
Sloping side-valve 557cc engine of 1932 Ariel SB32. Silencers and splayed frame suited the four as well

Top right
The twin-port model G Ariel of 1930 with 499cc ohv engine

Right
Edward Turner making a point about his Ariel Square Four 601cc 4F at a show of 1934 models

Below
Typical Ariel side-valve engine built for many years and in this case of 557cc and fitted in the model VA of 1933. Note Bowden carburettor

Far right,top
The 1938 Ariel Square Four 4G with the 995cc engine which replaced the earlier ohc type

Far right
1938 competition version of the Ariel 499cc model VH

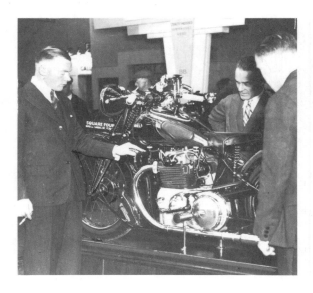

The most impressive new model was of course the Squariel as it was nicknamed. The design was Edward Turner's and the ohc engine layout unique. The prototype was exceptionally compact with all four cranks overhung with gears in the centre coupling the shafts and driving the three-speed gearbox built in unit with the engine.

This was a little too special for economic production at that time, so the left rear crank gained an outer web and this drove the four-speed gearbox. The engine was of 498cc and its single camshaft was chain driven with an ignition distributor on its left end and a magneto behind the block. Lubrication was by connecting rod dippers which picked up oil from sump troughs to feed the big-ends, plus a pump to feed the cam box. It was a compact unit and able to slot between the duplex downtubes of the sloper single frame and drive the same gearbox. The cycle parts were much as the rest of the range and included a tank-top instrument panel.

It ran on for 1932 joined by a 601cc version while most of the rest of the range was much as

before but a new name appeared, the Red Hunter which was a tuned sporting version of the four-valve 499cc model with vertical cylinder. It was a name to stay with the firm for many years and was finished to suit with red tank panels.

In January 1932 the company learnt that it had won the Maudes Trophy for the previous year in recognition of the Ariel Sevens test which ran seven models in tests that featured the same number. Despite this success the group had problems and during 1932 ran into financial trouble, but Jack Sangster, whose family had been involved with it from Victorian days, was determined to save it. He managed this and re-established Ariel with a slimmed-down workforce, factory and range.

The diversification of vertical and sloping engines was discontinued and all the singles settled into the mould they were to stay in for many years. The four continued in 601cc form only with the 498cc version available to order and its frame changed to a single downtube and common to the range, as were Burman gearboxes. The Red Hunter range was extended to add 248 and 346cc versions and in this way the firm ran on into 1936 with developments but no major changes.

For the singles there was no change for 1937 but the Four had a major revamp with the engine becoming of 995cc but with overhead valves. The crankshafts were coupled by gears and the top half in iron so it was a heavy unit but able to run smoothly from around 10mph up to some 95mph in top gear. At the same

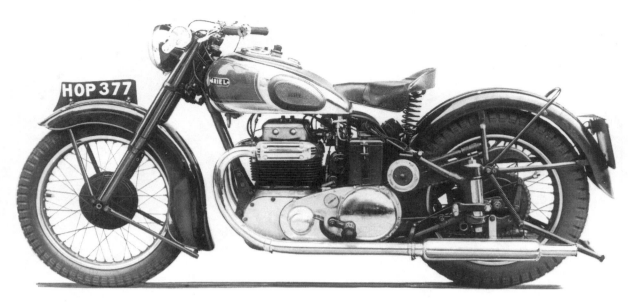

time a 599cc version of the four was proposed but, in the main, these machines seem to have been exported.

There was little real change from then on for what was a good range of tough singles in most common sizes, plus the unique four. Standard, de luxe, sports and competition versions of many models were listed and achieved by ringing the changes to the specifications and the 599cc Four reappeared for 1939. Also new for most models was a spring frame which used a linkage to connect the wheel spindle to the frame and to a plunger box on each side, this designed to give a constant chain tension. It was clever but introduced too many pivots which wore, and had limited wheel travel.

The whole range continued as it was for 1940, but the firm then concentrated on a service version of the 346cc ohv model for the duration plus a number of the 248cc ohv and a small batch of the 499cc sv from spares stocks. The services found the Ariel single just as tough and reliable as it had been in civilian life. Postwar, the firm continued with the 346 and 499cc ohv models in de luxe and Red Hunter forms, plus the 598cc sv single and the 995cc Square Four, all still with girder forks until mid-1946 when telescopics began to appear, along with the special rear suspension in 1947.

For 1948 a vertical twin-cylinder model was added, again listed in de luxe and Red Hunter forms, but otherwise based on the same design. This was of

Left top
The 1948 Ariel Square Four with its heavy iron engine in the sprung frame

Left bottom
Competition 1952 Ariel VCH model with an all-alloy engine in a rigid frame and with an odd exhaust-pipe run

Right top
Ariel 499cc vertical twin in 1950, when it was still built to KG or KH specification

Right bottom
Nice line of Ariel models at the 1950 New York motorcycle show, with the new, all-alloy Square Four at the front

499cc with ohv and of conventional construction, chain-driven camshafts to front and rear, iron head and block, single carburettor and magneto ignition. The rest of the machines was as for the singles with telescopic forks and either rigid or with the rear-link suspension as an option.

It was the turn of the Square Four to be changed for 1949 and this was to an all-alloy engine to reduce the weight and at the same time coil ignition was adopted. The result was considered by many to be the most handsome Squariel of all, with its chrome-plated tank with red panels and matching wheel rims.

For 1950 there was one new model in the form of the competition, all-alloy, 499cc Hunter, which could be supplied in trials or scrambles specification, but in

either case came with a racing magneto and alloy mudguards, but no lights. No rear suspension was offered and the rigid frame was special with a shorter wheelbase.

The de luxe twin was no longer listed in 1952, but there was a new single in the form of the all-alloy 499cc Red Hunter, and the next year brought an all-alloy Red Hunter twin finished in Wedgwood blue, a colour also used for other models that year when the Square Four took a Mark II form with four separate exhaust pipes to distinguish it from the earlier model.

The all-alloy single and twin, competition single and early Four were all dropped for 1954 when others appeared. Smallest was a 198cc ohv single based on a similar BSA and named the Colt. It was of simple con-

Top
The Ariel all-alloy VHA
was only built for 1953
and is seen here in the
sprung frame

Left
The four-pipe Ariel
Square Four, of 1953,
hitched to a sporting side-
car to make a fast road
outfit

struction with telescopic front and plunger rear suspension and a Brunswick green finish. At the other end of the scale was a 647cc ohv twin known as the Huntmaster, which simply used the BSA Golden Flash engine with the minimum of changes to disguise the fact. It also had a new frame with pivoted-fork rear suspension which was used by the smaller twin and ohv singles, the cycle parts and dualseat were to suit, and the finish was in deep claret. The other two new models both used the 499cc all-alloy engine and were for competition, one having a rigid frame with saddle for trials, and the other a pivoted-fork frame and dualseat for scrambles.

After this major redesign, it was no surprise that little was altered for 1955, while for 1956 there was just a headlamp cowl and full-width, light-alloy wheel hubs for most models. Otherwise it was detail changes only, although the trials model did go into a new frame with pivoted-fork rear suspension, but designed to retain the

short trials wheelbase and in 1957 it was joined by a 346cc version. This minimal activity was because the firm were close to some major changes of direction.

There was no immediate sign of these when the 1958 range was announced with no alterations, but the firm had been working and planning for some time on a new future. They made a major decision to design a radical machine for the next decade, using modern production techniques to reduce costs and keep quality high. Initial market research indicated that a 250cc twin two-stroke was the engine type to use and engineering sense dictated the use of pressings, mouldings and die-castings as much as possible, while the trend of the time lent towards enclosure.

So Val Page set to work, and the result was announced in July 1958 as the Ariel Leader. It was a sensation, for it not only used the suggested engine, but had a pressed-steel frame with full enclosure, legshields and windscreen, as for a scooter, but on motorcycle-size

Top
The Earles leading-link front forks tried out during 1953, but which never went into production and seen here on a KH twin

Right
Basic Ariel single in the form of a 346cc NH during a 1953 road test, when it demonstrated the tough nature of the type

wire-spoke wheels. The engine capacity was 247cc and its two cast-iron, parallel cylinders were inclined well forward and had alloy heads The cylinders went into a single, massive, lower-half casting which combined the crankcase, inner primary case and gearbox as one, but with space between the two major units. Into this went full-disc crankshafts, keyed at the centre, and the unit had an alternator, external flywheel and coil ignition while the gearbox was a four-speed Burman.

The engine unit was hung from the main frame beam, which contained the box-shaped petroil tank and extended down behind the gearbox to support both the box and the rear fork. The front suspension was by trailing links, the units and arms being concealed within the fork pressings and there was no top crown as such, so the handlebars were simply clamped to the top of the column. Both wheels had light-alloy, full-width hubs with 16in. rims and whitewall tyres.

The mechanics of the Leader were then hung with its clothes. A dummy tank, with parcel compartment, went on top of the main frame beam and extended back to form the seat base. The seat itself was hinged and beneath it were the tools and battery. The sides of the machine were enclosed by panels and to

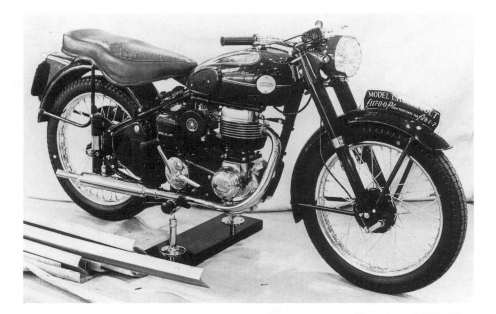

Left
The Ariel Colt, which owed much to the BSA C11G, but had a 198cc engine

Left
The scrambles HS model of 1954, on show at Earls Court and under close scrutiny

the rear of these there was a hinged section to blend with the seat base. There were also legshields and a windscreen with an instrument panel behind it and a cowl for the headlight in front while the front wheel had its own well valanced mudguard. The machine was conceived to have extras, which included panniers, indicators, clock and many more, rather in the scooter vein. They were available when the machine went on sale and combined with it to make the whole operation very successful.

Thus encouraged, Ariel decided on the major step of terminating their entire four-stroke range, which caused consternation among enthusiasts for the marque, and took place during 1958 and 1959. This left the Leader, which was unchanged for 1959, but for 1960 it was joined by the Arrow. This was a sports version, which dispensed with most of the enclosure, but kept

the basic engine unit, frame beam and forks. To this was added a dummy tank, rear mudguard and other details and the machine was an instant success.

Later on, in the 1960s, were to come the Golden Arrow and the smaller 200cc version, but in 1965 the parent group decided to stop production in a declining market. It was a tragic decision, for the formula could easily have been developed over many years, but it was not to be. Val Page had other ideas for the Leader, including a 700cc four-stroke tourer with in-line, four-cylinder engine laid down with the heads pointing to the left - just as the BMW K-series of 1983. Sadly, the parent group did not share his vision and let it all fall apart.

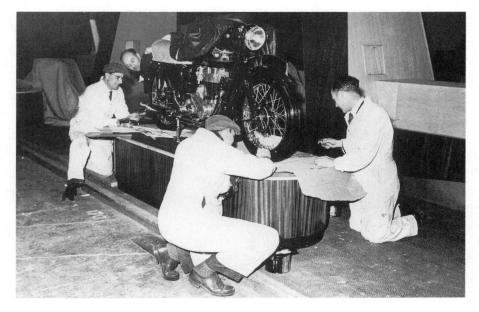

Right
Traditional Ariel single, in pivoted-fork frame, having its finishing touches applied for the late 1954 show at Earls Court

Left
The 1955 Ariel 598cc VB hitched to a double-adult Watsonian Maxstoke sidecar, and thus carrying out its traditional role

Right
Ariel Leader 247cc twin-cylinder two-stroke with all its enclosure and forward-looking engineering

BAC

These were the initials of the Bond Aircraft and Engineering Company, which built the Bond machines whose manufacture was taken over by Ellis of Leeds at the end of 1950. BAC then turned to new designs named Lilliput for 1951, these being machines in miniature using 99cc Villiers 1F or 125cc JAP engines.

These went into a loop frame with telescopic forks which ran on 20in. tyres and the lighting was direct. Only the 99cc engine was listed for 1952 when it was joined by the Gazelle scooter which used the 122cc 10D engine. The layout was in the scooter form but the style less so thanks to the grill set round the engine. At the end of the year the scooter was joined by another with the 1F engine while the firm also offered a light sidecar.

None of this made much impact, and by May 1953 the Gazelle had been taken over by Projects and Developments of Blackburn. They did some modifications but nothing further was heard of the machines.

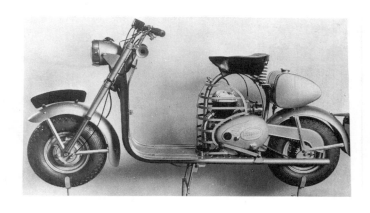

Above
The BAC Gazelle scooter, for 1952, with its 10D Villiers engine and odd enclosing 'cage'

BAKER

F.E. Baker was involved with motorcycles from Edwardian times but by 1930 was listing just six models, all Villiers powered. Smallest were the 172cc 55 and 65, next came the 196cc 50 and 58, while largest were the 247cc 60 and 343cc 62. A four-stroke was added in March 1930 using a 249cc sv James engine, but late that year Frank Baker sold out to James.

Below
A two-stroke Baker with auto-lube from 1929, possible with 247cc engine

54

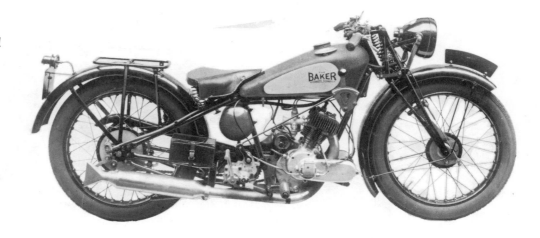

Left
*The Bantamoto cyclemotor unit, introduced for 1951,
had a gear-train drive to the rear wheel and remote
petroil tank*

BAUGHAN

H. P. Baughan was a trials man first and last, involved
for many years with the ACU Western Centre and
ISDT selection tests. This background through the
1920s served his business at Stroud, Gloucestershire,
well when they began building motorcycles in 1930 as
nearly all were produced for competition and normally
with sidecar.

Most of the outfits also had the sidecar wheel driven which helped them to be most successful and, as
production was always limited, the machines were really hand built to order.

Due to this a range of engines was listed from
300cc sv to 500cc ohv and could come from
Blackburne, JAP or Sturmey-Archer. The rest of the
machine was equally open to option, with the basic
frame, forks, tanks and wheels laid out with trials work
in mind. Not all machines were built as sidecars, but
when they were the drive to the wheel was incorporated and this had a simple dog clutch and a cross-shaft
with two fabric alignment joints.   It worked very well
and could be used to reach farm or cottage off the beat-
en track in addition to its trials competitions. On a
hard surface the dog clutch was disengaged as the outfit
would otherwise try hard to go straight on at the first
corner it came to.

BANTAMOTO

One of many cycle attachments and listed from 1951
for two years. It was made by Cyc-Auto, and the 38.5cc
two-stroke engine fitted to the left side of the rear
wheel which it drove via a gear train. It was a neat
unit, the positive drive preferred by some, while controls were simple and running costs minimal.

Above
*A solo Baughan from 1935 filled with a 348cc
Blackburne engine and full competition equipment*

Below
*The strange Berwick with its turned Villiers engine
and shaft drive. Note how rear mudguard section
acts as a frame member*

From then on a range of models was listed each
year with 250, 350 and 500cc engines from one or more
of the three firms and in either side or ohv form. Only
a dozen or so were built in a year but they continued in
this way until 1936.

BERWICK

This unusual machine was experimental and built to
appear at Olympia by the Berwick Motor Company of
Tweedmouth in Northumbria who then moved to
Banbury were production was to take place. The engine
was a 247 or 343cc Villiers turned to suit the use of
shaft drive with the clutch and three-speed gearbox
behind it. The unit went into a duplex frame fitted
with Brampton girders and the finish was in black with
gold lining for the tank, but sadly no more was heard of
this interesting design.

BIKOTOR

This was a simple and ingenious cycle attachment which came and went in 1951. It had a 47cc two-stroke engine designed for minimal weight and to drive the rear wheel by friction in the usual way. It was well made, but failed to catch on, so no more was heard of it.

Right
*The Bikotor clip-on unit of 1951, which
drive the rear wheel with a friction
roller and was of all-alloy construction*

BOND

Lawrence Bond was best known for the small three-wheeled cars that carried his name, but for 1950 he introduced a motorcycle that was just as unusual.

It was based on a large, tapered, oval-section alloy tube, which ran back from the headstock, was rolled from sheet and lap riveted on its underside. At the rear it was stiffened by a massive rear mudguard that enclosed more than half the wheel. From this frame was hung the engine, a 99cc Villiers 1F unit with two-speed gearbox, and this was flanked by footboards with deep legshields. The front mudguard was as large as the rear so is also concealed much of the wheel and the complete machine weighed in at 90lb. There was no springing, other than that provided by the saddle and balloon tyres, and the lighting was direct.

By July 1950 the forks had become telescopic, and for 1951 the machine was joined by a de luxe version powered by a 125cc JAP engine with three-speed

Above
*Bond P4 of 1960 with 197cc 9E
Villiers engine and improved lines at
the front*

Left
*The Bond motorcycle with its mono-
coque main beam and well enclosed
wheels in 1951*

gearbox. The machine was built by the Bond Aircraft and Engineering Company in Lancashire, but for 1951 manufacture was taken over by Ellis of Leeds, while the original firm produced another small range under the BAC label. There were some changes, but the models continued with their unique frames and a light-blue polychromatic paint finish to run on in this form for a year or two. Early in 1953 the smaller was dropped and production of the 125 ceased later that year.

However, it was not the end of the name, for the three-wheeler continued in production, and the company moved to a new factory in Preston, Lancashire, returning to two wheels in 1958. The new machine was a scooter listed as the P1 and powered by a fan-cooled, 148cc Villiers 31C engine with three-speed gearbox and Siba electric start. This went into a typical scooter frame with suspension front and rear by single, pivoted leading arms. The mechanics were enclosed by a plastic body with hinged dualseat over a plastic fuel tank. Styling was provided by a two-tone finish and the side panels, which were extended back to form small fins in the American car style. Two small portholes on each side highlighted this aspect.

In the middle of the year the P1 was joined by the P2, which used the 197cc Villiers 9E engine, still with fan cooling and Siba electric start, but with a four-speed gearbox. Otherwise, it was the same, and both continued for 1959 but were replaced by the P3 and P4 for 1960. These retained the same engines, but had the bodywork amended by dispensing with the rear panels and hinging the entire rear section from the tail. At the front the mudguard became part of the apron moulding and assumed a lighter and more graceful line but, despite the changes, the lines were really much as before, including the twin fins and portholes. The two models continued in production until 1962, after which the firm concentrated on its three-wheelers

BOWN

This 1920s firm built the Aberdale autocycle and then took it over under their own name in 1950 but revised the machine to used the 99cc Villiers 2F engine in place of the JDL. The frame was amended to suit and continued with blade girders, the whole finished in maroon with gold lining and listed as the Auto Roadster.

For 1951 it was joined by a motorcycle which used the Villiers 1F engine in a cradle frame with tubular girder forks. Direct or battery lights were offered and the finish was again in maroon. During 1952 the Tourist Trophy model was added, this using a 122cc 10D engine in similar cycle parts but with telescopic forks and the model continued the Welsh firm's reputation for well made, sturdy machines, all four models running on to the end of 1954 when production ceased.

Two years later the firm returned to the market with a typical moped powered by a 47.6cc Sachs engine in a rigid frame with trailing-link front forks. The next year it had plunger rear suspension, but then faded from the scene.

BRITAX

This accessory firm moved into the motorcycle field late in 1949 by importing the 48cc Ducati Cucciolo engine unit with two-speed gearbox. As in its Italian homeland, the engine, the name of which meant 'little pup', was sold as a bicycle attachment, and it was very successful with over a quarter million sold world-wide.

The engine unit was unusual in a number of ways, first for being a four-stroke in a two-stroke class,

Top left
*First of the P-series Bond
scooters at the start of the
1959 Isle of Man rally, with a
TWN behind it*

Top right
*The tank may say Aberdale,
but this is the model which
became the 1950 Bown autocycle with the 2F Villiers
engine*

Bottom right
*Bown 99cc motorcycle with
the two-speed 1F engine in a
nice duplex frame, but still
with girder forks*

next for having its overhead valves opened by pull-
rods, and for the gearbox which had preselector control. In other respects it was simple enough and the
assembly clamped to the cycle bottom bracket with
chain drive to the rear wheel. Less usual was for the
left-hand pedal to act as the gearchange lever, it being
positioned to suit and then the clutch operated.

In the middle of 1953 the firm moved on to a
complete machine, using the Ducati engine, simple
cycle parts and the girder forks from the lightweight
Royal Enfield model. It was joined for 1955 by two further models, one a scooter and the other a road racer,
and both retained the Ducati engine unit, rigid frame
and girder forks. The Scooterette was enclosed with
mainly flat panels and had a vast front mudguard plus
legshields, none of which did anything for its looks. Its
performance was adequate for the time but, despite this
and a competitive price, there were very few takers.

The racer was given the name Hurricane and was
notable for its aluminium full fairing. This 'dustbin', as
all such were called in the 1950s, was joined by further

extensive panelling, which enclosed the tank and ran
back to form a seat base and rear mudguard to shield
half the rear wheel. Under all this was the same Ducati
engine fitted with stronger valve springs and a megaphone exhaust system. The racing of 50cc machines
was in an embryonic stage in 1955, so the sight of a
number of Hurricanes at a Blandford race meeting
looked good, even if they failed to win.

There were minor improvements to the models
for 1956 but that was their last year as Ducati were
moving on to other matters and Britax went back to
accessories.

The Britax Hurricane road racer, which had a 48cc ohv Ducati engine under all the panelling. It had a short life in 50cc racing

BROUGH SUPERIOR

The Brough Superior was the machine of legends, an early superbike before the term was coined and 'The Rolls-Royce of Motorcycles'. George Brough was also a master of the art of publicity, grabbing the best parts for his machines and truly making the whole greater than the sum of its parts. Much of the legend came from performance by specific men and machines and from the show-stoppers George produced year after year for Olympia and Earls Court.

Another view is that George Brough made the machines he most liked to ride, which might account for the gradual move from out-and-out performance, in totally sporting style, to the high-speed sports tourer.

There is hardly such a thing as a standard Brough Superior as, for the price charged, there was very individual attention. The range was really just the starting point from which the customer could refine his choice to the specification desired. This made it expensive but it worked well and part of the expense came from the firm's practice of assembling each machine completely and getting every aspect right before anything was plated or painted. When correct, it was stripped, finished and reassembled for final testing.

With this background it is hardly surprising that the Brough story is peppered with show specials, works specials, customers' specials and modified models each with a name and a story. Best known owner outside the

world of motorcycling was T. E. Lawrence, who had a string of Broughs known as George I to VII, but there were many others.

George Brough was a perfectionist and, as a hard rider, one of the most stringent and critical inspectors of all the machines that carried his name. Many customers were personal friends and all would have their needs and wishes discussed before their machine was put in hand. Service and back-up was to the same standard for George knew only too well that if you charge high and exclusive prices then you must also keep the client happy.

The starting point for a machine in 1930 was the 680, SS80 or SS100 models. All used V-twin JAP engines and the first had a 677cc ohv which drove a three-speed gearbox in a rigid frame as stock but in Black Alpine form had four speeds and rear suspension plus an eggshell black tank finish. The other two machines were bigger, the SS80 being fitted with a 981cc side-valve engine and the SS100 with a 995cc ohv unit. Both pulled high gears.

All three machines were topped off by the famous Brough fuel tank, which gave them their distinctive air. It was made from many hand beaten pieces all soldered together and was a Brough trademark. Possibly it was

Left
The V-four Brough Superior on show at Olympia for 1927 with 994cc side-valve engine

Bottom
The working area of the Brough banking sidecar chassis showing the scroll formed in the back of the wheel which raised the chair body after a left bend

Left
Top view of the Austin-engined Brough Superior with its twin rear wheels and the prop-shaft running between them

the most important feature that George himself contributed aside from his demand for perfection from everyone.

A smaller model fitted with a 491cc ohv V-twin JAP joined the range for 1931 but was really too expensive for its class and only nine were built.

Aside from this it was time for another stunning special to grab the headlines and excite the customers. All Broughs were special in some way but these show models were more so and the most interesting were the fours. The first appeared in 1927 and had a 994cc, side-valve, 60-degree, V-four engine with the single camshaft in its centre, which drove straight back to the clutch and gearbox built in unit with it. Bevels turned the drive for the chain to the rear wheel. George came back in 1928 with an in-line four fitted with a 900cc Swiss-made MAG engine and similar transmission arrangements. This machine had a Bentley and Draper spring frame with the suspension spring horizontal under the saddle, the usual Castle forks and twin head-

lamps. It was smooth to ride, but had some engine problems, so no more were built.

The next four reflected George's opinion that a four was needed to give the smooth, quiet, Gran Turismo style he was beginning to seek. Water-cooling was thought necessary as a means of keeping the noise level low and from there it was only a short step to using an existing car engine. The obvious choice was the Austin 7, as it was small and light, so George set to work on Sir Herbert Austin.

This is thought to have been the most difficult part of the project, but in the end Sir Herbert agreed to supply engines bored to 800cc and fitted with an alloy cylinder head. Attached to it was the usual clutch, gearbox and a propeller shaft, which was of course on the centreline of the machine.

Most people would have solved this by shifting the engine or drive but George left the mechanics where they were and moved the wheel to one side. Then to balance it he fitted another, so there was just room for the shaft to pass between them, and declared

it a sidecar-only model. Only ten were built, all in 1932, but the last was not sold until two years later. Nearly all survive and some have been ridden solo.

The standard 680, SS80 and SS100 all continued in the lists with their options and extras, but for 1933 the SS80 was redesigned into a new frame and the range joined by the 11.50, which used a 1096cc side-valve JAP engine, and a side-valve 680 which failed to find much favour. It was dropped for 1934 as was the SS80 just for that year, while the SS100 was much modified and fitted with the 8/75 JAP engine in a new frame fitted with the Castle forks. It was guaranteed to do 110mph solo and 90 with a chair, but sadly the engine proved troublesome and not more than ten were built.

There was also a one-off banking sidecar chassis which used the outfit's momentum to lift the chair once it had gone down under its own weight, a peg locking it. The SS80 returned in July 1935 fitted with a Matchless 982cc V-twin engine marked as a Brough to join the 680, SS100 and 11.50, and the SS100 changed to an ohv Matchless engine for 1936, after which the 680 was dropped.

By 1938 it was time for the next show special and

with it came plunger rear suspension, which went on all models except the standard SS80. The special was less spectacular than the fours and was based on the SS80 engine with this set transversely across the frame. The drive side was extended back to the single plate Austin 7 clutch and a three-speed and reverse Austin 7 gearbox. At the rear of the gearbox went a spiral bevel pair which drove the rear wheel by chain and allowed the kickstart to operate in its normal plane. The

Top
Top of the line was always the SS100 Brough and this is the 1936 version

Centre
The side-valve Brough Superior mainstay for many years was the SS80 and this is the 1937 one

Bottom
The show special seen late in 1937 and based on the SS80 but turned to create a transverse V-twin housed in a frame with plunger rear suspension but with chain final drive

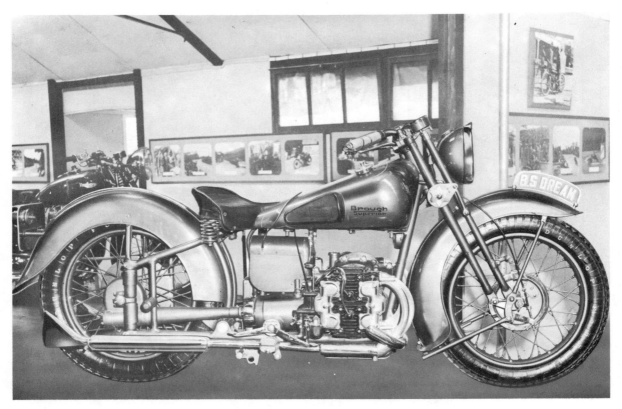

The 1938 Brough Superior Golden Dream pictured in the Beaulieu gallery in 1959. Very special flat-four engine with shaft drive

mechanics went into a frame based on the standard design but with plunger rear suspension.

The public showed limited interest in the transverse engine concept, so limited that only the show model was sold, but this hardly mattered to George for the twin was interim. He had his eyes on his dream - the Golden Dream for 1939, and it went on view at the show late in 1938. Two were built, one in the usual black and chrome for road testing and the other in gold for the show. Hence the Golden Dream name it gained before the week was a day old.

As usual it was the engine that set the Dream apart and for it George chose an ohv flat-four layout of unique type. The aims were to gain smooth power impulses, complete engine balance, no vibration and even cooling for all four cylinders. This usually meant water-cooling but not for George and his team. They arranged the four cylinders as two flat twins, one above the other, so all four exhausts had the same cooling draught available to them. The crankshafts lay along the machine and were geared together to rotate in opposite directions.

Two engines were built, with different camshaft drive systems, and capacities of 988 and 998cc. In both the pistons all moved from side to side in unison, for there was only one crankpin for each flat-twin pair of cylinders. Engine construction was on car lines with the light-alloy crankcase casting split on its vertical

centreline and extended out to form the cylinders which had iron liners. Twin Amals provided the mixture and ignition was by a special mag-dyno driven from the rear of the top crankshaft and incorporating a distributor to feed the sparking plugs.

A three-speed gearbox was bolted to the rear of the engine with a kickstarter on the black prototype and a hand start lever on the gold show model. There was also a four-speed box made but not finished off. From the box a shaft ran back within a tube to the rear wheel, and an underslung worm and wheel turned the drive round the corner. The frame and cycle parts were positively prosaic in comparison but well up to the usual Brough standard. Plunger rear suspension and specially widened Castle front forks looked after the ride and the details and finish incorporated all of George's ideas and ideals for his Dream machine.

Sadly, this innovative design was overtaken by the war and with it came the end of Brough Superior motorcycles. Right to the last days the three basic models continued to be listed, but from October 1939 the firm was committed to high-precision work.

It was perhaps only right that the company who used the slogan 'The Rolls-Royce of Motorcycles' should do much work for Rolls-Royce during the war and were one of the very few entrusted to machine Merlin crankshafts.

BSA

At one time during the 1930s the BSA slogan that 'One in Four is a BSA' was simply a fact. They dominated the market and were always well ahead of their rivals, one year building twice the machines of their closest.

They were successful in surviving the Depression because they concentrated their efforts on building machines the public would and could buy. There were very few excursions into the interesting, the innovative or the exciting, and this avoided the costs, the lack of sales or the commercial heartache so many others suffered.

BSA concentrated on a range of plain and straightforward models built in traditional sizes and without any signs of oddity in their specification or construction. What the customer got was a very well-made machine, reliable, sturdy, priced to a level he could afford and backed by a first-class chain of dealers for spares and service. In the 1930s this was what most buyers wanted because it was all they could afford.

Dreams might have been a Brough or even a car, then a real luxury item with heavy running costs, but reality was getting to work on time. For many a motorcycle became the way to do this in preference to the

Below left
1931 249cc side-valve single BSA model B31-1. Basic get-to-work transport, good and cheap to buy and run

Below right
BSA model G30-15, a 985cc V-twin from 1930

Bottom
The BSA Sloper model in its 1928 form, here without lights which would have been an extra

tram, bus or bicycle and at weekends it offered the countryside. BSA appreciated all this, so built their range of models to suit, and in 1930 it was an extensive one running to some 18 basic machines. In addition there were variations and options and accessories, so customers could easily turn their standard machine into something a little special and unique to them, a welcome fillip in those hard times.

On the smaller machines the specification could be important, for it naturally affected the weight and this could determine the taxation class. When the limit went from 200 to 224lb it helped, but could still be marginal. The effect in those Depression years was dramatic as the tax rose from 30s. to £3 in an era when you could buy a second-hand machine for less.

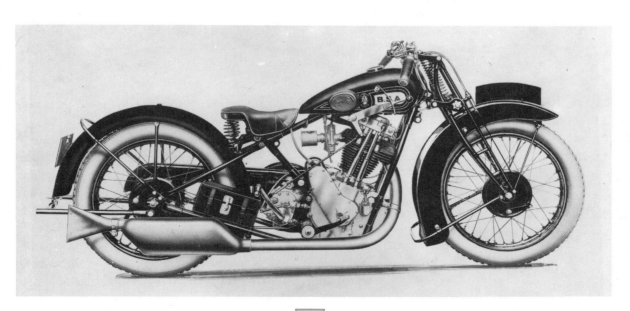

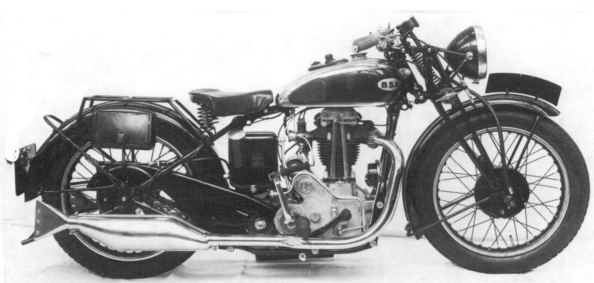

Top
J34-11 BSA or the 499cc ohv V-twin for 1934 which had first been designed for the War Office

Above
The BSA 499cc model with fluid flywheel in the crankcase and elaborate timing chest

One area of variation was the electrics, with magneto, mag-dyno or Maglita being available and machines offered without lights, with acetylene lamps and bulb horn or with a lighting set. The Maglita was a device that in theory acted as both dynamo and magneto in one unit, but as so often happens with compromises, it failed to do either job all that well.

The smallest machine in the range was a 174cc two-stroke built in unit with a two- or three-speed gearbox. It was their first two-stroke, was not a success so went at the end of the year, and they were to wait for

Above
*1934 499cc BSA Blue Star W34-9 with front
mag-dyno and sump cast in with the crankcase*

Below
*1935 149cc X35-0 model which looked after the
bottom end of the BSA ohv market*

the postwar Bantam before they tried that engine type
again.

For the rest it was a solid range of worthy and
conventional singles and twins with three or four
speeds and in rigid frames with girder forks. They ran
from 249 to 556cc in the singles and as 771 and 985cc
as twins, both of which had side valves. The singles
came with side or overhead valves, generally with vertical cylinder and front-mounted magneto, but some
were descended from the Sloper of 1927 and kept the
inclined cylinder and rear magneto of that model. Most
of the heavier machines had a frame with a forged steel
backbone running from steering head to saddle nose
that BSA would make much of up to 1936. The Sloper
was listed with many options and one was a tuned
engine. To distinguish it from the standard ones it had
a red star stencilled on the timing cover and from this
came the star theme that was to run through to gold
when times improved.

For 1931 the range was cut back to 12 models,
but the variations, options and extras continued so that
all customers could be satisfied. It was much the same
for 1932 but in that year tuned 348 and 499cc models
were given the name of Blue Star, being joined by a
248cc version in 1933. Other 250s were simpler and
really cut to the bone for the Depression, while, right at
the bottom, 1934 brought a new 149cc ohv model
much on the lines of the 250s. Improvements to existing models were mainly detail, but a sign of the slightly
improving times was that all models were supplied as
standard with full electrical equipment. The days of
scraping the barrel and acetylene lights were firmly put
in the past, while models with the mag-dyno mounted

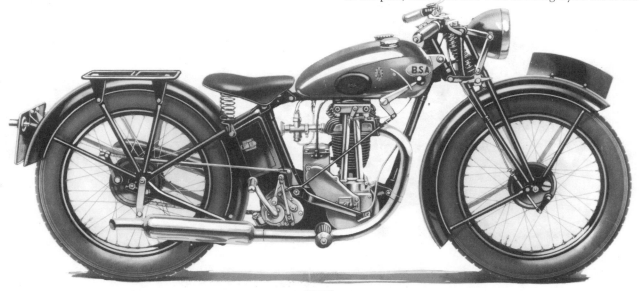

67

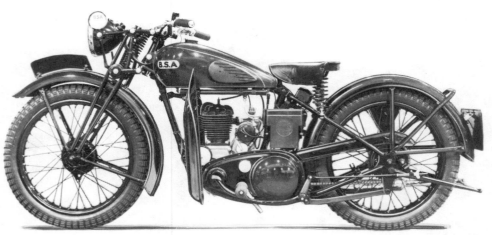

Left
The big V-twin for 1936,
the 985cc model G14 still
with handchange and
external oil pump

Left
Competition R19 from
the 1936 BSA range and
of 348cc with tyres, mud-
guards and crankcase
shield to suit its purpose

Left
For those who still want-
ed a magneto BSA listed
this 249cc B20 in 1938
as well as the C10

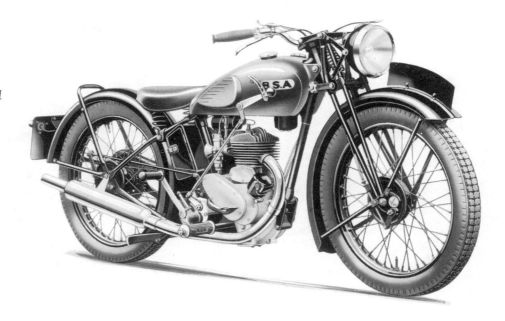

Right
*The much-maligned BSA
grey porridge C10 of 249cc
and side valves in its original
1938 guise*

Below
*The M23 Silver Star of
1939, 496cc and with the
option of a close-ratio gearbox*

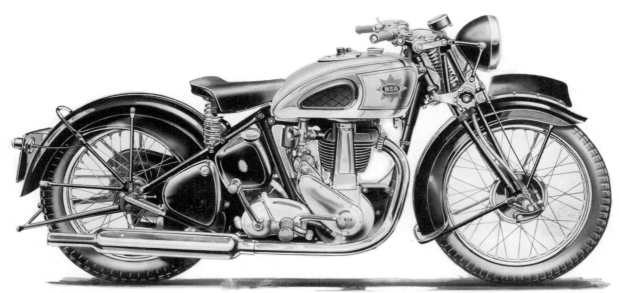

in front of the engine were provided with a shield to protect it.

Very new in the 500 class was the model FF, so named because its transmission comprised a fluid fly-wheel and pre-selector, three-speed gearbox and due to this the kickstarter turned the engine via gears in an extended timing cover. For the rest the model was much as the others of that capacity, but the new transmission dampened the normally good performance down to a humdrum level. The prototype was displayed at the 1933 Olympia Show, but the model never entered production.

Of more interest was a small 499cc ohv twin which joined the 985cc one, it having been originally designed for the War Office and then modified for civilian use. The range rolled on through 1934 and 1935 with some alterations while 1936 brought the Empire Star models to mark the Royal Silver Jubilee of

the previous year. Otherwise the list was much as before, covering most of the bases in the search for buy-ers and offering a good spread of specifications for each model size and type. One addition was a 748cc version of the ohv twin, much as the 500.

While the previous years had been ones of con-solidation, 1937 brought a major revamp to the singles, which were fully redesigned to reduce the confusing array of models and simplify production. The man responsible for the engineering was Val Page and the design was to continue post-war to the end of the pre-unit days.

The 150 was dropped and the rest of the singles were built as two ranges in one basic design. The light models were the B-range with 249 and 348cc engines with side or overhead valves while the heavy were the M-range with 349, 496 and 596cc engines and the same valve position choice. All had engines of typical

British design, drove three or four-speed gearboxes and went into rigid frames with girder forks. They were what BSA did best, worthy, dependable, solid but without much glamour as they were for working. The Empire Star models remained in their three sizes and to complete the range there were two of the V-twins, the 748cc ohv and the 985cc side-valve models, neither of which received any significant changes.

The new range was consolidated for 1938 with little alteration, but was joined by two new and significant models. The first was triggered off when Wal Handley came out of retirement to ride a specially prepared Empire Star at Brooklands in June 1937. He duly won his first race at over 100mph, so was awarded the usual Brooklands gold star, and from this exercise came the famous model of the same name.

For the catalogue it was prosaically typed the M24, but was a full sports machine with an all-alloy, bench-tested engine and TT carburettor. The gearbox

shell was cast in magnesium alloy and the frame was lighter and without sidecar lugs. Two additional versions were listed, one for competition and the other for track racing in Brooklands style. It is doubtful if any of the track models were built, but the competition one proved popular.

The second new model came at the opposite end of the range and was the 249cc C10 side-valve. It had an engine built on similar but simpler lines to the others but with the points for the coil ignition located in an angled housing on the timing cover. A separate three-speed, handchange gearbox was fitted in the simple cycle parts, but dry sump lubrication was retained, with the oil stored in a compartment in the petrol tank. The silencer had a cheeky uptilt to its tail and the machine was an adequate if basic performer.

In 1938 BSA won the Maudes Trophy using M21 and M23 models and for 1939 added the C11 to the range, an ohv version of the C10 using the same detail

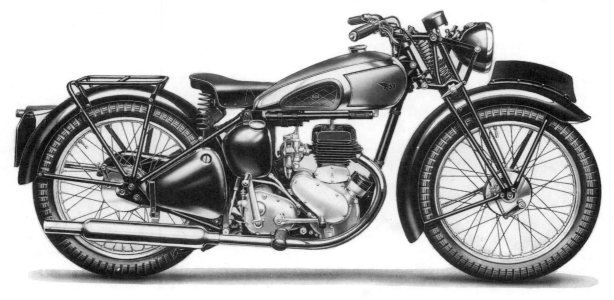

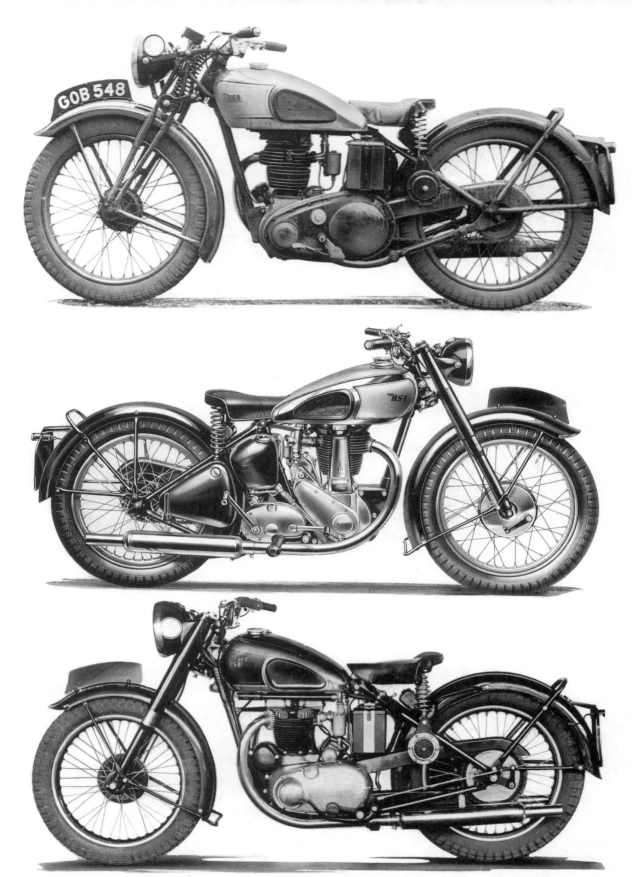

Top
Matching BSA C11 with ohv for the slightly more sporting rider, but little different from the side-valve model

Centre
For more serious work, BSA offered this 499cc

B33 in 1947, and it continued right up to 1960 with its solid and reliable performance

Bottom
The early BSA 495cc vertical twin, as in 1947, in a rigid frame and with a saddle

parts other than the engine top half. Of the others, there were detail changes and the sports models became Silver Stars to go with the Gold Star which continued only in its 496cc size. The range was completed as always by the massive 985cc V-twin, which was still much as it had been in 1930, its oil pump bolted to the outside of the timing chest and still with its sight glass. The auxiliary hand pump had, however, gone. The machine itself continued to fulfil its role of a sturdy plodder to pull a sidecar along and it did this as well as always.

Despite the stringencies of wartime, BSA had not one but two new models in their 1940 range although many older ones were dropped. The two new models were both of 348cc capacity and the more mundane was the C12, which had side valves and was modelled strongly on the C10. The second model was the B29 and the forerunner of the post-war big singles. It retained the usual BSA design but was based on the heavier M-series engine, had fully enclosed valve gear and hairpin valve springs It was a basically simple and sturdy engine that was tough and successful.

However, before BSA could really reap their reward with it they had to produce all manner of armaments for the Services, including some 126,000 motorcycles. Nearly all were the prosaic 496cc M20 which

Top
The 1948 BSA M33 model produced by fitting the 499cc ohv B33 engine into the heavy-duty cycle parts shared by the M20 and M21 side-valve models

Left
An M33 doing its duty attached to a single-seat sidecar, which it would haul along with little trouble

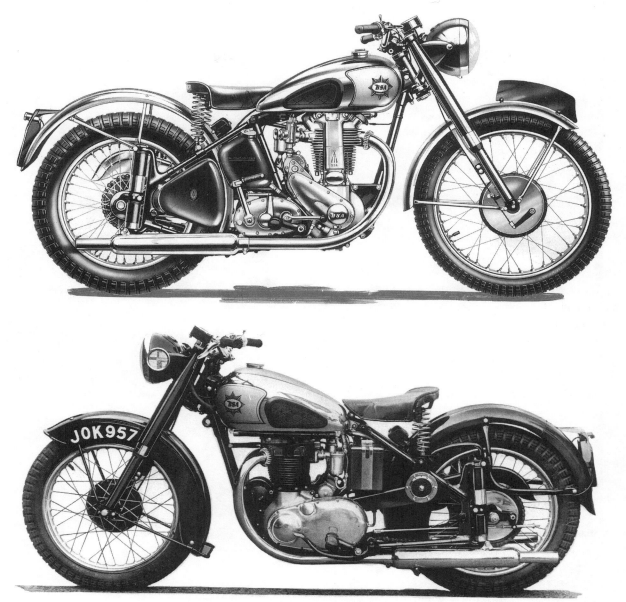

Top
*The first post-war Gold Star was this 1949 B32GS,
which set the style for the machine from then on*

Above
*First of the sports twins was this 1949 Star Twin, which had two
carburettors and was supplied in the plunger frame as standard*

was tough and reliable so just what the army needed. There were also a small number of C10s built for training purposes while the B29 was developed into the WB30 in answer to a call for a new service model that was lighter and more agile. However, the needs of wartime prevented it going into production but it was to lead to a major postwar range.

It was August 1945 when BSA announced their post-war range, which comprised just four models. However, these covered the learner, commuter, tourer and sidecar markets quite well, and within a few years the BSA range was to be the largest in the country. At first they just offered the C10, C11 and M20 from pre-war days but added one new model, the 348cc ohv B31 which was based on the B29. It alone had telescopic forks, the others retaining their girders but the C models did get a separate oil tank.

The four models formed the basis of much of the BSA single range for the next decade or so and before the end of the year were joined by the 591cc sv M21. Within a month the five had become six, with the appearance of the B32, a competition version of the B31. This was aimed at both the trials and scrambles rider and most of it was pure B31, but with a 21in. front wheel, competition tyres and much more chrome-plating.

In April 1946 the C-range machines received hydraulically-damped, telescopic front forks and in September that year BSA announced their new vertical twin-cylinder model, the A7, from which an extensive range was to come over the years. The 495cc engine was a 360-degree vertical twin, of mainly conventional construction, with an iron head and barrel. The layout utilised a single camshaft for all four valves, located at the rear of the crankcase and gear driven with the train extending on to the rear-mounted magneto. The dynamo was clamped to the front of the engine and had a chain drive, while the oil pump went in the timing case with a worm drive from the crankshaft.

The four-speed gearbox was a separate assembly that bolted to the rear of the crankcase, which was formed to suit. The effect was the same as unit construction, and the appearance was enhanced by a handsome, light-alloy chaincase, which enclosed the primary drive and included a tensioner for the chain. The engine unit went into a rigid frame with the standard telescopic forks and much of the remaining cycle parts were as for the B31, but adapted to the twin frame. A patented telescopic stand was fitted to the first few twins, but failed to inspire much confidence, for the result seemed unstable. The speedometer went into the top of the tank, which was chrome plated with black or Devon red panels, and the rest of the machine was finished in one of those two colours, and was matched by the rims.

The rest of the range continued as it was for 1947, joined by yet another new model, the B33 which was a 499cc version of the B31 and virtually identical. It was soon joined by a competition version, listed as the B34. For 1948 one further single was added by slotting the 499cc ohv B33 engine into the M20 frame and forks to make the M33. This had a brighter finish as standard and a little more pep for the sidecar driver, for whom it was intended.

In June 1948 one of the best known of all BSA models made its debut as the 123cc Bantam. This simple two-stroke was to become their most popular model, and it sold round the world in large numbers. The engine unit had been announced three months

Above
Looking over a Bantam in 1955 to see if it would meet their needs if a pillion seat was added

Below
The Beeza scooter shown late in 1955 at Earls Court, but not put into production

before and was, in fact, a mirror-image copy of the pre-war DKW RT125.

The engine was built in unit with its three-speed gearbox and was based on a vertically-split crankcase, in which ran the pressed-up crankshaft, a cast-iron barrel and an alloy head. The Wipac flywheel magneto and generator for the direct lights went on the left, the primary drive on the right to the very sturdy, three-plate clutch, which drove the cross-over gearbox. The gear pedal and kickstart went on the right on concentric shafts, and the design enabled the machine to be kicked over when in gear, a rare feature in Britain at that time.

The complete unit went into a rigid loop frame with light telescopic front forks. There was a petroil tank, saddle, rear carrier and toolbox, drum brakes, and a flat silencer that had a nice line to it. The front mudguard was sprung and deeply valanced, the bulb horn worked through the steering column, and the headlamp switch was cable operated from a handlebar lever.

The M-range was also in the news that month, for all three models were fitted with the telescopic front forks used by the A and B models.

By now the BSA empire was really getting into its post-war stride, and 1949 brought more new models and improved features for the existing ones. Foremost among the latter was the option of plunger rear suspension for the twin and the B-range singles. The most exciting news was the launch of the Gold Star to revive the 1938 name but in a new class with a 348cc engine. It was built in a super-sports style based on the B-range with an all-alloy engine, the usual gearbox and the plunger frame, but with chrome-plated mudguards.

There was a large range of options listed to suit road use, trials, scrambles or racing, for BSA had their eye on the TT Clubman's races. For this there was an

Assembly line of BSA Dandy machines in the Small Heath works around 1957

Below
The 1956 BSA B31 which retained its 1945 engine with little change, but now had a new frame, tank, seat and wheels

extension pipe to go with an open exhaust, then allowed, provision for a rev-counter, and a racing pad to go with the saddle. During the year the Gold Star, listed as the B32GS, was joined by a larger 499cc version which was built to the same specification and with the same options.

Left
*The C10L was the final form of the 249cc
BSA side-valve model*

Below centre
*By 1958 the A10 Golden Flash was only built
in pivoted-fork-frame form, even for sidecar
use, but it still made a nice outfit*

Right
*The DBD34 was the final form of the 499cc
Gold Star and is seen here in its 1958
Clubman build*

Bottom
*The first 172cc Bantam was the 1958 D5, and
this example is being made to work for its living by
the full load of AA gear it carries*

The final new model for 1949 was the A7 Star Twin, which was a sports version of the original with the plunger frame as standard and a brighter finish for its tank and wheel rims, making it a very handsome motorcycle.

There were two more models, various options and some detail changes for 1950, the most important being the 646cc A10 Golden Flash twin. On the surface this was an enlarged A7 but, in fact, the engine had been revised, using the original basic design simply as a starting point so few parts remained common. That aside, the machine was much like the old one, and the gearbox continued bolted to the back of the crankcase. Both rigid and plunger models were offered, and the model did have the benefit of an 8in. front brake from the start. The finish was new, being golden beige for all painted parts. This gave the machine its name. There was an all-black finish as well, which tended to be used for home market machines at first, but in time the beige became the norm and was generally preferred.

At the other end of the scale, a competition version of the Bantam appeared. This had a raised saddle, fatter rear tyre, tilted silencer, blade mudguards and a decompressor. It proved a handy tool, for its light weight made it easy to paddle through sections if things went wrong, which was better than stopping. There were options of plunger rear suspension for road or competition Bantams, and a Lucas alternator and battery lighting system. Either or both options could be taken, although most road models with the Lucas equipment would also have the plunger frame.

The A7 and Star Twin were revised in line with the A10 for 1951, so many components became common to both engine sizes. Both had a single Amal carburettor and, as before, the A7 was in a rigid frame with the plunger version being an option, but standard for the Star Twin. There were changes for the more prosaic models that year, with options of plunger rear suspension and a four-speed gearbox for the C10 and C11 machines, the plunger option also made available for the M-range.

The rigid-frame versions of the A7 and A10 were not continued into 1952 and for 1953 there was a headlamp cowl for the larger models, a dualseat option for the Bantam and C-ranges, and an 8in. front brake for the B33. The Gold Star machines went over to a frame with pivoted-fork, rear suspension, and in this form were known as the BB models, the earlier ones being designated ZB from the engine number prefix. For the export market there was a hotter twin in the form of the 646cc Super Flash which had a tuned engine but retained the plunger frame for which the power was really too much. Not sold in Britain, it was well suited to the long, straight American roads it was intended for.

During 1953 BSA joined the cyclemotor market, and their solution was the Winged Wheel, which was fitted in place of the standard rear wheel, the only other part the fuel tank, which was made as a flat carrier to fit above the wheel. Its simple 35cc two-stroke engine and gear transmission drove the full-width hub which also acted as the brake-drum surface.

There were major changes to most of the range for 1954, when the pivoted-fork frame came into more general use. The original user, the BB Gold Star, was joined by the CB model, which had a revised engine with much deeper finning and a swept-back exhaust pipe. The B31 and B33 followed suit with the frame, although the rigid and plunger models stayed in the range until the ends of 1954 and 1955 respectively. With the new frames came a dualseat, a slim oil tank tucked into the corner of the subframe on the right side, and a matching toolbox and battery on the left. The competition B32 and B34 went over to a rigid

The BSA C15 was based on the Triumph Cub and was to sire a whole range of models in the next decade

frame, had the all-alloy engine as standard, and were also listed with the pivoted-fork frame as an option, when they became very similar to the ZB Gold Star.

The new frame and all its matching features was also used by the twins, although the plunger-frame models continued for one more year, and the A10 until 1957 to keep the sidecar buyer happy. The touring twins in the new frame remained the A7 and A10, but the engine and gearbox became separate units. The sports models were the A7 Shooting Star and A10 Road Rocket, which had many common parts between them and the tourers, but had light-alloy cylinder heads. They kept to the single carburettor, but differed from the tourers in respect of their finish.

Among the smaller models, the Bantams with Lucas electrics were phased out, but the D1 model was still available in rigid or plunger frames, with direct or battery lighting, and in road or competition form. It was joined by the 148cc D3, which was produced by simply boring out the engine, but also had heavier front forks and a larger front brake. The road model had the plunger frame as standard, but either electric system, while the competition version had the choice of frames.

The C-range, too, was altered from 1954 with a change to alternator electrics. The side-valve model became the C10L, using some Bantam cycle parts, and only came with three speeds and a plunger frame. The ohv machine was the C11G. The rigid-frame version of this came with three speeds, but the plunger one with three or four. Following all these changes, there was little alteration for 1955, but a DB version of the Gold Star joined the BB and CB versions.

At the end of the year there was a major reduction in the number of models, along with news of some new ones, and this simplified the range. Out went the

Winged Wheel, the rigid and competition Bantams, while the D3 engine went into a new frame with pivoted-fork rear suspension. In the 250 class, the C10L acquired a four-speed gearbox and continued with the plunger frame, while the C11G was replaced by the C12 which had the same engine, four speeds and a pivoted-fork frame. The B31 and B33 also changed to full-width, light alloy hubs that came from the Ariel range, but the plunger-frame versions were no more. It was the same with the rigid competition models, and the B32 and B34 were only listed with the pivoted-fork frame.

The Gold Star line-up was simplified, being reduced to the two DB versions, which were joined by the DBD in the 499cc size only, this very similar. All had the option of the 190mm, full-width front hub and a five-gallon alloy tank added to the list. The Gold Stars were only built in road, scrambles, road racing and Clubman's forms that year, the first being phased out that season. The side-valve range lost the M20 and the M33 in rigid form, but the M21 with either frame and the plunger M33 were given the 8in. front brake, while the twins stayed much as they were.

Two new models were shown at the end of 1955, one being a 70cc scooterette and the other a 200cc scooter. The former was called the Dandy and had a moped-style, pressed-steel beam frame with short, leading-link front forks, and a pivoted fork for the rear wheel. The engine and gearbox were built as part of this rear fork, and it was this area that was both the clever part and the flaw in the design as the ignition points were buried in the middle of the engine and the gearbox had a preselector control which was much more trouble than the type by then common on continental mopeds.

The scooter was called the Beeza and had a side-valve engine laid across the frame, so it drove back to a four-speed gearbox and then by shaft to the rear wheel. All the mechanics were fitted into a series of alloy castings and the assembly pivoted to provide rear suspension. At the front were short leading-link forks, while the works were enclosed in scooter style and electric starting was standard. The machine appeared to have potential, but by then the market was used to light, zippy Italian scooters with two-stroke engines, so a side-valve plodder was unlikely to find much favour and BSA did not proceed with it.

The Dandy did not appear until 1957 when it was the only new machine for the firm was nearing the end of an era and approaching some major changes. This was highlighted at the end of the season by the disappearance of a number of old favourites from the range. Out went the C10L, for a new 250cc range was in development, and the M33 and plunger A10, to leave only the M21 for the sidecar man. This old stager was now mainly sold to the AA and the services, for there were few private owners left for such machines. The competition singles were dropped, for the trend was to smaller and lighter machines for trials or scrambles. Out went the DB Gold Stars, so only the DBD remained, and solely in scrambles and Clubman's form as a 500.

The D3 and A10 Road Rocket were replaced by new versions for 1958, and the smaller was enlarged to 172cc, becoming the D5, but the D1 continued. The sports A10 became the Super Rocket with detail improvements. The other three twins continued and were joined by the 646cc Rocket Scrambler, which was built in street-scrambler form for the USA with open, waist-level exhaust pipes, no lights and off-road cycle parts. Among the singles, the C12 continued as it was,

and the Dandy ran on with some detail changes while the B31 and B33 went over to alternator electrics and coil ignition.

In September 1958 BSA launched the first of a new series of unit-construction singles, which were to run on to the end of the company. The machine was the 247cc C15, and while presented as new, it was, in truth, a stretched Tiger Cub and repeated many of the features of this model in its engine design and four-speed gearbox. The engine unit went into a simple loop frame with telescopic front and pivoted-fork rear suspension. Full-width drum brakes, similar to the others of the range, were fitted, along with a headlamp nacelle and dualseat. The oil tank and toolbox were blended into one by a central panel, which carried the ignition switch, while the lighting switch went into the headlamp.

With the advent of the C15, the C12 was dropped, and for 1959 the D5 gave way to the D7. This used the same engine unit with an extra cover to streamline the generator, but in a revised frame and new forks based on those used by the Tiger Cub. The two B models continued, although both had gone by the end of 1960, and the M21 was to special order and only in the plunger frame. The Gold Star was only in DBD form and as a Clubman's or scrambles model.

The twins in A7 and A10 forms continued, as did the Dandy, which was joined by a trio of scooters, but these were sold under the Sunbeam label. Once the road C15 was underway, it was joined in the New Year by two competition versions, listed as the C15S for scrambles and C15T for trials. These had minor changes inside the engine, raised exhaust systems and competition wheels and tyres, but retained much from the standard model.

Late B33 with alternator electrics, as built from 1958 and shown here with the optional full rear chaincase

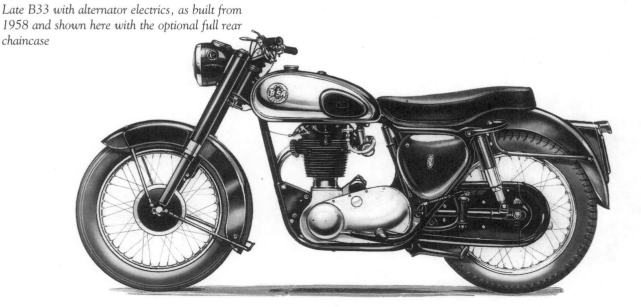

In this form, the BSA range entered the 1960s. The company was flush with success and sure it was set for a long period of prosperity. For this, they revamped the twins in 1962, expanded the unit-single range, and kept the Bantam, at least in 172cc form, for many years. It was, however, the beginning of a decline but, regardless of what was to come, BSA could look back on many years of producing some of the best motorcycles for all classes of user.

CALTHORPE

First seen before World War 1, this marque name was best known by one machine, the Ivory Calthorpe, by the end of the 1920s, thanks to the distinctive finish it had for its petrol tank and mudguards which made it stand out from the many sombre black machines of the times.

Introduced for 1929, it became Ivory the Second for 1930 with a new inclined 348cc ohv engine which had the magneto at the rear and dynamo at front. It drove a three-speed gearbox while the rest of the cycle side was conventional with girder forks.

For 1931 it became the Ivory III, with a four-speed gearbox, the option of coil or magneto ignition and a tank-top instrument panel. It was joined by the Ivory IV in 1932, and this was of 494cc but in other respects the same and also offered with the choice of ignition systems. Competition versions of the III and IV were also listed. At the show a third Calthorpe appeared as the 247cc Ivory Minor and this differed from the others in having a two-stroke engine based on a Villiers with auto-lube, but with the oil tank cast into the front of the crankcase. It retained the finish but was otherwise a basic lightweight.

A full range was announced for 1933 but in the event only the 494cc Ivory Major was built. It continued unchanged for 1934 when it was joined by the 247cc ohv Minor built in the same form. The 348cc

Ivory Junior returned in 1935 and the two larger engines had new heads with enclosed valve gear for 1936 when the competition versions reappeared.

For 1937 Calthorpe became one of the ranges sold exclusively by London dealers Pride & Clarke. For this purpose they lost their old colour and became the Red Calthorpe, which somehow lacked the same ring. The range itself stayed as it was with three road and two competition models with few alterations. It was the same for 1938 plus an option in green, but sales were not enough and the firm went into liquidation.

It was sold to Bruce Douglas, a member of the motorcycling family of Bristol, and in May 1939 a new range was announced. There were three models with 245, 348 and 497cc ohv Matchless engines with vertical cylinders but it is unlikely that any other than a prototype or two were ever built before war preparations led to the new company being given notice to quit their premises at Bristol Airport.

Post-war the Calthorpe name revived briefly, but was for a machine built by the firm that became DMW. This built a 122cc Villiers lightweight shown in prototype form as the Calthorpe-DMW in October 1947 but as a DMW when production began late in 1950.

CARLTON

A transient make which used bought-in components and first appeared in the early 1920s to sell in small numbers. For 1930 they offered their 500DP with Sturmey-Archer engine, handchange and chrome-plated tank.

They then dropped from sight to reappear in 1937 as one of many using the 122cc Villiers engine for a lightweight machine. It was much as others but sold well enough to continue to 1940 when production ceased.

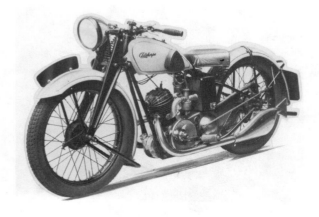

Left
Ivory Minor Calthorpe of 1932 fitted with a 247cc two-stroke engine and finished in the same style as the larger models

CHATER-LEA

Chater-Lea began by making bicycle parts and then motorcycle items for other firms but started to build complete machines in Edwardian times. In the 1920s they broke world records and became a leader in style, fitting saddle tanks as early as 1924.

In the mid-1920s the firm designed their own camshaft engine and the result was a 348cc face cam type that was still in use in 1936. The bottom half was conventional, but with a bevel gear to drive a vertical shaft which carried the two face cams. A cap went in the top of the shaft housing to give access to the cams, while the shaft itself was extended below the bevel gear to an oil pump in the crankcase. Both magneto and dynamo, when fitted, went in front of the crankcase and the engine went into a diamond frame with girder forks and rather vintage lines.

In 1928 the firm moved from London to Letchworth Garden City, then a development town,

and for the following year offered two other machines as well as the 348cc Camshaft Super Sports. One had a 545cc side-valve engine much on the lines of the ohc and which dated from the early 1920s and was sold as the Sports model. The other had a 247cc Villiers engine in a bolted-up frame and was listed as the Super Sportlette.

Only the four-strokes continued for 1931 and in 1932 the model names became Camshaft and Side-valve, but otherwise the two machines continued in their rather vintage style from year to year. The last camshaft model left the works in March 1935 and, along with the rest of the final batch, had a four-speed gearbox with footchange. The final Side-valve went to the AA in July 1936 as one of some 1200 combinations supplied over the years.

The company continued in business at Letchworth and half a century later they were still there in business.

CHELL

This Wolverhampton company announced two models for the 1939 season using the 98 and 122cc Villiers engines in loop frames which were much as others of the time except that there was the option of rear suspension. Production only lasted a few months, after which the make vanished from the lists with few machines built.

COMMANDER

A dramatic appearance on a stand at Earls Court late in 1952 introduced this new make and a range of three models with styling in total contrast to the norm of the time. They were made by the General Steel Group of Hayes, Middlesex, and all used the same beam frame with pivoted-fork rear and short leading-link front suspension. On to this basic structure went the startling bodywork, more expected at the Paris show than in Britain, with panels that flared and swept from end to end and a grill that enclosed the engine while the finish was in ivory and a choice of light blue, dark blue or maroon depending on model.

Rather sadly, all that was under this exciting styling were the prosaic Villiers 2F, 1F and 10D engines, in 99 and 122cc sizes, to give the models as Commanders I, II and III, with the same numbers of transmission speeds. The enterprise really deserved something a little better. Whether this was the reason or not, the make left the market as quickly as it arrived, and no more was heard of it.

Top
Later 122cc Carlton with Villiers engine and built from 1937-40, this being from its first year

Top right
1930 Chater-Lea Camshaft model with 348cc engine

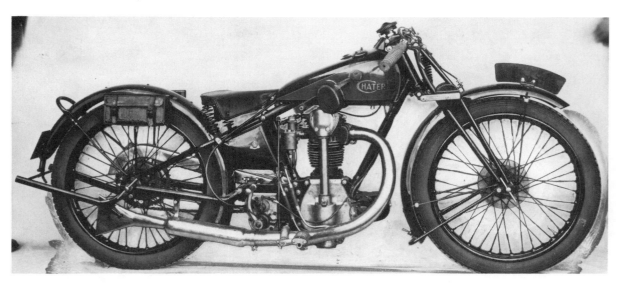

Centre
545cc Chater-Lea called the Sports model in 1930

Bottom
*1930 Super Sports Chater-Lea two-stroke with
247cc Villiers engine*

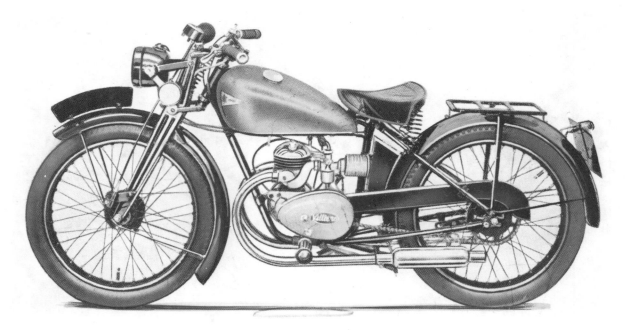

CORGI

The notion of a small motorcycle that can be folded up for easy transit when not in use has been around for a long time, and the Corgi was such a machine. It was developed from the wartime Welbike, which was built for parachute drops and used a 98cc Villiers engine to propel its very basic chassis.

The Welbike was made by Excelsior and proved useful in both its original role for the paratroops, and for short-distance duties on camps and airfields around the globe. After the war the design was made more suitable for the civilian market, and the results often confused with the Welbike. The Corgi, as the post-war model was called, used a 98cc Excelsior Spryt engine, but was made by Brockhouse Engineering of Southport, who also built the engine under licence.

The first news of the machine came in 1946, although it was 1948 before supplies reached the public. The engine was a two-stroke, much as the Villiers Junior de Luxe, with horizontal cylinder and countershaft with clutch. It went into a duplex cradle frame with the petroil tank on top and the saddle on a pillar

Above
1939 Chell with 122cc Villiers engine

Right
The Commander range on show at Earls Court in late 1952, when the machine's strange styling created great interest

so that it could be lowered for storage. The forks were
rigid and the handlebars could also be folded down
while the wheels were small, the lighting direct and the
rider had to push start the engine.

It might have been crude transport but it was
available so sold well for shopping and trips to work.
During 1948 a kickstart was added along with a dog
clutch to provide a neutral for starting and this model
became the Mark II, the original the Mark I. As a further asset, a sidecar platform became available with a
steel box and canvas top. This proved very handy for
taking parcels to the post or when collecting the shopping.

During 1949 a two-speed gearbox and telescopic
forks became available as options and in 1950 an
enclosed bodywork was offered which turned the
machine into a scooter but prevented it being folded.
There was also a banking sidecar for this version, which
was intended for carrying loads and not a person.

By 1952 the Corgi, in Mark IV form, was fitted
with the gearbox and forks as standard, and had a
weather shield and luggage grid added. It continued
like this for two more years, but the advent of the
moped and improvements in standards brought it to an
end late in 1954. It had been a useful method of transport, but its day had run.

Below
*The Corgi, which was developed from the wartime Welbike,
but had an Excelsior 98cc Spryt engine*

COTTON

The Cotton hailed from Gloucester, and from their
start in 1920 was hallmarked by its frame. This dated
back a further seven years to when Francis Willoughby
Cotton first laid down his triangulated design that was
still little changed in 1939. He was also a trained
lawyer so well able to fend off any attempts to poach
the design, and during the 1920s the temptation was
certainly there.

The worth of the frame was shown by success in
the TT and this served to establish the small firm in
the public's eye. This worked well up to the Depression,
but by 1930 the effect was wearing off and they ran
into harder times. To cope they offered an extensive
range of models using proprietary engines, but always in
their very stiff, rigid and light frame.

Engines were Blackburne or the slightly cheaper
JAP plus one Sturmey-Archer and one Villiers two-
stroke. The models were numerous, but all had a
Burman gearbox, and in 1930 the ohv machines had
saddle tanks while the others retained the older style
with it between the top frame rails.

The two-stroke was of 247cc, while the side-valve

machines came in 295, 348 and 495cc sizes, all with Blackburne engines. The 495cc had the engine inclined, but the other three were installed vertically. All the ohv machines had their engines at the slope and were listed with Blackburne and JAP engines in 348 and 495cc sizes, plus a 242cc JAP. Most continued for 1931 while 1932 saw all models with saddle tanks and more JAP engines plus Rudge ones and Villiers and JAP 150s. More 250s were added for 1933 to bring the range up to 17 models with two more for the next year, all still in the distinctive triangulated frame.

It was much the same for the next two years but 1937 saw the range reduced and using Villiers engines for the small two-strokes and JAP ones for the rest, some of these new with a high camshaft. This kept the firm going for the next two years with little changed although that year brought a new type of JAP engine whose fins gave it the looks of a two-stroke. Also new that year was a model with a 9D 122cc Villiers engine to sell at a low price, but it still kept the triangulated frame.

While never a large company Cotton certainty stood out from the crowd of runners using similar engines due to their frames and their TT successes and during the war supplied a few machines to the services. These were the 1939 500 fitted with the JAP engine of two-stroke appearance and they proved durable under heavy loads.

The firm returned to motorcycles during 1954 with a simple lightweight called the Vulcan. This used the 197cc Villiers 8E engine in a rigid frame, built on the triangulated principles of the past with light telescopic forks. There was a dualseat, battery lighting and electric horn to complete a neat, if conventional, machine.

For 1955 the Vulcan was joined by the Cotanza, which used the 242cc British Anzani engine in a new frame with pivoted-fork rear suspension and during 1955 this was used for another version of the Vulcan, but fitted with the three-speed 9E engine. For 1956 it was also offered with four speeds, and the Cotanza with the 322cc Anzani twin engine added. One further model was the Trials, which used the 9E engine, four-speed gearbox and pivoted-fork frame. The cycle parts were altered to suit its job, with competition tyres, no lights and a saddle.

During 1956 the original Vulcan was dropped, and for 1957 the whole range continued with one addition. This was the Villiers Twin model, which had the 2T engine in the Cotanza cycle parts. The complete range then continued for 1958. The whole range had Armstrong leading-link forks for 1959, when it remained unchanged, except for the Villiers Twin. This was renamed the Herald and given a rather crude

design of rear enclosure which emphasised the limited resources of the small company and their need to produce such parts with the minimum of costly tooling. They did add another model to the list that year, in the form of the Messenger, which was powered by the 324cc Villiers 3T twin-cylinder engine. The cycle parts were mainly the same as for the Herald, other than for a 21in. front wheel and bigger brakes.

The use of the Villiers twin engine made the Anzani ones redundant, so for 1960 the Cotanzas were only listed to special order. The other models continued as they were and were joined by a Scrambler, powered by a 246cc Villiers 33A engine. From then on, the Cotton range expanded greatly, a sports 249cc twin, the Double Gloucester, arriving in March 1960, and all manner of road, trials, scrambles and road-racing models during the 1960s.

Above
JAP-powered Cotton from 1937 and typical of the marque throughout the decade

Right
The 242cc British Anzani twin engine, with rotary valve, installed in a Cotton Cotanza and fitted with a siamesed exhaust system

Right
*Cotton trials model
based on an 8E engine,
the pivoted-fork frame
and leading-link forks.
In production, in
1956, the 9E was used*

Right
*The 1959 Cotton
Herald with the 249cc
Villiers 2T engine and
rather crude rear enclo-
sure*

COVENTRY EAGLE

This company was located in Coventry and had its
roots in Victorian times with bicycles and early powered tricycles. They always used proprietary parts, but
in a neat assembly with a good finish, so they survived
longer than some of their competitors.

During the 1920s they introduced their Flying 8
series with big V-twin JAP engines and very stylish
tanks, somewhat like the Brough, and at the other end
of the scale came utility models. The latter went into
pressed-steel frames from 1928, which was novel in
England even if more common for Europe.

The beginning of the 1930s saw Coventry Eagle
offering a good range of models to cover most people's
aspirations. All were in their traditional finish of black

with cream tank panels and a carmine tank nose, which gave them a distinctive air.

At the lower end of the range were four machines with 147, 172 and 196cc Villiers engines in the duplex, pressed-steel, channel frame. This had the fuel tank perched on top and pressed-steel forks as well. The rest of the range had tubular frames and four of these had vertically-mounted JAP engines, two side-valves of 300 and 346cc, the other two ohv and of 346 and 490cc. There was also one with a 482cc side-valve, inclined engine. The other three singles had Sturmey-Archer engines, either sloping as in the case of the 495cc sv or just inclined a little for the ohv 348 and 495cc ones. At the head of the range came the three Flying 8 models with V-twin, 1-litre, JAP engines, two with side valves and one ohv.

The range was thinned down a little for 1931 and some more the next year as the firm concentrated on what sold best to keep them going. This meant dropping the Flying 8 models and concentrating on two-strokes in the main. Most interest centred on the Silent Superb model, which had a 147cc Coventry Eagle engine and was built with a full luxury specification. The engine was actually made by the Levis factory and had very extensive silencing with expansion box and twin silencers to keep it quiet. The frame was an improved version of the pressed-steel type, fitted with blade girder forks and the machine came fitted with massive legshields that curled under the rider's feet to give ample protection.

The Silent Superb was excellent value at £23 10s., but for those who could not stretch to this there was the Eclipse, which was simpler and cheaper. Even cheaper was the Marvel that used a 98cc Villiers engine with two-speed gearbox in a tubular frame. For all that it still had legshields.

Below
1931 Coventry Eagle Flying Eight with side-valve V-twin engine

Bottom
The pressed-steel frame of the Coventry Eagle was a feature for many years and is here seen on a 1931 example with a 196cc engine

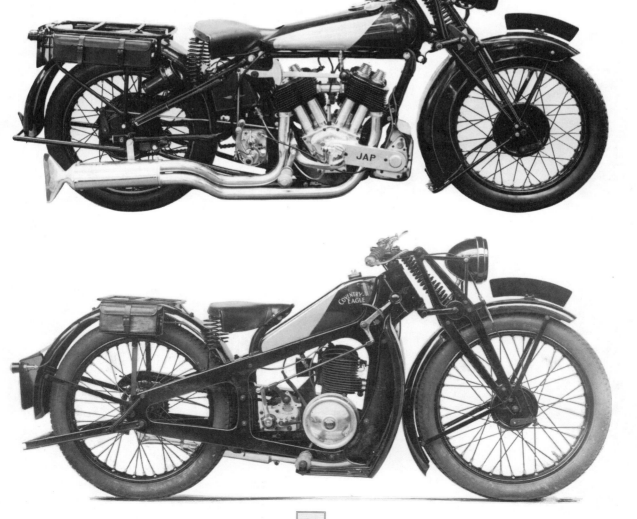

Above
Very basic 1932 98cc H16 Coventry Eagle Marvel

Below
*249cc Coventry Eagle Pullman model N11 of 1937 with
semi-elliptic rear springs and massive cast-alloy silencer*

There were only three models for 1933, for trading was very hard in those times. Sensibly the firm dropped the four-strokes and concentrated on their two-strokes although they dropped the Coventry Eagle engines, which had proved unsatisfactory, these being replaced by Villiers. This left the 148cc Wonder which used the pressed-steel frame, plus the Silent Superbs in 147 and 247cc forms, still with extensive silencing. During the year these were joined by another with the 148cc engine. For 1934 most continued and the larger was also listed complete with a sidecar or in competition form. There were also two new models with 245cc ohv JAP engines in the pressed-steel frame but different specifications.

There was little change for 1935 or 1936, but late in the year, at the Olympia show, the firm caused a sensation when they launched three new models as Pullman Two-seaters. These used either 247 or 249cc Villiers engines or a 246cc ohv Blackburne. It was the chassis that was special and it was an extension of the

pressed-steel design. For the Pullman, the frame had two deep channel-section members that extended to the tail of the rear mudguard and were cross-braced for rigidity and to carry the engine and gearbox. There were also legshields and access panels where needed, while at the rear went a massive rear mudguard-cum-valance which completely enclosed the wheel down to the frame. The frame extension was due to the rear suspension which was unusual in fitting semi-elliptic springs which lay outside the frame members. Front suspension was by girders and silencing was extensive with cast-aluminium chambers and a silencer.

There was one further model with a 249cc Villiers engine for that year but it was dropped for 1937 along with the Pullmans with the 247cc Villiers or

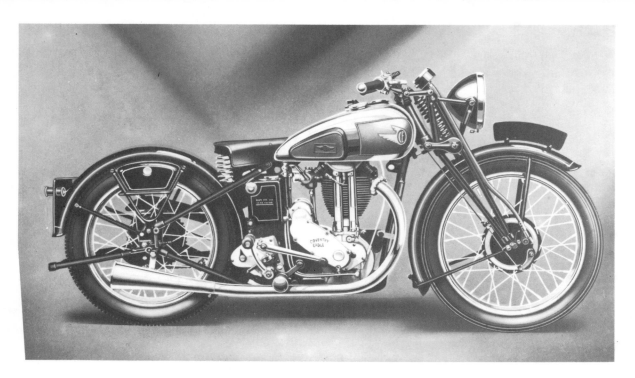

Top
*1938 P50 Coventry Eagle with 497cc Matchless
engine and natty megaphone silencer*

Above
*The model Q9 Coventry Eagle of 1939 with 98cc
Villiers engine and plunger rear suspension*

Blackburn engines which just left the 249cc one which had its rear springs moved to inside the frame members. The 148cc and 247cc Silent Superbs continued much as they were in their pressed-steel frames. Four versions of the larger model were still listed with direct lighting, dynamo, de luxe or with high-level exhausts.

New for 1937 were three four-strokes listed as Flying models with ohv Matchless engines of 245, 348 or 497cc vertically mounted in the tubular frame which had Webb forks and a four-speed gearbox. 1938 brought two new models, both called Cadets and with 122cc and, for export, 98cc Villiers engines in a simple tubular frame with blade girders. Both offered basic utilitarian motorcycling.

Right
*Coventry Eagle R14 98cc autocycle of
1940 with neat side shields to enclose
the engine and protect the rider*

The six Silent Superbs continued with few changes for 1939 as did the two Cadets and three Flying models, but the Pullman was no longer listed. New were two more Cadets with plunger rear suspension. At the show Coventry Eagle had one further model to offer, the Auto-ette. This was an autocycle propelled by a 98cc Villiers Junior engine and much as others of its ilk with simple frame and heavy-duty, rigid cycle forks.

A reduced range was announced for 1940 with two Silent Superbs with 148 and 247cc engines and these were joined by a 98cc version using the smallest Villiers engine. Two Flying models were listed, and the range was completed by the Auto-ette. In March this was joined by a version which had neat side shields added to enclose the engine unit and made in one piece with the chainguards on each side of the machine. Like the rest of the range it was well thought out but like many others, the marque failed to survive the war.

COVENTRY-VICTOR

This firm began to build flat-twin engines for sale in 1911 and a complete machine in 1919. By 1930 they offered two models using this engine type as the 499cc ohv Royal Sports and 688cc sv Super Six. Both had similar cycle parts with a three-speed Sturmey-Archer gearbox under the engine, duplex frame and similar

style. They also built a speedway model using the smaller engine and this had a shorter wheelbase frame that was adopted for the road models in 1931.

For 1932 the three models continued and the speedway machine was offered with a 600cc ohv engineas well as the 499cc one. This larger engine went into the Speed Six in 1933 but by the next year the range was down to the 499cc ohv and 688cc sv road models and only the later for 1935. After that the vintage-style solos were dropped and the firm built three-wheelers up to 1938.

CYC-AUTO

This machine was a pioneer of the pre-war autocycle and post-war clip-on and moped, built to provide basic powered transport at minimal cost. It was announced in March 1934 and was unusual in having a worm drive from its 98cc two-stroke engine. For the rest it was bicycle and listed as the model A, joined in 1935 by the open-framed B.

For 1937 they became models C and D, joined by the CV and DV, which had a Villiers engine. This continued for 1938, during when the firm ran into money problems and sold out to the Scott company who revised the engine unit to add a clutch while continuing to offer the Villiers at a lower price.

For 1939 the engines were made at the Scott works and the machines offered in Ladies' or Gents' form, both models also available in de luxe form with a

sprung fork. A tradesman carrier version was listed and in these forms the Cyc-Auto ran up to the war before production ceased until the end of hostilities.

Postwar, its production remained in Yorkshire, although the machine itself was built in London. For 1949 the Cyc-Auto was joined by the Carrier model, aimed at the delivery market and fitted out to suit. In 1950 the Carrier model continued as it was, but the other became the Superior, and for 1952 the Carrier was fitted with the blade girders. From then on the two models continued as they were, but were no longer listed by 1955.

CYCLAID

This cycle attachment differed from others sat over the rear wheel in that the drive was by V-belt. It was made by British Salmson at Raynes Park, London, and first appeared during 1950. The engine was a 31cc two-stroke of conventional form but all-alloy to keep its weight down. It drove a countershaft which carried the belt pulley while the controls were of the simplest. The engine worked well, so the Cyclaid remained in production until 1955, which was as long as most.

Far left, top
Coventry-Victor 688cc Super Six showing the old-fashioned lines and the flat-twin engine they used in side- and overhead-valve forms

Far left
The 1935 Cyc-Auto in its early A model form with its own make of engine and unusual worm gear in the frame bottom bracket

Top
1939 edition of the Cyc-Auto Ladies model with the Scott engine

Above
The Cyc-Auto in its 1940 form, which was continued in the early post-war years

CYCLEMASTER

One of the better known attachments but which came as a complete rear wheel to replace the stock one. It was made by EMI at Haynes, Middlesex, and appeared in 1950. The engine and transmission were all contained within a large drum which formed the wheel hub and was vented for cooling. The engine was a simple 25.7cc two-stroke with disc valve induction but otherwise conventional and the transmission was by chain in stages. The petroil tank fitted in the upper part of the drum and covers concealed the mechanism.

The unit sold well, and was bored out to 32.6cc for 1952. At the same time, lighting coils were added to

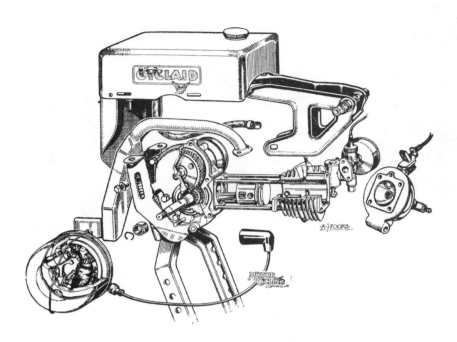

the flywheel magneto and the finish changed to grey. In
the middle of 1953, Cyclemaster offered complete
machines, one even with a pillion pad, plus the
Roundsman built as a delivery bicycle with small front
wheel and large carrier. It was ideal for a tradesman,
especially if the roads were hilly or the wind inclined to
blow hard.

The next move came for 1955, when the
Cyclemate was created in the moped image with the
engine mounted ahead of the bottom bracket of a frame
built by the Norman company. It was a good attempt,
but lacked the style of the mopeds then beginning to
arrive in Britain. Despite this, the firm continued to
build the Cyclemate and the wheel unit for several
more years.

Before then, in 1956, the firm tried another tack
with an unorthodox small scooter called the Piatti,
after its Italian designer. The machine was low-built
with a monocoque body which concealed the mechanics, there being two small access panels, but for anything else the machine was laid on its side.

The 124cc two-stroke engine unit, complete with
transmission and rear wheel, was pivoted to the body to
act as the rear suspension arm and a leading arm went
at the front. Both standard and de luxe versions were
built, but only up to 1958, after which just the
Cyclemate trickled on to 1960.

Left
Cyclemaster taking the hard work out of riding a bicycle against the wind and on hills, whether carrying a load or not

Below
The Cyclemate, which appeared in 1955 to combine the Cyclemaster engine with a Norman cycle built for it

CYMOTA

This 1950 clip-on had a conventional, 45cc two-stroke engine, which drove the front wheel with a friction-roller. The unit sat above the wheel, ahead of the steering column, and was nicely styled with a louvred cowling, in which a small headlamp was fitted. The Cymota came and went in two short years, for even by 1951 the clip-on era was beginning to show signs of age.

DAYTON

Dayton were a bicycle firm who occasionally produced powered machines prewar. Their first came in 1913, but soon lapsed, and they reappeared in 1939 with an autocycle which was of typical construction and powered by a 98cc Villiers engine. It was only built for that one short season.

On their fiftieth anniversary as a bicycle maker, in 1955, the firm entered the scooter market with a luxury model they called the Albatross. It was powered by the 224cc Villiers 1H engine and was larger and heavier than the popular Italian models, so it was also more expensive.

Construction was typical for the type with a tubular frame, leading-link front and pivoted-fork rear suspension, wheels with split rims and drum brakes. On

Top
A Piatti scooter, as built under licence by Cyclemaster from 1956, but only until 1958

Right
The Cymota clip-on went over the front wheel and had a bonnet that carried a headlight powered by the engine magneto

Top
Dayton autocycle with 98cc Villiers engine as built for 1939, its only year in production

Above
Dayton Albatross in 1955 with Villiers 224cc 1H engine unit

this went a body with apron, floor with deep tunnel and rear section with panels for access and a hinged dualseat over the petroil tank.

In 1957 the scooter was joined by the Albatross Twin which used the 249cc Villiers 2T engine but was otherwise the same. Both had a new front mudguard for 1958 which improved the looks, but in March the twin changed its name to Empire and the two were joined by four others, two still using the 2T engine and two the 246cc 2H single. All kept the Albatross name as a prefix which made some clumsy. The new models had

some revisions to the body and other details to enhance the luxury specification.

The range was down to four for 1959, comprising two twins, the 246cc single and a new 174cc Flamenco model which was lighter in style and concept with its Villiers 2L engine. The new frame and body were shared with Panther and Sun to reduce costs and each styled the result to suit themselves.

The Flamenco was far more in the style of the scooter world than the original Albatross, despite a rather heavy appearance to the front mudguard. It continued for 1960 with the Twin, the Single to special order only, but at the end of that season the make went out of production.

DIAMOND

A minor make from before World War 1 to 1928, who reappeared in 1930 with just one model which had a 247cc Villiers engine in a set of conventional cycle parts. For 1931 this was joined by 245 and 346cc models with ohv JAP engines and a 346cc Villiers one. The two-stroke models and the larger ohv continued for 1932, plus one with a 490cc sv JAP engine.

There was no range given for 1933, but the firm did continue, and added a 148cc Villiers model to suit the new taxation limit, using a simple frame much as many others. From then on the company turned to trailers and milk floats, although late in 1935 it was suggested that they would make motorcycles to use Villiers engines to special order.

DKR

This scooter was built in Wolverhampton and launched in July 1957 as the Dove. It was typical of the type in design although the appearance was somewhat heavy. The engine was the 147cc Villiers 30C with fan cooling and the model was as well-equipped as others of the time. In February 1958 the Dove was joined by two more models using the same body to create the Pegasus with the 148cc Villiers 31C unit and the Defiant with the 197cc 9E engine.

They were joined in 1959 by the Manx with the 249cc Villiers 2T engine and late that year the Dove II replaced the original using the 31C engine. In the same way the Pegasus II took over with the 174cc 2L engine in 1960 but the two smaller models were dropped at the end of that year when the firm launched the lighter-looking Capella series which took them on to 1966.

Far left, top
The Albatross for 1956, but still with rather unfortunate front end. The name did nothing to help, either

Far left, bottom
148cc Diamond from 1933, the final year the firm was listed

Below
DKR Dove in 1957 with heavy front end due to the forward mounting of the fuel tank

DMW

This firm was briefly associated with the Calthorpe name just after the war, when a small prototype was built, using a 122cc Villiers engine fitted into a rigid frame with telescopic forks. Its most noticeable feature was a saddle mounted on a single post, bicycle style, which, thus, was adjustable for height.

It was April 1950 before any more was heard of the Sedgely firm, but then came news of a small range of lightweights. The machines were available with Villiers 1F, 10D or 6E engines, and the two larger with rigid frames or plunger rear suspension. All had MP telescopic forks, which the firm themselves had developed and were to sell to other companies for many years, and the machines were nicely finished in turquoise blue.

The smallest model was dropped during 1951 when the others were built to various specifications including a new one using frames built from square-section tubing. For 1952 these became the standard, the tubular frames being dropped, and competition models based on the road ones added. Plunger frames were standard for 1953 but the 122cc rigid model was listed as the Coronation to mark the event of that year.

There was a considerable change to the model line-up for 1954, as DMW established a link with the

Above
*The 1952 competition DMW with square-tube frame,
plunger rear stroke engine unit and offered for 1954*

Below
*The basic DMW 200 Mk VIII with Villers 8E engine
in tubular frame as listed for 1957*

French AMC engine company. This was Ateliers de Mécanique du Centre, nothing to do with the Plumstead group, who produced a nice line of single-cylinder, four-stroke engines. The largest of these was of 249cc and had a chain-driven, single overhead camshaft, hairpin valve springs, gear primary drive and unit construction of its four-speed gearbox. The other two engines, of 125 and 170cc capacity, had overhead valves.

There was also a new frame, the P-type, which had some square-section tubes, a rear half comprised of pressings welded together, and pivoted-fork rear suspension. The pressings also formed the rear mudguard and number plate while accommodating the battery and tools in compartments. This frame was used by the Dolomite model, which had the 249cc AMC engine,

one with the 170cc AMC, and three using Villiers power. Of these, the Cortina had the 224cc 1H, the De Luxe the 197cc 8E, and the Moto Cross the similar-sized 7E. The plunger frame remained for two other 197cc models. Other models using the AMC engines were either short-lived or failed to reach production. One that was a show surprise at Earls Court late in 1953 was the Hornet which had a twin-overhead-camshaft 125cc engine and was built for road racing. It had style but little more was heard of it.

All these models continued for 1955, when they offered the option of the Earles forks in place of the usual telescopics, and were joined by a 147cc replacement for the 125 model, listed as the Leda. After then the AMC engines were dropped and only Villiers used from then on.

Above
DMW fitted with the French 170cc ohv AMC four-stroke engine unit and offered for 1954

Below
The DMW Bambi scooter launched in 1957 and fitted with a Villiers 4F engine with two-speed gearbox

From 1956 the accent was more on competition models although road ones continued to be listed. The first were the Moto Cross and Trials using 197cc engines, as did the De Luxe, while the Cortina kept the 1H and the Leda the 29C. This last was dropped for 1957 when the road machines used the 148 and 174cc engines as well as the 197cc, the competition models ran on with a variety of specifications, and the Dolomite returned with a 249cc 2T engine.

The final new 1957 model was totally different, for it was a scooter that used the 99cc Villiers 4F engine with two-speed gearbox and was called the Bambi. The frame was a monocoque, built up from steel pressings in scooter style and the front forks were of the Earles pattern, but with a stirrup linking the fork arms to a helical spring concealed within the steering column. A well valanced mudguard concealed most of the supporting members and the pivoted-fork carried the engine unit so the whole became a major assembly while there were disc 15in. wheels, larger than usual for a scooter.

The range was well thinned out for 1958, only four models remaining, plus a newcomer. Left were the Bambi scooter, two 197cc road models and the Dolomite twin. New was a competition model available for trials or scrambles and powered by a tuned 2T engine, hardly the most suitable type for that use.

The older 197cc road model was dropped for 1959 when a further Dolomite twin was added with the 324cc 3T engine. Late in the year a competition model appeared fitted with the 246cc 32A engine for trials or the similar 33A from scrambles. In 1960 these were joined by two more with suitable 197cc engines and the rest of the range ran on as it was into the new

decade when they continued until 1967. During that time they built the unique Deemster, which was part scooter and part motorcycle.

DOT

Devoid of Trouble it was said and the make was five years established when Harry Reed, the founder, won the 1908 twin-cylinder TT. He was also second in the 1924 sidecar TT, in which decade they built some interesting models, but by 1930 the range was down to a pair with 196cc Villiers engines and one with a 346cc ohv JAP engine, all built on conventional lines.

In May 1930 a 247cc Villiers-powered model was added and this alone went on into 1931 when it was joined by another using a 343cc Villiers engine and a four-stroke with a 349cc ohv Bradshaw. Later came a model with a 98cc Villiers engine in very basic cycle parts but with the usual Dot finish of red with light tank panels. These models were then joined by others with 147 and 346cc Villiers engines.

For 1932 there were just three models listed as the 98cc Midget, the 147cc Minor and the 148cc Major, the last fully equipped although all were still basic machines. This small range was not enough to sustain the works and during 1932 they turned to other products. This led to the building of three-wheeled delivery trucks, powered by Villiers engines, and eventually, in 1949, back to motorcycles.

Their first postwar motorcycle was a road model which used the Villiers 6E engine in a rigid frame with girder forks. Equipment included a battery, saddle and centre stand, making a neat machine. For 1950 two

Far left
The Dolomite II with 249cc 2T engine in the DMW P-type frame with pressed-steel rear section

Top
Trials version of the Mk X with 2T engine, Earles forks and increased ground clearance

Bottom
A 1931 Dot V31 with 247cc Villiers engine with auto-lube

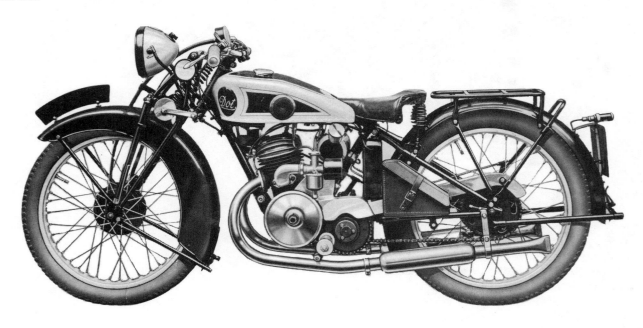

Top
*Dot Mancunian with 9E engine, which was one of the few road
models built by this competition-oriented firm*

Above
*A Dot 246cc scrambler of 1960 with the inevitable Villiers A-
series engine*

versions were offered with direct or battery lighting, and for 1951 these were fitted with telescopic front forks. They were joined by the Scrambler model, which had alloy mudguards, trials tyres and a waist-level exhaust system but was supplied with lights, which could be easily removed, and a silencer. During 1951 the firm introduced a road-going 250, which used the 248cc Brockhouse side-valve engine.

In 1952 the range began to take the shape it was to keep for the rest of the decade with a variety of models which used the same basic parts. The two road models remained up to 1953 but were then dropped as the firm concentrated on a series of competition machines in frames with pivoted-fork rear suspension. These were built for scrambles and trials, each available with road equipment, direct lighting or stripped for action. At first there was the option of a rigid frame which soon went, but there were also options of three or four speeds and telescopic or leading-link forks. These machines all used the 197cc 6E engine at first, but changed to the 8E for 1954 and then moved on to the 9E from 1957. From 1959 they were also listed with 246cc engines, using the 31A for moto-cross and the 32A for trials.

In 1956 a road model reappeared as the Mancunian which used the 9E engine and the leading-link forks plus a cowl for the headlamp and some enclosure, but it was only listed for three years. However, early in 1957 the firm began to import the Italian Vivi machines, produced by Viberti of Turin. All brought in had a 50cc two-stroke engine and two-speed gearbox and were built as moped, racer and scooterette and helped to augment the company's cash flow.

For 1959 there were also three new models with twin-cylinder engines, two built for scrambles and the third for the road. The first competition model used the 249cc 2T engine but the second fitted the 349cc RCA unit. This unit was of advanced construction, with horizontally-split crankcase and full flywheels, twin Amals and a four-speed gearbox and the third twin also used the RCA engine and was a road machine, named the Sportsman's Roadster.

This range, less the 2T scrambler, ran on for 1960 when the firm also imported some motorcycles from the Guazzoni range. Much of the range was then dropped and from then on they offered a reduced selection of models until 1968, after which they were forced to use foreign engine units.

DOUGLAS

The Douglas firm was well established before World War 1 and even by then was famous for its flat-twin engines, a type they used for nearly all their models. In the 1930s they continued, with one exception, to be installed along the frame. This always meant that the front plug suffered from mud and water, while the rear's problems were overheating and access. The company also went through many financial hard times despite, or because of, excursions into other realms.

By 1930 the firm was in a sound position with good sales, new models designed by Freddie Dixon and some very successful dirt-track machines. However, despite the adoption of saddle tanks, the machine's appearance was rather vintage due to the length inherent in the engine type and layout. Also the speedway JAP was about to begin its long reign of the tight ovals.

All the 1930 models had flat-twin engines of 348, 499 and 596cc with side valves and the two larger with ohv. Their construction followed the lines established by the firm so the valve gear went on the right, the magneto on top and the oil in a sump while the mixture was supplied by a single carburettor for the side valves and two for the ohv. All drove a three-speed gearbox but for the ohv machines this went over the rear cylinder to keep the wheelbase to a reasonable length. Chain adjustment was by moving the engine forward and rear wheel back, a variation of the normal method. The clutch, as usual with a Douglas, was built into the outside engine flywheel but not fitted to the dirt-track models, for that sport used a rolling start in those days.

The frame design was straightforward with girder front forks and rigid rear. The wheels had hubs with separate 8in. diameter drums and inside these went Douglas patent semi-servo brakes, a design which dated from 1925 and would be used right up to 1939. The dirt-track models came minus brakes, left footrest, silencer or full mudguards, but all these were supplied for the speed models, which could thus be ridden on the road to competition events.

For 1931 Douglas adopted tartan borders to their petrol tank panels and kept their range much the same but near the end of 1931 the company was sold off by the family and became a public firm. For a brief while they were involved with the Dynasphere, which used a Douglas engine to drive the one enormous wheel in which the rider sat along with the mechanics.

New for 1932 were 348cc ohv and 750cc sv models along with other variants on the existing machines

Above
Douglas Terrier model A32 from 1932 with a 348cc engine and a tartan border to its tank panels

Below
The 1934 Douglas model Z of 596cc with the usual flat-twin engine associated with the marque

with short-stroke engines. This was only a passing phase and by June the new company had announced its range, which was some of the existing models with detail changes, reduced prices and the name of a breed of dog for each one. This produced the 348cc Terrier, 499cc Bulldog, 596cc Greyhound and Airedale and 750cc Mastiff with side valves, but no ohv models at all.

This did nothing to remove the financial problems that had already afflicted the new company, but despite these a 1933 programme was prepared and in it were two interesting new models, but only one ever went into production. This model broke Douglas traditions by using a 148cc Villiers engine set horizontally in the frame. It drove a three-speed Albion gearbox, and this plus engine and dynamo were all mounted on a

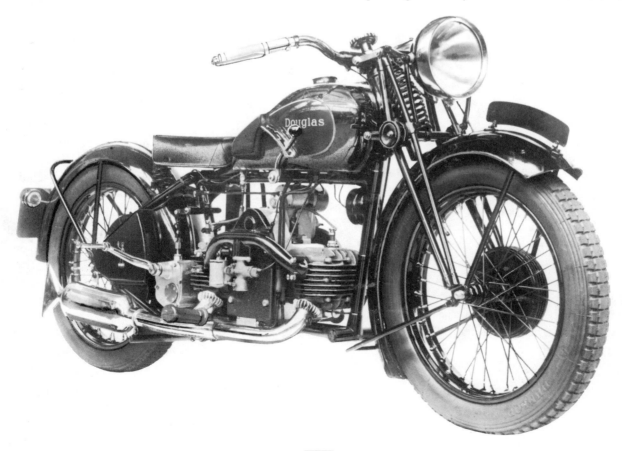

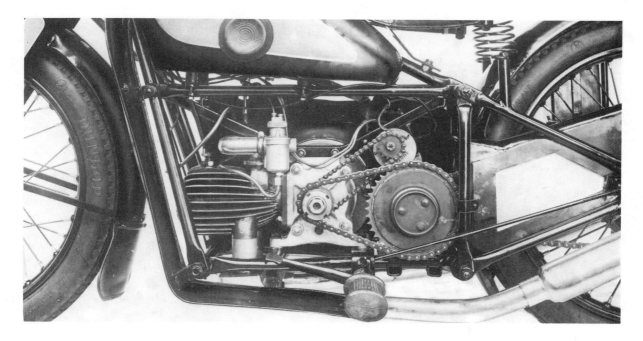

Above
The engine room under the panels of the Douglas model X of 1934 which was first sold as the Bantam the year before A rare single for the make

Below
Speed Special Douglas model 5OW1 from 1935. 596cc with ohv and the gearbox above the rear cylinder

baseplate which in turn was rubber-mounted to the bolted-up tubular frame with blade girder forks and was enclosed by side panels that hid it entirely. Legshields and the petroil tank completed the job of keeping the mechanics out of sight. It was called the Bantam.

1933 was a bad year for the firm as their financial troubles worsened and an official receiver was appointed. In September the company was reformed, but for that season there seems to have been little or no motorcycle production. For 1934 the two-stroke was fitted with a Douglas engine Next came a run of five sidevalve twins on the lines of earlier models in 245, 348, 489, 596 and 744cc sizes, the larger two fitted with four-speed gearboxes. There were also two with ohv

and of 499 and 596cc with four speeds.

In 1935 Douglas played safe on most models, but sprang a surprise with the Endeavour, their first real transverse twin. This used a new 500cc engine which was also fitted to a more conventional model with fore and aft cylinders. The range were given names as well as numbers and there were detail improvements. The two-strokes retained the Bantam name, while the 245cc sv became the Comet and the 348cc sv the Cotswold. The 596cc was the Wessex and the 744cc the Powerflow, while the two ohv machines became Speed Specials.

The 494cc sv became the Blue Chief, and had light alloy heads and barrels, the latter with iron liners.

This same unit was turned round for the Endeavour model, in which it drove back to a four-speed hand-change gearbox and then by shaft to the rear wheel bevel box. The remainder of the machine followed Douglas practice with some good detail points, but its price when launched was rather high.

By the middle of the year the firm was in financial trouble once more and was rescued by the British Aircraft Company, who re-formed them as Aero Engines. The idea was to use the facilities to make aircraft engines, and so Pride & Clarke in London became sole agents for Douglas machines, which were assembled from stock to clear out the stores. In this way the 1936 range comprised the 245, 348, 494 and 596cc side-valve models from the previous year, all with the name Aero, plus the Endeavour at a reduced price. There was no 750, no two-stroke and no ohv models. There were also no changes until some parts dried up and others were substituted, resulting in hybrids reaching the market.

This situation continued into 1937 with just 348, 494 and 596cc Aero models while for 1938 these were replaced by a two-model range and the Aero prefix was dropped. One model had a 148cc two-stroke engine

Left
*The post-war 348cc flat-
twin Douglas T35, as
first seen in 1946 with its
leading-link forks and
torsion-bar rear suspen-
sion*

Below
*The T350, or Mk III,
road tested during 1948,
when the superb suspen-
sion was greatly and
rightly praised*

and three-speed gearbox while the other was of 585cc
with a sv flat-twin engine, four speeds and BTH magneto and pancake generator.

Only the larger was built in 1939 and then only
in small numbers until war broke out and the works
turned to defence contracts. This built the company up
once more and during the war they did produce a prototype design, the DV60. This had a 602cc side-valve,
flat-twin engine set transversely in the frame to drive

Far left. top
*1935 Douglas Endeavour with transverse flat-
twin engine, a style they were to adopt post-war*

Far left, bottom
*Douglas CL38, a 148cc two-stroke built for
1938 and not in their normal mould*

Above
The 1948 Sports model Douglas introduced during that year

Below
First signs of the Vespa came at the late 1949 Earls Court show, where this early model with mudguard-mounted headlamp was shown

Far right, top
The production Vespa differed in the headlamp location and is seen here in 1951, outside Victoria bus station in London

Far right, bottom
The Douglas Dragonfly, which kept the essence of the past in a new frame and forks with an unusual fuel tank

back to a three-speed gearbox from where bevel gears and a chain took the power to the rear wheel. The rest of the machine was strictly functional to suit the services but did include leading-link forks, called Radiadraulic by Douglas, which had a substantial wheel movement and hydraulic damping.

Some of this went into their postwar model, first described in September 1945, which had a transverse, 348cc, ohv, flat-twin engine built in unit with its four-speed gearbox and with chain final drive. The crankshaft was built up with roller big-end bearings, there were twin camshafts beneath the crankshaft, and the valve gear was totally enclosed. Both heads and barrels were in cast iron, but the rockers were concealed by a polished alloy cover, and there was an Amal for each side. The timing gears were at the front of the engine, under a large polished cover, and the drive was extended up to a Lucas mag-dyno mounted on top of the alloy crankcase. This item was extended downwards to form the sump for the oil system.

The engine and gearbox unit was mounted in a duplex frame with pivoted-fork rear suspension and short leading links at the front. The rear was unusual in that the suspension medium was torsion bars which ran along inside the lower frame tubes. The front end was locked with an arm splined to the bars, while a lever at the rear connected to the fork with a short link. The front suspension was by the Radiadraulic fork, which had the short leading links connected to compression springs within the fork legs. The springs were taper ground to give a variable-rate action over the total 6in. of movement. A deep rear mudguard was supported by a subframe, and the machine came with full electrical equipment, a saddle and a centre stand. In this form, the machine was known a the T35, or Mk I, and even-

tually reached production in 1947.

For 1948 there were improvements and the result called the Mk III, joined during the year by another with upswept exhaust, slimmer mudguards and listed as the Sports. Both continued for 1949 but took a Mk IV form the next year when they were joined by three new versions. Of most interest to the enthusiast were the 80 Plus and 90 Plus models, which were built as sports machines, although the second could be obtained in Clubman's form, stripped for racing. The engines had deeper finning and were worked on to raise the power output. They were bench tested and anything over 25bhp became a 90 Plus, while the failures were used for the 80 Plus.

On the cycle side, both models were much as the

Mk IV, except that the exhausts ran straight back to the silencers, the front brake was a massive 9in. diameter, and its hub was spoked into a 21in. rim. The finish was maroon for the 80 Plus and gold for the 90 Plus, which made them stand out. In competition form the 90 Plus came with racing magneto and tyres, close-ratio gears, rev-counter, alloy guards and a dualseat of uncomfortable appearance. The final new 1950 machine was the Competition model, which was built for trials use so the frame was new and rigid, there was more ground clearance and the wheels, tyres, gearing and exhaust were to suit.

The standard and Sports models became a single model for 1951, listed as the Mk V, which was much as before, as were the two Plus models and the

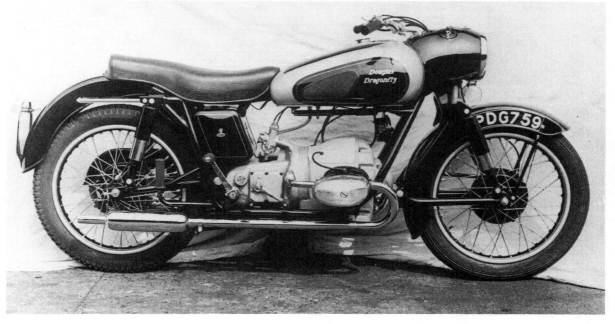

Competition. Of equal importance to the firm was the launch of the Douglas Vespa scooter for 1951, following an earlier showing at Earls Court. At that time, scooters were viewed disparagingly by the British industry in general, but Douglas had the good sense to see which way the tide was running. They came to an arrangement with the Italian Piaggio firm of Genoa to make the Vespa under licence, and the official launch took place in March 1951.

The design was brilliant, the concept of a monocoque frame with a compact engine and gearbox unit running on for many years. There was no frame in the accepted sense, for the Vespa followed car practice and combined this with the body panels to save weight, while retaining rigidity. Thus, the apron and floor were one pressing which carried the rear suspension arm with its single right leg. A rear body was welded to the main section to form the seat mounting, enclose the petroil tank and act as a rear mudguard. Large blister cowlings on each side gave a balanced appearance; the right-hand one enclosed the engine, while that on the left was used to conceal the battery and tools. On top

went the saddle and the rear carrier, which could have a mounting for a spare wheel added to it, while the cables and wiring harness were all located within the body shell.

The front suspension was by a single trailing arm, and the front mudguard was mounted on the steering column, so it was sprung and turned with the bars. In Italy it had the headlight mounted on top of it, as on the 1945 Piaggio original, but this was too low for the British height regulations, so it was moved up and on to the apron. The wheels were of the split-rim type with 8in. tyres, and were interchangeable, so the spare was a real asset. There were drum brakes in the hubs and studs for the wheel mounting.

The 125cc two-stroke engine and three-speed gearbox were built as a very compact unit, which was mounted to the rear pivoted arm. Thus, it was very easy to detach the wiring, controls and rear unit, pull out the arm's pivot bolt and wheel the whole assembly to the bench for maintenance. Thanks to the compact design and need for a minimum number of bearings and seals, the Vespa was always a lively performer, which usually had the edge over the rival Italian Lambretta. As the Vespas were made in the Douglas Bristol works, they featured British components from Amal, BTH, Lucas and others. There were plenty of options to catch the scooterist's fancy while the machine had a centre stand that was easy to use, and the offset engine weight did not seem to worry riders.

The Douglas Competition model was dropped at the end of 1951, to leave the three flat twins and the Vespa with little change. At the show, there was a

Far left
A Douglas Vespa on tour in Glencoe, Scotland, and high-lighting something of what two-wheeled transport is about

Below, centre
1930 Dunelt model T with 249cc ohc Sturmey-Archer engine with face cams at the top of the vertical shaft. Their working face was at an angle to the shaft to match the rockers and valves

Bottom
The 1931 Dunelt Vulture with 348cc Sturmey-Archer engine. Few model names can have been as unfortunate

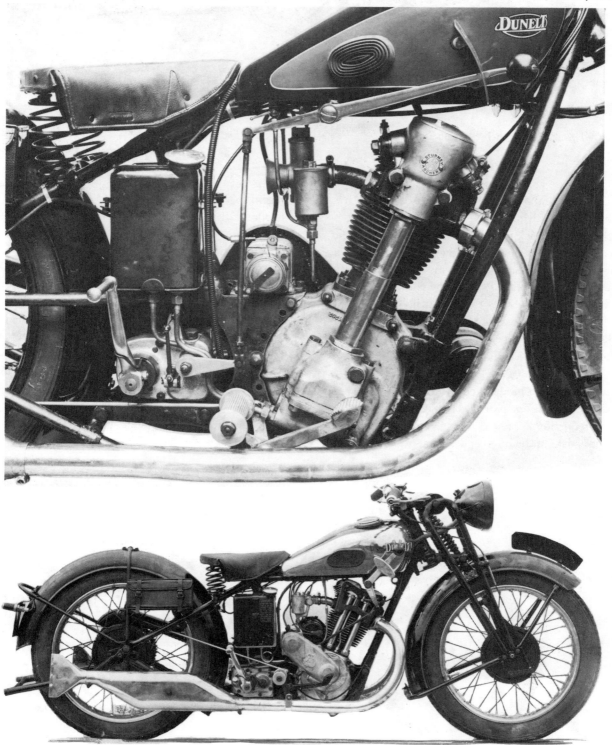

Above
Dunelt V1 from 1933 with 148cc Villiers engine

Below
The Dunelt 50cc moped, which made the briefest of appearances on the market in 1957

489cc prototype that was based on the existing design, but had the mag-dyno enclosed by a finned cover, which extended back to include the air cleaner. It went into a frame with sidecar lugs and was exhibited with a chair attached. The production twins had an external Vokes oil filter added for 1953, at the end of which the 80 Plus was dropped. The other two twins continued for 1954 without change, but the Vespa became the model G, the gearchange being controlled by twin cables in place of the earlier rod system.

It was all change for 1955, as a new flat-twin replaced the earlier models and the Vespa had a revamped engine. The twin was first called the Dart, but in production became the Dragonfly. It represented a major update of the original design, especially with

regard to the frame and suspension. The engine and transmission were basically as before, but most components were revised in some way or other. The frame was duplex with a single top tube, and its pivoted rear fork was controlled by Girling suspension units as were the Earles-type leading-link forks which went at the front. The most distinctive feature of the model was the headlamp mounting, which was flared back to the fuel tank, so the lamp did not turn with the bars. The tank itself held over five gallons of petrol, so the model was a true tourer in that respect. The Vespa had some major engine changes and alterations to the cycle parts including a dualseat option. Early in the year it was joined by the 145cc GS model which had a four-speed gearbox and was an import built entirely in Italy.

Unfortunately, time ran out for Douglas and they were unable to develop the Dragonfly, which had become known as being too slow for sports riding and too noisy and fussy for touring. Sales were poor, and late in 1956 the company was taken over by Westinghouse Brake and Signal. By March 1957 production at Bristol had ceased and the flat-twins were no more. The Vespa continued as an import, but to devotees of the marque, it was the end. Only the old sales slogan remained: 'A twin is best, and Douglas is the best twin'.

DUNELT

Dunelt won the Maudes Trophy in 1929 and 1930 but before then were best known for a 500cc single-cylinder two-stroke with a double diameter piston. They were built in Birmingham, although the firm, Dunford and Elliott, were steel makers in Sheffield who had come into the motorcycle industry in 1919.

Several of their 1930 models fitted inclined ohv Sturmey-Archer engines, these being the 348cc Montlhéry and 495cc Majestic, plus the 495cc model SD with dry sump lubrication. The others were of 249cc with one powered by a two-stroke engine with double diameter piston, while the other had a four-stroke with a face cam for the valve operation. They were formed as bevelled discs and the rockers followed their form and were laid over to lie across the head to reach the valve tops.

The face cam was too noisy to be a success, so was dropped for 1931 when the range used Sturmey-Archer engines and the models had bird's names. While Cygnet for the 297cc side-valve machine and Drake for the 495cc ohv one were nice, the choice of Vulture for the 348cc ohv seems to have been a marketing error. The fourth model was the 598cc side-valve Heron and all had inclined engines. Early in the year they were joined by the Monarch which fitted a 346cc Villiers.

Late in the year manufacture was transferred to the main works and for a time the machines were called Sheffield-Dunelt to highlight this point. For 1932 the names were replaced by numbers and the smallest used the 148cc Villiers engine to join the 346cc version. The two ohv Sturmey-Archer models continued as did the 598cc side-valve one. Most ran on for 1933 but the 346cc Villiers was changed for a 249cc one and one with a 248cc ohv Rudge engine was introduced.

Only Villiers or Rudge engines were used for 1934 with 148 and 249cc of the first and 248 and 499cc of

the second. The Villiers ran on for 1935 but the four-stroke engines became 245 and 490cc JAP units and the year proved to be the last prewar season for Dunelt and from then on they kept to their main job of making steel for others to use.

They did return for the briefest of spells in 1957, when the name was revived for a 50cc moped. This was typical of the type with two-stroke engine, two-speed gearbox, telescopic front and pivoted-fork rear suspension and direct lighting. It came and went in months, with virtually no record nor any impact on the market. At that time, there were scores of continental mopeds of all styles, so there was little call for yet another marque.

DUNKLEY

This make came and went in three short years, leaving barely a mark on the industry but, for all that, represented a good attempt to break into the market. The models often had continental lines, but were mainly made at Hounslow on the outskirts of West London.

They came on to the market in 1957 with the Whippet 60 Scooterette, which had a 61cc ohv engine built in unit with a two-speed gearbox and controlled by a left-hand twistgrip. This engine unit went into a spine frame with telescopic front and pivoted rear suspension. Later in the year, it was joined by the Super Sports 65 which had the engine stretched to 64cc and a raised compression ratio. The two-speed gearbox remained, but the frame took on a very continental look and was made from two pressings in spine form.

For 1958 these two models were joined by the S65 Scooter, which retained the 64cc engine in a new set of cycle parts in the scooter style. The body, including the apron, was a single assembly, which was hinged from the top of the apron to give access to the engine and rear wheel.

The Super Sports 65 became the Whippet Sports for 1959 and the other two models ran on with two new but similar names, the 49.6cc Popular Scooter and 64cc Popular Major Scooter. They had a rigid frame with the fan-cooled engine set well back, telescopic forks and a simple body to enclose the mechanics. The result was somewhat stark, but functional. The larger-capacity machine had some additional trim to enable it to carry a de luxe tag, but otherwise they were the same.

At the end of 1959 the firm dropped the entire range, and the marque vanished as quickly as it had come. Maybe they had a premonition about the next decade.

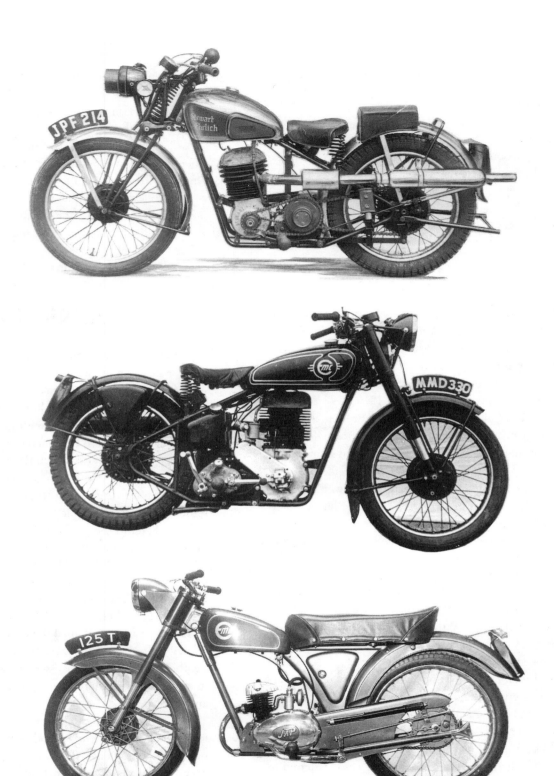

Top
The machine Joe Ehrlich was showing to the press in 1939 with its 240cc split-single engine

Centre
The post-war 345cc EMC split-single engine installed in a rigid frame with Dowty Oleomatic forks

Bottom
The EMC exhibited at the 1952 show with a 125cc JAP engine, spine frame and downtube suspension unit

EMC

Josef Ehrlich came to Britain in 1937, and by 1939 had an engine of his own manufacture installed in an old Francis-Barnett for road and track testing. He was Austrian, so it was hardly surprising that his interest lay in two-strokes and that these were of the split-single type, favoured by Puch and the German DKW. The 1939 engine was a 240cc split-single with the cylinders one behind the other and sharing a common combustion chamber.

Centre
1933 water-cooled C6 Excelsior with 249cc Villiers

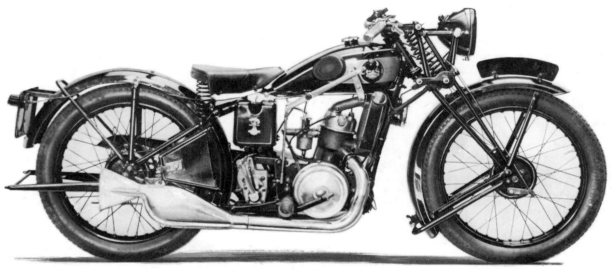

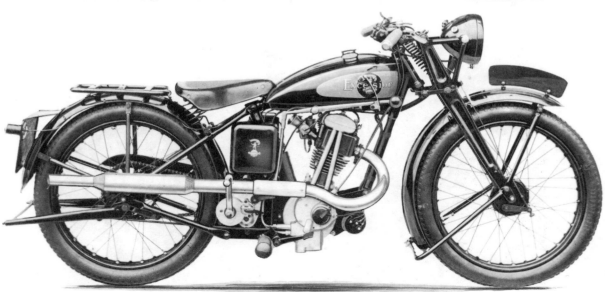

Above
The 1935 Powerplus E10 Excelsior with 490cc twin-port JAP engine

Below
The famous Excelsior Manxman on show in 1935 when it was listed in sports and racing forms. This was its first year

Far right, top
The fully-enclosed 1935 Viking model E9 with its 249cc water-cooled engine

Far right, bottom
1938 Excelsior Autobyk with the 98cc Villiers Junior engine and typical of its type

After the war, Ehrlich set up in business to produce his EMC machines, which were launched in 1947. The engine had grown to 345cc, but remained a split-single with its own style thanks to the arrangement of cooling fins, and drove a four-speed gearbox. These went into a rigid frame with Dowty oleo-pneumatic telescopic front forks. The machine was highly geared, and Ehrlich claimed over 100mpg in advertising, which was an important point in those days of petrol rationing. Owners, however, found it difficult to achieve half that figure and spoke of vibration at the 70mph top speed, while they were expensive machines.

In the early 1950s Ehrlich became linked with the Puch firm, and one outcome was a neat 125cc racing model. This used the split-single Puch engine with

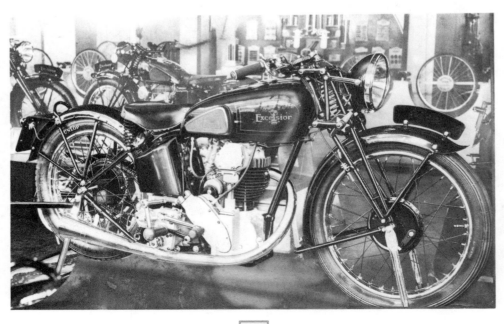

its unit-construction, four-speed gearbox, twin carburettors and twin exhaust pipes and megaphones. The engine went into a simple loop frame with telescopic forks and a Puch rear fork constructed from pressings welded together. They performed quite well and were on offer for two or three years.

A 500cc split-single was spoken of, and a 125cc road model with a JAP engine was shown at Earls Court. It had a spine frame and the pivoted rear fork was extended forward to carry the engine unit and fixed to what looked like the downtube but was actually a long suspension unit, while the rear fork tubes also doubled as exhaust pipes. There was a move to sell the Puch 250cc road model with EMC badges, but this did not last for long, for the firm was wound up in 1953. Puch later set up their own organisation, while Joe Ehrlich went on to fresh pastures, but remained with motorcycle racing for a good few years.

EXCELSIOR

This company dated from 1874 in its original form, when it made penny-farthings, and it became involved with motorcycles in 1896. From the turn of the century they appeared in track races and later ran at Brooklands and in the TT. Their machines were mainly utility ones, but, like many in the early days, they would build just about anything if there was a chance of selling it.

In 1929, they had their first Lightweight TT victory and so entered the new decade on a high note with 14 models using 147, 196 and 247cc Villiers, 300 and 490cc sv JAP and 245 and 490cc ohv JAP engines. All these plus various gearboxes, frames and forks covered most needs and included a TT replica

Models came and went for 1931 as the company sought sales, including a couple within the 224lb weight limit despite their ohv engines. During that year

Excelsior created some kind of record by introducing their 98cc Universal at a mere 14 guineas, the lowest price anyone was to reach. For that money the rider got a Villiers engine, two-speed gearbox with rocking pedal foot control, simple tubular frame and blade girders. Lights were an extra with the choice of direct or acetylene and later a 147cc version was added.

There were more variations for 1932 and 1933 but that year did bring a 149cc ohv model with an Excelsior engine which was joined by a 246cc version soon after. In June 1933 the racing world was introduced to the works 250, which became known as the Mechanical Marvel. The engine, which was the special feature of the machine, was in fact made by Blackburne and had a single vertical cylinder with four radial valves and a rather complex system to open them using high mounted camshafts, plus twin carburettors. The overall result won the TT that year, but proved troublesome to keep in tune and was much less successful in 1934.

Despite this, it was listed in the 1934 range while most of the others were there with names as the 98cc Universal, 148cc Empire, 196cc Service, 249cc Scout and Water-cooled all with Villiers two-strokes, the 149cc Bantam, 246cc Pathfinder and Chieftain, 346cc Warrior and 490cc Powerplus with ohv and the 346cc sv Marathon, plus the Mechanical Marvel, of course. Following on the general announcement came one that the water-cooled model was also to be available with total enclosure as the 249cc Viking, fully panelled from its legshields to the rear number plate, and a second 149cc ohv model would be listed as the Wasp.

Right
*Early Talisman Twin with
its 243cc two-stroke engine
and Excelsior form of
plunger rear suspension*

Left
*One of the two Excelsior
autocycles in 1951, both of
which had their own make of
98cc engine with one
or two speeds*

The 1935 range brought the first mention of the famous Manxman models that did much to lift the firm's name above those who built similar small models with Villiers engines. Most of these ran on but there were new names such as Pioneer, Meritor and Dictator.

The two Manxman models were launched at the show in 246 and 349cc sizes. They shared a common stroke and were of straightforward but massive design with a single overhead camshaft driven by shaft and bevels on the right. The valve gear was fully enclosed with just two valves and the top bevel box cover carried the Three Legs of Man insignia. The mag-dyno went behind the cylinder, where it was driven by a train of gears and these also turned the two gear-type oil pumps and a rev-counter. The cycle parts were also obviously intended for racing as well as sports use with a cradle frame, four-speed gearbox, footchange and large brakes and petrol tank. The models were to be listed in sports or racing form and for the latter there were rearsets, bigger tanks, narrower mudguards, different engine internals and an oil drain from the cambox.

The bewildering list of two-strokes was pruned down for 1936 and all the four-strokes had overhead valves, and new were the 246cc Norseman, 344cc Warrior and Clubman which offered a sporting performance without the complexities of the camshaft engine. The Manxman range was extended to include a larger 496cc version and this closely followed the lines of the two smaller models. The road machines aped the racers with megaphone silencers, but had spiral baffles inside them. Early in the New Year a new Universal Model was announced with a 122cc Villiers engine. It was a basic machine with simple loop frame and a wedge-shaped tank fitted under the top tube. Blade girders and useful legshields were fitted as standard along with direct lighting and a rear carrier. It continued the Excelsior tradition of utilitarian models.

1937 saw the range stabilised with a few deletions, revised camshaft engines and a super sporting one in the 496cc capacity, it having a bronze head, raised compression ratio, racing-type mag-dyno, close-ratio gears and quickly detachable lights. Little altered

Left, top
The 1957 Excelsior Consort F4 with 99cc engine, two speeds and girder forks to provide minimal transport

Left, below
The Excelsior Skutabyk, as it appeared in 1957 based on a Consort with enclosure panels

Far right, top
The Excelsior scooter, which was launched in 1959 in two forms, both powered by the firm's 147cc engine. It shared body pressings with DKR

Far right, bottom
Excelsior Roadmaster R10, of 1959, with Villiers 9E engine in conventional cycle parts

for 1938 but the range was joined by the Autobyk, which was an autocycle fitted with a 98cc Villiers Junior engine and the usual pedalling gear but without enclosure or legshields.

It continued in the 1939 list along with the Universal, which had a longer frame, larger fuel tank and was listed with either 98 or 122cc engine. Most of the rest ran on with minor changes while the Manxman range adopted hairpin valve springs and Girling cable brakes with wedge operation. The racing versions were improved, with the gearbox bolted directly to the crankcase and a duplex primary chain, and made available in the rigid frame or with plunger rear suspension. The 249 and 349cc Manxman range was then further extended by special versions of the road models fitted with many of the racing parts in the engine. This provided a super sports machine or race replica for the clubman racer.

The three basic road Manxman models were list-

ed in the 1940 range with no changes along with the pairs of 148 and 247cc two-stroke models and the 122cc. The Autobyk completed the range and was joined by a de luxe version with the JDL engine and front forks in the form of fork blades that could move as telescopics against a single central spring. Later in the year it was fitted with side shields in the usual auto-cycle style. On that note they concentrated on their wartime production and built the Welbike, from which the Corgi sprang, but after that, restricted themselves to lightweight models.

There were just two of these for 1946; one the Autobyk and the other the Universal model O with a 122cc 9D unit and three-speed gearbox in a rigid frame with girder forks. It was a neat machine, but its oddest feature was the hand gearchange which worked in a gate set in the top of the petroil tank. For 1947 the Autobyk was joined by a Super version fitted with an Excelsior 98cc Goblin engine with two-speed gearbox,

and later by the de luxe with the single-speed, 98cc Excelsior Spryt engine.

All ran on for 1948 and 1949 but the 122cc model was changed to use the 10D engine for the latter year and during it was fitted with telescopic front forks. At the same time the firm added models with the 197cc 6E engine as the Roadmaster, all in two forms with direct or battery lighting. Two further models were added at the same time as the Minor and were miniature motorcycles with loop frame and blade girders, but with a wedge-shaped tank hung beneath the top tube. Both models had Excelsior engines, one the 98cc Goblin, and the other a 123cc version, both with the two-speed gearbox.

The Minor models were dropped for 1950 along with the Autobyk and the 122 and 197cc models were given plunger rear suspension that year. They were joined by what was, perhaps, the best known post-war

Excelsior - the Talisman Twin. For this, the firm built their own 243cc, twin-cylinder, two-stroke engine which was of conventional form, and drove a four-speed gearbox. The unit went into a loop frame, with plunger rear suspension and telescopic front forks, as used by the other motorcycles and the fittings were either common or similar.

There were no changes for 1951 but a Sports version of the twin with twin carburettors was added for the next year. The 1953 range showed some change, for the Universal models were replaced by the Courier which had a 147cc Excelsior engine, much in the Villiers mould, other than the Wipac generator and Amal carburettor. The cycle parts were as before, and as still used by the Roadmaster models. The two Autobyks were still there, and the range was expanded in April 1953 with the Consort, which was a small motorcycle fitted with the 99cc Villiers 4F engine with

two-speed gearbox which went into a rigid frame with light girder forks, and basic equipment.

The whole range continued for 1954, with a change to the 8E engine for the Roadmaster models and five new machines, four in a new frame with pivoted-fork rear suspension and a dualseat. The first two models were the Roadmaster with the 8E engine and direct or battery lighting respectively, while the other two were twins, in Talisman and Sports versions. The final new model was the Condor which was effectively the Consort fitted with a 122cc Villiers 13D engine, but it was only built for 1954, at the end of which it and the plunger framed machines were all dropped.

For 1955 this left the two Autobyks, the two Consorts, one Roadmaster, and the two twins who were joined by a Courier fitted with a 147cc Excelsior engine and three-speed gearbox, two revised Roadmasters which used the Courier frame, a Popular version of the Talisman in the new frame, and the Special Equipment Sports Talisman Twin which had full-width alloy hubs.

There were more revisions and new models for 1956, when the Consort changed to the 6F engine and was joined by a Consort with plunger rear suspension. Only one Roadmaster continued, but it was joined by the Autocrat, which fitted the 9E Villiers engine with four-speed gearbox. Also new was the Condex with 147cc Villiers 30C engine and three-speed gearbox, which used the Consort spring frame with telescopic front forks. Among the twins, the Special was dropped, to leave the Talisman and Sports models. That year, the firm also moved into the scooter and moped market by importing the Heinkel products, which served them for a few years.

The Courier was joined by the Convoy in April 1956 and, like it, used the 147cc Excelsior engine but was lower in price and replaced the Courier in 1957 by when the Autobyks had been dropped along with some others. The two Consort models continued for 1957, along with the two twins. New was the Skutabyk which, in a sense, replaced the Autobyk. It was based on an Consort, but had added extensive enclosure panels, legshields and footboards.

The Consorts, as such, were dropped at the end of the year, although the Skutabyk continued and a new Consort joined it. This had a pivoted-fork frame with telescopic forks, in which to accommodate the 6F engine, while the rider was provided with a dualseat. A new Universal model fitted with a 147cc Villiers 30C engine replaced the Convoy and had a similar specification. The Talisman Sports twins continued and were joined by a larger 328cc Super Talisman, much as the Sports Twin, with twin carburettors and the same set of cycle parts, including 6in. brakes in full-width hubs. The S8 engine had been developed to suit the light three-wheelers then on the market, and late that year this idea was taken one step further. The result was a 491cc, three-cylinder engine with Siba electric start and suitable Albion gearbox.

Below
The Irish-built Fagan, produced in Dublin using British components including a 148cc Villiers engine, this being a 1936 model

Most of the range continued for 1959 with the Consort, Universal, Skutabyk, Talisman and Super Talisman, but not the Sports Twin model. In its place, there was a new Special Talisman, but this used the 328cc engine and was distinguished by full enclosure of the rear end down to wheel-spindle level. The early form of the Consort reappeared in April 1959 much as before, complete with rigid frame and girder forks. A week later, the firm announced a two-model scooter range, and achieved this by dint of using DKR cycle and body parts but their own 147cc engine. The result was called the Monarch, came with kick or electric start, and was hard to tell from the DKR, other than by the badges they wore.

The scooters continued for 1960, when the Roadmaster model returned with 9E engine and four-speed gearbox, along with the Talisman models in both sizes, the Consorts and the Universal which changed to a 148cc 31C engine. In this way, the long established firm entered the 1960s, but soon began to flag. After 1962 the range was down to just two models, and the last of these went in 1965 to remove one more famous name from the role of British manufacturers.

FAGAN

This obscure make hailed from Dublin, Ireland, and was assembled using British components in order to avoid the tariff that existed on imported machines in the 1930s. It was around for 1935 and 1936. The single model used a 148cc Villiers engine fitted into a frame made by Diamond Motors. The other parts were conventional and the result priced at £27 but few seem to have sold, hence the short model life.

FEDERATION

Millions of people shopped at the Co-op and collected dividend stamps, tin plate coins in the 1930s, and for a while the Co-operative Wholesale Society, or CWS, put up the money for a range of motorcycles which were built at the Federal Works in Tyseley, Birmingham. The 1930 range was conventional with four models with JAP sv engines of 300, 346 and 498cc plus a 346cc ohv. An ohv of 490cc was added for 1931 plus a 677cc sv V-twin to round the range out.

A model with a Villiers 147cc engine appeared for 1932 and was joined by a 148cc version the next year when the only JAP engine was the 490cc ohv, later joined by a 245cc ohv. By 1935 there was just the 148cc Villiers and the 245 and 490cc ohv JAP engines in use and only the two smaller for 1937, after when the Co-op dropped two-wheelers and concentrated on its groceries.

FLM

This was Frank Leach Manufacturing of Leeds, who entered the lightweight market in 1951 with a machine that looked like many others, but differed a good deal. Unlike most, they used the 125cc JAP engine with three-speed gearbox, installing it in a frame with pivoted-fork rear suspension and constructed from channel-section steel.

At the front were telescopic forks, and both wheels had drum brakes and well valanced mudguards. The machine had a dualseat and was called the Glideride. It was offered for 1952, and during the year a second prototype machine was seen with a Villiers 6E

Top
1934 Francis-Barnett Falcon 38 with 196cc engine

Bottom
1934 249cc Cruiser 39 model Francis-Barnett

engine but this failed to reach production. During 1953 supplies of the JAP engine began to dry up so the firm decided to stop production.

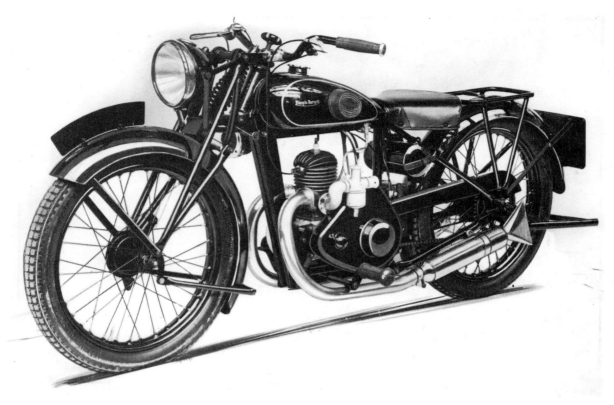

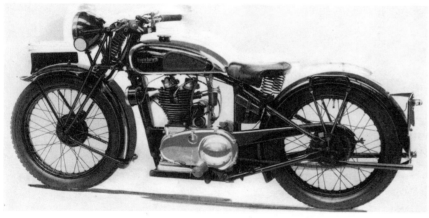

Top
Francis-Barnett 1935 Plover 41 with 148cc engine in frame with built-up downtube

Centre
The Stag F/44 model with 247cc ohv Blackburne engine in 1936. A rare four-stroke Francis-Barnett

Bottom
The simple Francis-Barnett 122cc Snipe J48 of 1939 which gave basic transport. Note the built-up frame

FRANCIS-BARNETT

The first machine carrying this name was built in 1920, but both founders had been involved from pre-World War 1 days. In 1923 they produced their triangulated frame and from then on were known mainly for light-weight machines.

The frame was the essence of simplicity and comprised six pairs of straight tubes and one pair with a small kink. Each was identified with a stamped-on letter and, given the listing, assembly was a matter of min-

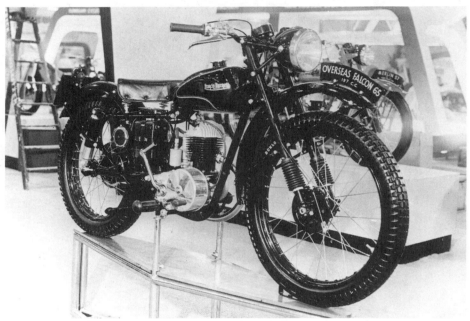

Top
A 1951 Francis-Barnett 55 with 197cc 6E engine in rigid frame

Centre
The export Falcon 65 Francis-Barnett with 8E engine, an early trail machine

Bottom
The Francis-Barnett Cruiser 68 with 224cc Villiers 1H engine in a built-up frame

utes. The system was still going strong in 1930 and the firm claimed not to have had a breakage except in accidents.

Into the frame went a run of Villiers engines of 147, 172, 196, 247 and 343cc with two or three speeds and auto-lube in one case. The larger were listed as the Empire and Dominion but the next year saw the start of the use of bird's names relating to specific engine sizes with the two 196cc models listed as Black Hawk and Falcon.

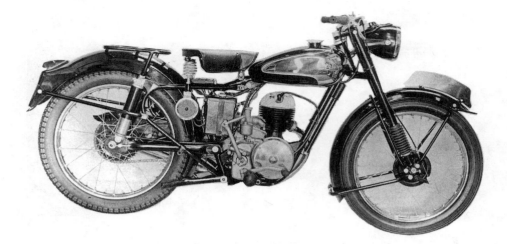

Top
The 1953 pivoted-fork frame
Francis-Barnett, which was
built as the model 57 with
10D engine, and as the 58
with the 6E

Models also took numbers, a practice that would continue throughout the rest of the firm's life. By 1932 the 147cc machines were the Merlin or Kestral, the 148cc one the Lapwing, and the 172cc the Condor, some to continue for the hard days of 1933.

Completely new, and launched in the first week of 1933, was the Cruiser, a 249cc machine with full enclosure and a different form of frame construction. This comprised a forging, channel sections, flitch plates, tubes and stays plus an undershield for bracing. At the front went blade girders and all the mechanism other than the top half of the cylinder was enclosed by a curved panel on each side which were easily removed for servicing. At the rear, fixed panels filled in the area between the chainstays and matched to the sides. At the front what appeared to be a bulbous panel was in fact a cast-alloy expansion box which fed a second silencer. Both mudguards were large and valanced, and legshields were built in, the whole machine designed to keep the rider clean and free from road dirt.

There was little change for 1934 but major changes came for 1935 along with a four-stroke. This was the Stag and it had a 247cc engine made for it by Blackburne, this having an unusual valve gear layout, as the push rods crossed over and the rockers lay across the head. Ignition was by magneto and lubrication was wet sump with the oil carried in a casting bolted to the base of the crankcase. The frame was similar to that of the Cruiser with forging, tubes, angle sections and girder forks. The Cruiser and a single Black Hawk were little altered, but the two 148cc and two 249cc models all had a new form of bolted-up frame of a more usual appearance to become Plovers and Seagulls

Little was altered for 1936 or 1937 except for a second ohv model listed as the Red Stag for the latter year, but there were no Stags in the 1938 list, Blackburne having ceased engine production. For that year the Plover, Cruiser and Seagull all ran on with

minor changes and were joined by the Snipe which had either a 98 or 122cc Villiers engine and was aimed at export markets in Norway and Holland, where capacity or weight limits gave tax concessions. Again, the frame was unusual with channel sections, angles and tubes, all bolted together.

It was no change for 1939 but plus the Powerbike, an autocycle with a 98cc Villiers engine fully shielded and with a simple form of front suspension. The 1940 range was unchanged but then added a Powerbike with the JDL engine.

After the war. they returned to the market with just two models for 1946, one the Powerbike and the other the model 51 Merlin with 122cc Villiers 9D engine and three-speed handchange gearbox in a rigid frame with girder forks. In 1947 the firm became part of the AMC group, but it was some time before this had any great effect. Meanwhile, the two models continued, the Powerbike changing to tubular girders with rubber-band springing for 1948.

For 1949 the Merlin changed to a 10D engine and was joined by the Falcon which had the 197cc 6E unit. All had the rigid frame but with telescopic forks and could have direct or battery lighting. During the year a new version of the Powerbike appeared with the 99cc Villiers 2F engine in a new loop frame. The front forks continued to be girders, while the remainder of the machine stayed in the autocycle style with saddle, carrier and engine enclosure. These five models continued for the next two years with no real alteration, except that for 1951 the motorcycles were offered in an azure blue finish as an option. Quite a change for a utility range.

At the end of 1951 the Powerbike was dropped, and for 1952 the four motorcycles were joined by four more using the same engines and names. Two of these had a new frame with pivoted-fork rear suspension controlled by hydraulically-damped rear units made by the

Right
*Early Francis-Barnett
scrambler with the 249cc
AMC single engine, which led
to the model 82, but no real
success*

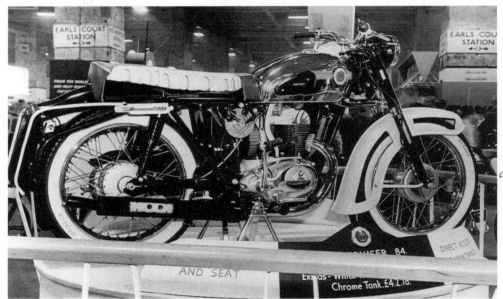

Left
*Cut-away show model of the
Francis-Barnett Cruiser 84, of
1959, with 249cc AMC engine
and normally fully enclosed with
panels*

firm. The same names and engines were also used by a
pair of machines built for competition with rigid frame
and suitable cycle parts, but these two were replaced by
four more purpose-built models for 1953, a Merlin and
Falcon each for trials and scrambles, the first in a rigid
frame and the second with pivoted rear fork, while the
Falcons fitted the 7E engine. Around the same time the
road models of 197cc changed to the 8E engine and
were joined by an Overseas Falcon which was in effect
a trail bike.

Only the models with rear suspension went on for
1954 but without the Merlins. New was the Kestral
which fitted the 122cc 13D engine into a frame with
plunger rear suspension to offer low-cost commuter
transport. A little later the firm announced a new
model with an old name, the Cruiser, and gave this the
224cc 1H Villiers engine with its four-speed gearbox.
The frame continued built up from tubes and pressings
allied to a degree of enclosure which gave the model a
neat appearance. The mudguards were deeply valanced,

and the finish was in a very nice dark green, set off
with gold tank lining.

There were only five models for 1955, all with a
new front fork with hydraulic damping. The road
Falcon was given a new pivoted-fork frame, while the
Cruiser gained full-width hubs, and the scrambles and
trials models went to four-speed gearboxes with suitable
ratios, the trial one still in its rigid frame. The Kestral
was revised to use the 147cc 30C engine but kept the
plunger frame and became the Plover for 1956 with a
new frame with tubular front, but pressed-steel rear sections. The pressing supported the pivoted rear fork,
concealed its rear suspension units, and housed the
tools, battery and electrics, with a single seat for the
rider. The four others all ran on much as they were
except that the competition ones had a new frame.

The existing models were little changed for 1957
but were joined by a second Cruiser, which was the first
Francis-Barnett to be fitted with the unhappy AMC
two-stroke engine. It used the 249cc version, which was

the first to appear and presented a smooth shape to the world. Smooth would also seem to apply to the Italian designer, who accepted his brief and fee, but departed for home before his work was either developed or fully tested.

The engine followed the lines of the Villiers 1H, with the four-speed gearbox bolted to the rear of the crankcase and the castings blended together. The main odd feature was the head, barrel and piston assembly, for there were no transfer ports, only depressions in the cylinder walls. To guide the mixture, the long piston had ports in its skirt and a tall crown shaped to match the head. This was different from most in having sunburst radial fins and internal downward projections to match the piston. In use, this design was to prove poor in operation and reliability, while weak gear-selector parts and poor electrics did nothing to enhance its rep-

utation. In keeping with their traditions, AMC never took the obvious way out with a new top half, but persevered with their troublesome design well into the 1960s. For the Cruiser, this engine was fitted into the existing frame, with minor alterations, which included Girling rear units.

The older Cruiser was dropped for 1958, to leave the AMC-powered one, which continued with the Plover. For the 200cc class, the Falcon changed to the more streamlined 10E engine, and the trials and scrambles Falcons were both dropped, for AMC had fully committed themselves to their new engine, but it was April before a new competition machine appeared.

This was the Scrambler, which used a tuned version of the 249cc AMC engine in a nice frame with Norton front forks. There were Girlings to control the rear end, and the whole package was very neat, except

Above
1932 Gloria with 98cc Villiers engine, a Triumph model that they preferred not to be known for

Below
The larger 147cc Gloria of 1933, the final year of production

133

Above
Greeves 20D road model, from 1955, with 8E
engine and four-speed gearbox in original frame with
rubber suspension at both ends

Below
The 1957 Greeves Fleetmaster with 322cc British
Anzani twin engine in standard frame with revised forks

for the engine. The heart of the problem was the strange piston design and its poor ring sealing, but this was aggravated by the Wipac energy-transfer ignition system.

A month after the Scrambler, the second road model appeared with the AMC engine. This was the 171cc Light Cruiser, whose engine was simply a smaller edition of the 249cc version and the cycle side was similar to the Cruiser. The centre-section enclosure was even larger, extending forward to the carburettor and along the subframe down to footrest level.

All the models continued for 1959, when the Trials model with the 249cc AMC engine joined them. This used the same frame and forks as the Scrambler, but had a long silencer tucked inside the right-hand subframe tube and rear unit. Also new was a further Cruiser, which created great interest due to its extensive enclosure and legshields fitted as standard. It con-

tinued with the 249cc AMC engine, but was fully enclosed from the cylinder to the rear number plate, and down well below wheel spindle height. It made an impressive machine.

The two Cruiser models ran on for 1960, along with the Light Cruiser and the two competition machines. The last two machines in the range with Villiers engines were changed to AMC units to make the 149cc Plover and 199cc Falcon, but in later years the company had to eat its words and ask Villiers for both engines and technical assistance.

As it was, the 1960 range ran on into the new decade, minus the model Light Cruiser, and, with later changes, on to the company's end in 1966. It was a sad fate for a firm that had lived through some hard times by building good reliable machines, and from them gaining a reputation of producing some of the better utility motorcycles.

GLORIA

Triumph used this name from their car side when they introduced this cut-price lightweight in 1932. It was aimed at the bottom of the market and was much as many others in using a 98cc Villiers engine in simple cycle parts. The result amounted to 124lb and was priced at 16 guineas. For 1933 it was joined by a 147cc version while Triumph included their own 148cc ohv model in their range and added a 148cc Villiers powered machine in 1934. This rather removed the reason for the Gloria so it quickly vanished after two brief seasons.

Top
Greeves trials model 20T with 9E engine, as in 1957, with saddle and tilted silencer

Bottom
Fleetwing 25D Greeves with 2T Villiers twin engine, as in 1958

GREEVES

Bert Greeves came into the motorcycle industry because his cousin, Derry Preston Cobb, was paralysed from birth. Bert made him more mobile by fitting a small engine to his wheelchair, and this led to the foundation of Invacar to build powered invalid carriages.

Derry joined in this enterprise as salesman and buyer for the Southend-based firm and, despite his handicap, often travelled about the country, either selling or attending sports meetings once the Greeves name was established. At a later date, his invalid car was powered by a well-tuned Villiers engine, which must have surprised a few people.

Invacar built up a good business after the war, serving the needs of the disabled, and in 1951 began their move into motorcycles by setting up a development programme, mainly centred on suspension using rubber bushes in torsion. The basis of these came from the invalid carriages, but the first prototype had some

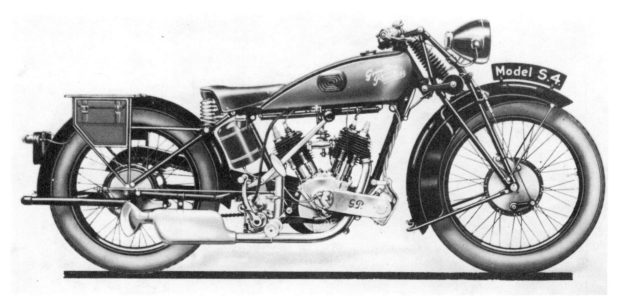

Above
1930 Grindlay-Peerless built in 680 and 750cc sizes

Below
*1933 Grindlay-Peerless Speed Chief with a 499cc
Ulster Rudge engine under the Python label and built
as a road-racing machine*

odd looks. due to its trailing-link front forks. Both
these, and the pivoted-fork rear suspension used the
rubber bushes with suitable links.

Late in 1953 the marque launched its range and
all used the 197cc 8E engine installed in a unique
frame. This was part tubular but had a cast-alloy beam
which ran from the headstock to the front of the
engine and which was cast round the welded tubular
section which, consequently, was totally locked to it for
all time. Further deep alloy sections ran under the
engine unit and were bolted to the main beam and to
the rear end of the top tube. Suspensions front and rear
used the rubber bushes which had friction dampers
built into them and the front had become by leading-
links with a tubular stay to connect them for rigidity.

There were two road models, with three or four
speeds, and two competition ones for trials and scrambles. Later, these were joined by another for the road

with a 242cc British Anzani twin two-stroke engine
and listed as the Fleetwing, and in 1955 a further twin
with the same engine in a tubular frame and two of
197cc in that frame. Also new for 1955 was a twin with
the 322cc British Anzani engine in the cast-alloy
frame.

By 1956 all the models had dropped the rubber
bushes and had conventional suspension units with
hydraulic damping and most of the 197cc machines
changed to the 9E engine and its four-speed gearbox.
The range ran on for 1957 with a new Fleetwing using
the 249cc Villiers 2T engine and by 1958 the Anzani
engines had gone and only 9E or 2T engines were in
use. The twin was used for competition machines for
that year alone but in 1959 these were replaced by
246cc 31A singles.

By then the top trials model was the Scottish
Trials Special and the top scrambler the Hawkstone

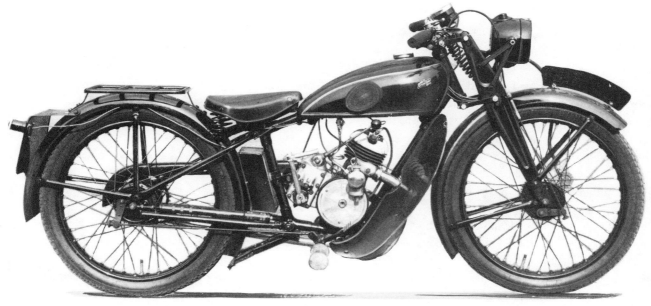

Special, both representing the best available for their sports and most successful. There were just two road models still in the range, both using the same cycle parts and either the 31A or 2T engines. In 1960 the first was changed to a 32A engine and the second joined by a further twin powered by the 324cc 3T Villiers engine. For that year the 197cc models stayed with the 9E engine but the 246cc ones went to the 32A for trials and 33A for scrambles, the latter also having a new frame.

With this range, Greeves ran into the 1960s to more success, road racing and their own engine.

GRINDLAY-PEERLESS

This firm first built sidecars and added motorcycles to their product range in 1923, achieving some records and successes at Brooklands during the 1920s. They entered the next decade with a range powered by Villiers and JAP engines and could offer great variety as the machines were hand-built so changes were easy to accommodate.

The Villiers engines used were of 172, 196 and 247cc, while side-valve JAP units were the 490cc single and 680 and 750cc V-twins. With ohv the singles came in 245, two versions of 346 and three versions of 490cc. This gave standard, sports and, for the largest, a TT model and there was also a 680cc ohv V-twin. Diamond and loop frames and Brampton bottom-link forks were used for the 350 and 500 twin-port models.

In 1931 the Villiers and V-twin engines were no longer listed and there were just four JAP-powered

models, all with ohv in 346 and 490cc sizes. In addition there were three models powered by Rudge engines, one of 348cc and the others 499cc. There were only three models for 1932 and all used Rudge engines with the cheapest 499cc listed as the Tiger. The other of that size had either an Ulster or a racing engine, four speeds and better equipment and was called the Tiger Chief. Third was the Tiger Cub and this used the 248cc

engine but kept the four speeds while all models had a similar finish with chrome-plated petrol tank with a black top panel.

They continued for 1933 and were joined by two more, based on them. One was the 248cc Speed Cub which had magneto ignition, and the other was the 499cc Speed Chief which was very fully equipped. There was also a road-racing version fitted with a Replica engine, four-speed gearbox, Brampton Monarch bottom link forks, racing fitments and Avon racing tyres.

All except the Speed Cub continued with little alteration for 1934, so there was one 248 and four 499cc models but this was their last season, for during the year motorcycle production ceased, although the company continued with other lines.

GROSESPUR

Another of the many lightweights that appeared to use the 122cc Villiers engine, this one made by the Carlton company for George Grose, a large retail dealer at Ludgate Circus in London. It was similar to the Carlton and appeared in 1938 with simple frame and girder forks, ran quietly and came complete with legshields. It remained on offer for 1939 and 1940 but then went, not to return.

GYS

Another 50cc, two-stroke, all-alloy cyclemotor attachment which mounted over the front wheel of a stock bicycle. It was made in Bournemouth and first sold as the GYS in June 1949, but by the end of the year a firm in Lancashire was making them under licence. Distribution was by the Cairns Cycle firm, who sold bicycles complete with the GYS attachment.

In 1951 a kit became available from Cobli, a London firm, which mounted the engine below the saddle to drive the rear wheel. The GYS became the Motomite for 1951, but then changed its name again to become the Mocyc for 1952. It kept this name until 1955, when it was withdrawn from the market.

HARPER

Some makes never really got off the ground, and this was one of them. The intention was to build an all-British scooter at the Harper Aircraft works at Exeter Airport, and the prototype was first seen in March 1954. It had low, wide lines, so both rider and passenger sat in the bodywork, rather than on the machine, and this style was accentuated by the twin headlamps. Its general construction followed scooter lines while the engine was to be a 122 or 197cc Villiers with electric starting.

Left
The Harper scooter, of 1954, with its futuristic lines, which enclosed the inevitable Villiers engine and was a good try

Far right, top
HEC Power Cycle of 1939 with 80cc engine and a little different to the usual autocycle

Far right bottom
The Her-cu-motor, as sold for 1957 and fitted with a small in-line JAP engine with two-speed gearbox

Above
*The Hercules Corvette in 1960, but really an
imported French Lavalette given new tank transfers*

Development continued during 1954, and the machine was shown at Earls Court, but a year later, work was still in progress and few machines were ever made. Then, in 1957, the name was used by a Surrey-based firm making an invalid carriage, and that was the end of the Harper scooter.

HEC

This autocycle first appeared at the Earls Court Show late in 1938 and was made by the Hepburn Engineering Company of King's Cross, London. It differed in a good many ways from the usual autocycle and used an 80cc two-stroke engine of its own design but manufactured by Levis. Also, while the frame was the open bicycle type, the engine sat above the bottom bracket and not ahead of it as was more usual. The fuel tank went between the frame members above the engine and the rest of the machine was heavy-duty bicycle with rigid

forks and drum brakes. The whole engine unit was held at three points and could be quickly and easily removed to leave the basic bicycle should this be needed.

By May 1939 the makers had moved to Birmingham while for 1940 the engine and cycle side were modified. During the war, HEC merged with Levis and turned to making air compressors.

HERCULES

This was an all-British moped, built by one of the largest bicycle firms in the country, launched at the Earls Court show late in 1955 and sold as the Grey Wolf. Its finish matched its name and the 49cc two-stroke engine was made by the JAP company with its crankshaft set along the machine to drive back to the clutch and two-speed gearbox. This hung from the spine frame which had leading-link front forks and both wheels had 23in. tyres.

The Grey Wolf name was soon dropped, and the machine became the Her-cu-motor. It ran well and cruised best at 25mph, the main problems being electrical. The model was listed as a Mk II for 1958, but

around that time production came to a halt when the JAP engine supply dried up.

However, the firm continued and in 1960 introduced the Corvette moped, which used a 49cc French Lavalette engine. This had V-belt primary drive and automatic clutch, and a simple rigid moped frame with telescopic forks. Its appearance was similar to the earlier machine, but it was withdrawn at the end of 1961.

HJH

H.J. Hulsman gave his initials to this small Welsh firm, which was based at Neath, in Glamorgan. There, in 1954, he began production of a conventional lightweight, which was called the Dragon, for all its prosaic Villiers 8E engine and three speeds.

The frame was a loop type built of square-section tubing with plunger rear and telescopic front suspension. Equipment included a dualseat and twin toolboxes, while the machine was nicely finished in maroon and silver with chrome-plated tank and mudguards.

For 1955 the Dragon was joined by the Super Dragon which had Earles forks, the Dragon Major with a 224cc Villiers 1H engine in a pivoted-fork frame with

Earles forks, the Dragonette with a 147cc 30C engine, rigid frame and telescopics, and the Trials which used a 7E engine in a rigid frame. For 1956 the engines, frames and suspensions were changed around for some models but this extensive programme was altogether too much for a small firm, and it ran into financial problems that year. There were other difficulties of lack of capital and obtaining local skilled labour, so by June, production had ceased, and in October, Henry William James John Granville Hulsman admitted a deficit of £5800 at a bankruptcy hearing. The HJH era was over.

HUMBER

Humber had their roots in bicycles and were involved early with powered machines to have their moment of glory in the TT, when P. J. Evans won the 1911 Junior. Despite this and some Brooklands successes, they were not a dominant make in the 1920s. By 1930 their range comprised three 349cc models, one with overhead camshaft introduced in 1928. It had the usual bevels and vertical shaft then common and conventional cycle parts. The other models were the OHV and the

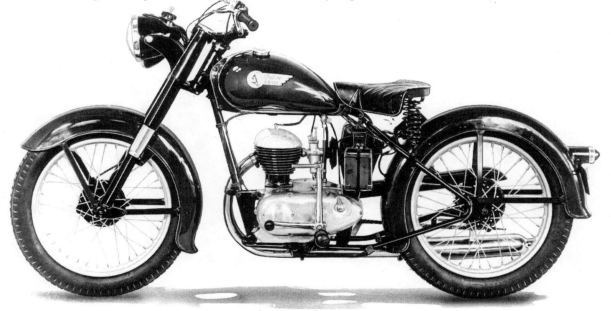

SV with valve gear to suit and these used the same
detail parts. This proved to be the final year as the firm
decided to concentrate on cars, so they stopped making
motorcycles and later sold the bicycle side to Raleigh.

Above
*The later model S Indian Brave with spring frame, but
otherwise little altered*

Below
1931 James Flying Ace C1 with 499cc James twin

INDIAN

An important American make which had a number of
links with British firms in the postwar era. These
included Royal Enfield, AMC and Velocette, but the
first on the scene were Brockhouse at Southport,
Lancashire, who were already producing the Corgi
when they became involved with Indian in the early
post-war years. Between them, they decided they needed a model to fit between the tiny Corgi and the heavy
V-twins, and the outcome was the 248cc Indian Brave.

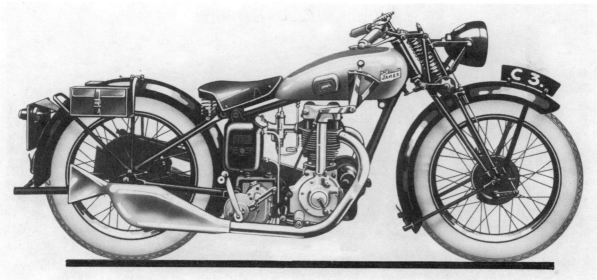

Top
1931 James C3 single with 493cc Rudge engine

Below
*The 1936 H9 James model with petroil-lubricated
249cc Villiers engine*

The machine was built on British lines for its
cycle parts, but the engine less so. It was a side-valve
type but with unit construction, an alternator and wet-sump
lubrication, while the transmission was on the
right and the pedals on the left to suit the American
market. The unit went into a loop frame with telescopic
forks and only a prop stand was provided, awkward
for dealing with a puncture.

Some of the specification was advanced for 1950
when it was built for export only and performed to the
same level as its contemporaries. Its real problem was
poor assembly and a lack of reliability so it failed to
make any real impact in the USA, and by 1952 became
available in the sterling area, although still not in its
home country.

This situation changed in 1954, when a second
model was introduced with pivoted-fork rear suspension
but sales remained poor and at the end of 1955
production ceased. Within two years Indian were selling
Royal Enfields with their name on the tank.

IXION

The Ixion company folded in the late 1920s, but the
name was revived by New Hudson for 1930, to clear
stocks of a slow-selling model. This had a 249cc side-valve
engine and three-speed gearbox fitted into a dia-mond
frame. The magneto location was between the
engine and gearbox, so was well protected but none too
accessible. Tubular girder forks went at the front and
the cycle parts were conventional in form. Lighting was
by acetylene or could be by dynamo, which was an
option. Once the existing stock was sold, the operation
closed down and the Ixion name returned to oblivion.

JAMES

To post-World War 2 riders the James was a utility two-stroke, but to earlier enthusiasts it was a Jimmy James V-twin or four-stroke single. The firm had its origins in 1880 and built its first motorcycle in 1902. From the start it was innovative and successful, although in 1920 it received a setback when the factory burnt down.

It took two years to get back on the market, but during the rest of the 1920s a succession of well-designed and well-made singles and V-twins left the premises. They were not built in large numbers for they lacked the cachet of a TT win or the bark of a tuned exhaust, but those that bought them were well pleased.

The range for 1930 included machines with James and Villiers engines, for the firm had seen the way business was drifting and the small machines were a hedge for the future. They ranged from 172 to 196 and 247cc and were conventional in form with rigid frame, girder forks and the accepted level of equipment for a utility model of the times. The rest of the range had James four-stroke engines, and these were a 249cc side-valve, 349cc with sv or ohv, and four 499cc V-twins, two each with sv and ohv, one of the latter for dirt-track use.

While the 1929 twins had fitted four-speed gearboxes as standard it was back to three for 1930 and 1931 with four speeds an option. At the end of the year James bought the Baker firm and began to use that

Top
1939 James 122cc model K17 which went to war as the Military Lightweight officially and as the 'Clockwork Mouse' by popular vote
Left
James Superlux autocycle of 1948 powered by the Villiers 98cc JDL engine installed in typical frame with girder forks
Top, right
Very basic transport in the form of a 1953 James Comet J10 with 1F engine, two speeds and simple girder forks for the rigid frame
Right
The 1951 James Cadet with 122cc Villiers 10D engine in a rigid frame with light telescopic forks

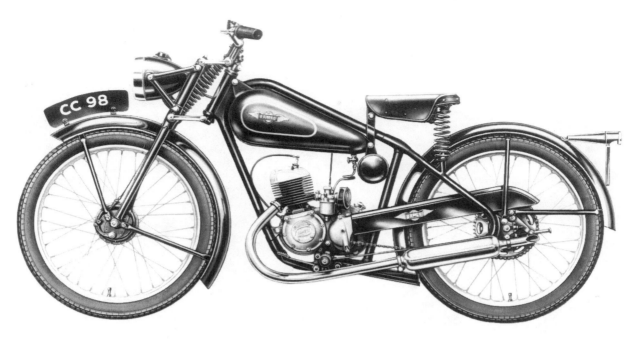

marque's frame for some of its models. It was of a bolted-up design with all straight tubes.

The range was similar for 1931 but it was joined by one model with a 249cc ohv engine and another with a 499cc four-valve Rudge engine. Only two twins were left and the 499cc sv was given a light grey finish with blue lining and tank-top panel to be called the Grey Ghost model the other took the name Flying Ace. Two models with 148cc James engines were added for 1932 but the Rudge one was dropped.

The 148s continued into 1933 as the Utility and Comet, while the single petroil-lubricated 196cc became the Terrier but with a James designed-and-built engine fitted with a four-speed gearbox. The 250 changed to the long-stroke Villiers engine, while the 249 sv became the Mercury, which seems to strain the buyer's credulity. The 249cc ohv was called the Shooting Star and it and the Mercury had four speeds. The sv twin became the Flying Ghost, so the range was smaller and less exciting than in the past.

The whole range continued for 1934 with a chrome tank with green panels, except on the Utility, which had an all-green tank. It was the same for 1935 but for 1936 it was two-strokes only, so the delightful V-twin was no more. The two with 148cc James engines ran on with the 196cc version, but the other two models used Villiers engines and were of 249cc. In June 1936 they were joined by a 122cc machine of very simple design with tubular frame, blade girders and a cast-alloy expansion box in front of the crankcase. Its frame top tube ran above the tank.

For 1937 it was acknowledged that all the power

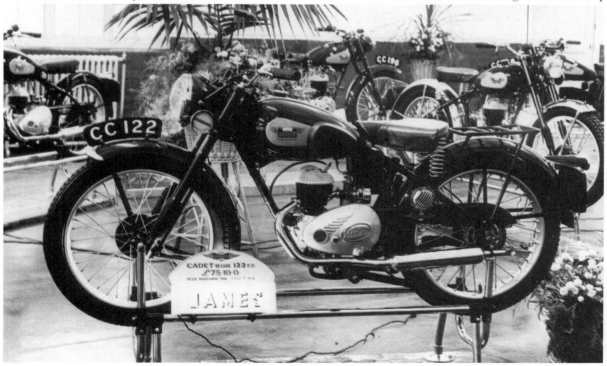

units came from Villiers and the range adopted a black and gold finish. It comprised the 122, two 148s, a 196 and two 249s, all of which ran on for 1938 plus an autocycle with a 98cc engine in a strengthened bicycle frame with rigid forks. It was very basic transport. 1939 brought a number of changes with all models, except the autocycle, having a new simple loop frame and a new tank finished in black and silver with gold lining. The utility 122cc was also offered with a 98cc engine to suit some countries' tax laws and there was one new model which used the new 197cc Villiers 3E engine in the loop frame.

The whole range was listed for 1940 and was joined by a de luxe edition of the autocycle which had a JDL engine, rubber-mounted handlebars and engine shields among its improvements over the standard model. Then Jimmy James went to war using the 122cc model as the basis of a light machine for the airborne forces. It was known as the Clockwork Mouse (officially, the Military Lightweight) and did sterling service. Their factory was badly bombed in 1940 but the ML was built from 1943 on, nearly 6000 being produced in all.

Post-war, the ML formed one half of their programme with a maroon and silver tank finish and the addition of a rear carrier. It was joined by the Superlux autocycle, to give a minimal range, but met the urgent needs of the times for transport of any sort. Both machines continued in production until the end of 1948.

The autocycle ran on into 1949, but the ML was replaced by a small range of machines in three capacities. Smallest was the Comet, built in standard or de

luxe form, and both used the new 99cc Villiers 1F engine with two-speed gearbox controlled by a handlebar lever, and this went into a simple rigid loop frame. At the front were girder forks with single tubes on each side to give the appearance, at least, of telescopics, and both wheels had small drum brakes.

Next in size were standard and de luxe Cadet models, which used the 122cc Villiers 10D engine in similar cycle parts, and finally, for the road, there was the de luxe Captain with 197cc Villiers 6E engine in the Cadet cycle parts, and with battery lighting as standard. Unlisted, but built in small numbers, were competition models using either the 10D or 6E engine with suitably modified frame, forks and wheels.

During March 1949 the autocycle was redesigned to use the 99cc Villiers 2F single-speed engine unit, but retained its Superlux name. The same month saw telescopic front forks appearing for the 122 and 197cc road models which used Dunlop rubber cushions as the suspension medium.

In general, the range continued as it was for 1950, with the autocycle, two each of the Comet and Cadet, plus the Captain, a second version of this with plunger rear suspension being listed, the suspension an option for the 122cc competition model. All models, other than the autocycle, now had the telescopic front forks. There was little change for 1951, but there was one new model, the 99cc Commodore, which was really a Comet, with 1F engine and enclosure panels. These ran from the downtube to the rear axle, and up from the footrest to the cylinder head, with legshields at the front. The whole range continued for 1952, the 197cc competition machines being replaced by a single

model with rigid frame as the Colonel Competition.

Things changed more for 1953, although the autocycle continued as before as the Superlux. In the 122cc class, the standard Cadet and competition models were dropped and the de luxe Cadet was joined by the one which used the 13D engine with three speeds in a new frame with plunger rear suspension. The Captain models remained, but with coil spring forks, also used on the 122cc models, and the competition version became the Commando, kept the rigid frame, but had a 7E engine and telescopic forks with two-way hydraulic damping.

For 1954 the Comet moved to telescopic forks, plunger rear suspension and the 4F engine. Only one 122cc model continued, while there was a new 197cc Captain with an 8E engine in a pivoted-fork frame, a dualseat and neat toolboxes under its nose, so was much more modern in its appearance. Similar cycle parts were also used by the Colonel, which was powered by the 224cc Villiers 1H engine, had larger brakes, but otherwise the style was the same. Finally, there was the Cotswold scrambler with 7E engine, four speeds, pivoted-fork frame and suitable wheels and tyres. The autocycle was dropped during the year, but most of the range ran on for 1955. New was a Cadet with a 147cc Villiers 30C engine in place of the 13D. but still in the plunger frame.

The Cadet had a major change for 1956, when it kept the 30C engine, but this went into a completely new frame with pressed-steel rear section and pivoted rear fork. This was controlled by coil springs, set far enough forward to be concealed by the very deep valance of the rear guard, which was formed as part of the pressing. Light telescopic forks went at the front,

and there was a short dualseat for just one person. Also new was the Comet, which used the new Cadet frame and forks to house the 4F engine, and the Commando, which replaced the older model but kept the 7E engine and housed it in the pivoted-fork frame. Both the Captain and Colonel ran on with 18in. wheels in place of the earlier 19in. ones.

The range continued as it was for 1957 with two additions. One was simply the option of the 6F engine in the Comet, in place of the 4F which remained available. The model kept its single seat, but a dualseat became an option for the Cadet. The second model was a more major addition and was the 249cc Commodore with AMC engine. This reflected that James, along with Francis-Barnett, had become part of the AMC group which led to some badge engineering between the two marques as well as their use of the AMC two-stroke engines.

The Commodore was the first James to use the engine and it followed the Cadet in the design of its frame. Thus, the front section was tubular, but the centre section was built up from pressings, carried the pivoted fork and housed the electrics, while the deep rear mudguard was bolted to it. The machine had stylish side covers, a deeply valanced front mudguard and a dualseat.

The firm switched more to the AMC engines for 1958, when the Commodore was joined by the 171cc Cavalier which was much in the manner of the Comet and Cadet, which both continued, as did the Captain, although that was fitted with a 10E engine in place of the older 8E. There were no competition models listed at all at first, but trials one made a brief reappearance during the year, when it, too, was fitted with a 10E engine. Otherwise, it was much as before, with pivoted-fork frame and suitable equipment for trials use. It was only listed for a few months.

For 1959 the Comet, Cadet, Cavalier, Captain and Commodore ran on and were joined by two new competition models. Both were powered by the 249cc AMC engine, modified to suit the intended use. The pivoted-fork frame was common to both, but the trials model used James forks, whereas the scrambler had AMC Teledraulic forks. The fixtures and fittings were to suit each machine's respective role.

During that last year of the decade, James made even greater use of the AMC engine by fitting it in the Flying Cadet model, which used the 149cc version in the Cadet cycle parts. For 1960 only the Comet kept to Villiers power, now with the 6F as standard, and the other models were dropped. This left the roadster and two competition models, with the 249cc AMC engine, and the Flying Cadet, but not the Cavalier, which had also gone. For the 200cc class, there was a new Captain with the 199cc AMC engine in cycle parts that followed the style of the Commodore. On this note, James entered the new decade. That year, they added a scooter to their list, and later came twins and a return to Villiers power for other models, after the trials and tribulations of the AMC units.

JONES

This was the prototype of the autocycles built by many companies before and after the war. It was designed by G.H. Jones around 1936 and built in conjunction with Villiers. The engine was of 98cc, single-geared, with

Top
Engine unit of the Jones was bolted to the frame

Bottom
Jones machine, the forerunner of the autocycle

auxiliary pedalling gear and drove back to a clutch, contained within an extension of the crankcase casting. The clutch shaft was hollow to allow the pedal shaft to pass through it and the whole unit bolted to the bicycle frame which had a special bottom bracket to take it. Otherwise it was stock but had sprung forks.

The design was quickly taken up by a number of firms, but in the production versions the engine omitted the concentric clutch and pedal shaft, and the pedalling mechanism passed through a cycle-type bottom bracket on the frame.

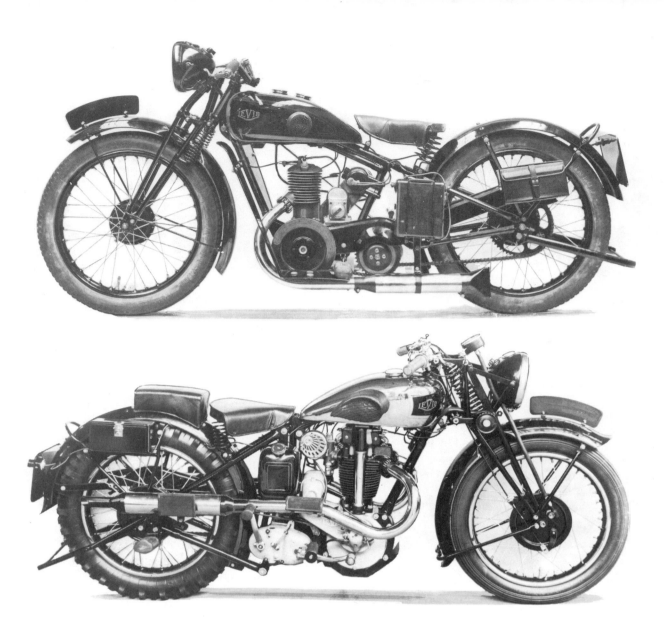

LEVIS

This firm dated from 1911 and in its early years was best known for its two-strokes with which they had many racing success in the early 1920s. By the end of the decade the effects of this were wearing off, but for 1930 the range still included the 247cc Six-port model as well as the model Z of the same size. There were also four-strokes listed, as 247cc sv and ohv singles plus a 346cc ohv single available in single or twin-port forms.

The range was much the same for 1931 but dropped the two-strokes and the side-valve for 1932, adding a 498cc ohv single the next year, all models having options available to increase their sales appeal. They ran on for 1934 to be joined by two diverse 247cc models, one a revival from the past in the form of the Two-stroke which was conventional but did have an oil pump. The other was quite different for it was a four-stroke with a chain-driven overhead camshaft and it retained the total-loss lubrication system they used for all their four-strokes. They advertised the use of fresh, clean oil as a benefit to reduce wear, which is borne out

Top
Levis model Z from 1931 with 247cc engine
Bottom
1935 model D Special Levis of 498cc. The engine has ohv although the pushrod tunnel gives the appearance of ohc

by the condition of engines half a century later.

This range continued into 1935, in fact it was nearly then before the ohc model reached production, and then into 1936, by when the camshaft engine was an option. New were a trio of Light models which lost weight, but were otherwise as the three ohv singles.

For 1937 the smallest Light model was dropped but a second 247cc two-stroke was added as the Baby and a 591cc ohv single appeared at the other end of the scale. The Baby went the following year by when the four-strokes all had enclosed valve gear, but the range expanded again for 1939 when the second two-stroke returned and both were listed as Master Two-stroke, a

Left
*The real overhead camshaft
Levis, the 247cc model CB
from 1935*

Bottom
*1939 Levis SF500 of 498cc
with plunger frame. The two
sides were linked by hydraulic
pipe and to friction damping
pads*

slogan the firm had used prior to World War 1. The other models were all there plus two competition machines using the 346 and 498cc ohv engines, and a 346cc side-valve model. The 346 and 498cc singles were also listed in a new frame with plunger rear suspension which had the two sides connected by a hydraulic pipe to balance the loads and provide some measure of damping.

The range was the same for 1940 with little or no change, but that year saw the end of the marque.

LGC

Another small Birmingham company that used others' engines to build its machines. For 1930 there was one with a 247cc Villiers engine listed as the TS/1 while the other three had JAP engines and were the 300cc sv S1, the 346cc ohv single-port 0/1 and the 346cc twin-port 0/2.

All except the last continued into 1931, but that was their final year. Len Gundle, the owner, went back to making butchers' cycles and ice-cream trikes.

LOHMANN

This was a German make of clip-on engine, but is included because it was handled in the United Kingdom by Britax and because of its sheer novelty. It was a mere 18cc in capacity, but even more unusual was the fact that it was a compression-ignition two-stroke with variable compression ratio.

The engine was first seen in 1949, but it was late 1952 before it reached the Britax lists. It could push a cycle along at 15mph on the flat and to deal with steep hills. but clip-on buyers looked for a little more performance and preferred an engine type they understood better.

Below
The 346cc LGC model 0/1, in this case from 1928

MAJESTIC

This make was a second string of the OK Supreme company and came about when the AJS concern was sold in 1931. While the bulk of the equipment moved south some parts stock was bought up by OK.

Three models were announced in January 1933 with 249, 348 or 499cc inclined ohv engines in conventional cycle parts. A week after the description had appeared, there was a note that the company would operate separately from OK Supreme but there was no further mention of them, so it would seem that this venture failed to get off the ground.

Right
The Majestic of 1933 which went as quickly as it came

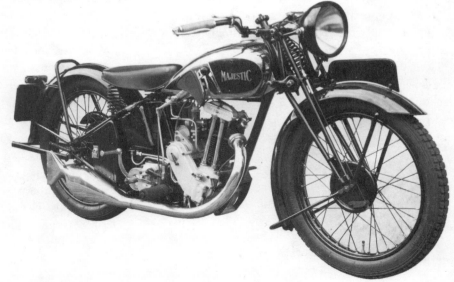

MARTIN-COMERFORD

When dirt-track racing came to England in 1928 all manner of machines were pressed into service at first and many firms listed a dirt-track model, but within a year or so Rudge and Douglas dominated.

Then late in 1930 the JAP factory produced an engine designed just for speedway and George Wallis came up with a frame for it. This combination won on its debut and the JAP engine went on to totally dominate speedway racing for four decades. The Wallis design was taken up successfully by Comerfords, the big dealers at Thames Ditton in Surrey and sold well, at first as the Comerford-Wallis.

It was typical of the type with short wheelbase, engine well forward, curved downtube and strutted forks which were normally Webb and in effect bridged telescopics with only about 1in. of travel. In time it became known as the Martin-Comerford as it developed, but most alterations were carried out to improve reliability or to aid the riders in their dash from meeting to meeting.

When the JAP engine took over, the speedway machine became standardised. It may have taken something away that existed briefly in the early exciting years when experimentation raged, but its simple efficiency was what won races.

Top
A Martin-Rudge from 1939 fitted with the usual JAP engine and set up for speedway

MERCURY

This name was used before and after the war by two totally different firms. Prewar, it was a special built for grand touring, the result of some dissatisfaction and came from a small Scott tuning shop and, in the end, five machines were built, the first in 1937.

They used the 596cc Scott engine and three-speed gearbox fitted into a frame constructed from Duralumin extrusions bolted together. Both wheels had suspension but neither was conventional. The front looked to be telescopics but was a combination of this plus a duplex steering system similar to that used by OEC which made it very self-centring. The rear had a system of pivots and guide plates to keep the rear chain tension constant and neither system was damped.

To suit its job, the sides of the frame were enclosed by panels, comfort was assisted by fat tyres, and both wheels had alloy hubs and big brakes. There was also a stepped-level dualseat, a rarity among a sea of saddles, and a five-gallon petrol tank mounted on rubber and with a toolbox plus glove compartment set in its top panel. Only three machines were completed prewar and the final, fifth one was not finished until 1959 but all five still existed into the 1980s.

The Mercury name was revived postwar by a bicycle firm for two models. Both were a little unusual, for one was a moped, but with an ohv engine, while the other was a small scooter with motorcycle-size wheels. The moped was the Mercette, which had a 48cc engine built in unit with a two-speed gearbox mounted in a rigid frame with telescopic forks. The scooter was the Hermes and had a 49cc ILO two-stroke engine with two speeds which also went into a rigid frame but its wheels were 20in. diameter, while the scooter bodywork implied rear suspension.

These two were joined by three more for 1957, two with 99cc Villiers engines. One used the 6F unit with footchange in a motorcycle named Grey Streak and fitted with front and rear suspension. The other was the Dolphin scooter and used the 4F engine while the third newcomer was the Whippet 60 which was an enlarged Mercette.

Only the Mercette and Grey Streak continued for 1958, while the scooters were replaced by the Pippin which stayed with the 4F engine and had a more conventional body. It proved an adequate performer but the firm found limited demand for its products, and during the year ceased production of its powered models.

MINI-MOTOR

This was perhaps the best known of the British clip-on engines and, although of Italian origin, when it appeared in 1949 it was built in Croydon. There was nothing exceptional about the unit, but it was well made and available at a time when anything was better than nothing.

The 49.9cc two-stroke engine sat above the bicycle rear wheel, which it drove with a friction-roller and was quite conventional in design with the petroil tank mounted above it. It could drive a bicycle at 30mph, which was adequate, and thousands found them ideal for short trips, whether to station, office or shops. Some were even fitted to tandems, where they proved equal to the task of hauling two people along at 20mph.

The unit ran on until 1955, but by then the moped was taking over and the Mini-Motor was no more.

Below
Mini-Motor at the end of the 1953
National Rally at Weston-Super-Mare - a
long ride for owner D.J. Anderson

MONTGOMERY

This was another fringe make that relied on proprietary parts, and found the 1930s hard going, but survived by offering a massive range based on Villiers and JAP engines fitted into just two frames but with every model available in standard and de luxe form. At the bottom came a 247cc Villiers engine but then there were JAP side-valve engines of 300, 346, 490 and 600cc plus a 750cc V-twin and ohv engines in 245, 346 and 490cc sizes.

They added the sporting Greyhound models for 1931, all with ohv engines plus one new one with a 677cc ohv V-twin. There was also a 994cc side-valve

Above
The Montgomery Greyhound of 1931 with 680 ohv JAP engine and a nice line to its exhaust systems

model for sidecar work. They changed premises late that year which resulted in a curtailed 1932 range but the numbers were up again a year later and included a 148cc Villiers model.

The range continued in this manner as year followed year, losing some and gaining other models which included a 122cc Villiers for 1936 but always in the strong Montgomery frame and with the various options to met the market demands. By 1939 there was plunger rear suspension for some models and by then

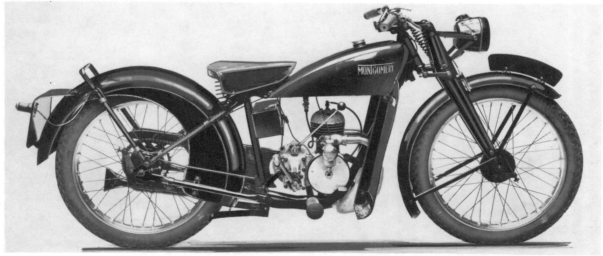

Above
1937 Montgomery Terrier de luxe with 122cc Villiers engine and simple cycle parts

Left
The Greyhound model MDL Montgomery of 1939 with 499cc JAP engine with continuous fins all the way up both barrel and head

the range was down to 98 and 122cc Villiers plus 245, 346 and 499cc ohv JAPs in standard and with rear suspension, the largest still with the Greyhound name, the others called Terriers.

Much of this went forward as a 1940 range but with the advent of war, production ceased, not to start again.

NEW COMET

This marque had its roots in supplying components and was first built in Edwardian times in Birmingham. Production was spasmodic, but began again in 1930 with a single lightweight using a 172cc Villiers engine in conventional cycle parts. For 1931 it was replaced by a 196cc unit and called the Super Sports, but from then on the firm found it better business to be suppliers to the trade and returned to making components.

NEW GERRARD

Jock Porter won two TT races in the 1920s on the New Gerrard machines which he built in Edinburgh, and this gave the name good publicity. The machines were built up from bought-in parts aside from the frame and throughout the 1930s the range was a single model with a 346cc ohv JAP engine. It was otherwise conventional, developed over the decade and remained in the lists to 1940, when production ceased.

NEW HENLEY

This was another small firm who assembled machines using bought-in parts. Engines were Villiers or JAP by 1930 and these went into a variety of frames with Burman or Albion three-speed gearboxes and fittings

much as many others.

The Villiers machines were the 172cc V1, the 196cc V2 and the 247cc Bryn, the last in a channel-steel frame. JAP ohv engines were of 346 or 490cc, the sv of 490cc and the twin a sv 750cc. The smallest was dropped for 1931 but three others appeared as TT or sports models but during the year the make ceased trading and became one more victim of the Depression.

Top
In 1940 the New Hudson name reappeared on a 98cc autocycle

Bottom
A 1931 496cc New Hudson with enclosure panels

Right
The 1950 New Hudson autocycle with Villiers 2F

NEW HUDSON

New Hudson made their own engines or used proprietary ones over the years from their beginning in 1903
and in 1930 had a good line of conventional singles on
offer. These all had vertical cylinders, dry sump lubrication, saddle tanks and a high standard of finish and
equipment.

There was an sv and ohv model in each traditional capacity of 249, 346 and 496cc and also models
in the two larger sizes with Power Plus-tuned engines.

The range was totally revised for 1931 to four
models with inclined engines and partial enclosure of
the lower engine and gearbox. The engines were 346cc
sv or ohv, 496cc ohv and 548cc sv. To prove the new
designs the firm ran a 548cc machine plus sidecar over
a long distance but this failed to help them over a bad
patch. There had been some problems with the engines
and enclosure had not caught on as predicted but they
were stuck with it.

There were revisions for 1932 but the enclosure
remained and sales continued depressed on into 1933 as
few buyers were prepared to risk scarce pennies on a
model with a whisper of a problem, even after it had
gone away. Fortunately for New Hudson, in that year
they were approached to make Girling brakes and suspension parts, which is precisely what they did from
then on.

In March 1940 the name reappeared on the side
of an autocycle which was typical of the type with a
98cc Villiers JDL engine and rigid frame and forks.
During the war the name was taken over by BSA and
they revived it postwar, building the same model from
1946. It gained girder forks for 1948 but was much

altered for the next year when it changed to a 99cc 2F
engine which called for a major frame change. Despite
this, the looks were little altered thanks to the conceal-
ing engine shields and the model ran on in this form
into 1956.

In May that year it was revamped with a new
frame, tubular forks which kept the girder action, and
had the tank and side panels restyled in a modern form
to give a new line. It was a good attempt to update an
old design but underneath was still the 2F engine and
by then the moped was taking over from the autocycle,
offering similar performance for a lower running cost
and better styling. The machine continued to be listed
until 1958, but that year saw the end of the 2F engine,
so the New Hudson also left the market.

NEW IMPERIAL

In their time New Imperial won six TT races, most in
the 250 class, and the last in 1936, the company having
been founded in 1892. During the 1930s they built
some innovative machines.

The 1930 range was simple with six models, two
344cc and one 499cc with side valves, and one each of
245, 346 and 499cc and ohv. They continued for 1931
plus Blue Prince models in the two larger ohv sizes but
only two from the range went on into 1932. That was
the year the firm took their first step along the road to
unit construction, then something held to impede servicing and not to be encouraged.

The unit construction models were announced in

August 1931 and had a remarkably modern specification. In addition to a common base for both engine and gearbox they also had wet sump lubrication with the oil carried within a compartment formed in the crankcase. On the cycle side there was rear suspension with a pivoted rear fork and the springs under the saddle in monoshock style.

The models were built in 344 and 499cc sizes and both had twin-port heads, inclined cylinders and fully enclosed valve gear. While the concept was novel the actual construction followed the ways of the period so transmission was by chain and there were only three speeds in the gearbox. However, cast-alloy case enclosed the primary chain. The remainder of the range was little altered and included many options on the basic machines.

A third unit construction model appeared at the show late in 1931 and for all its small size was of great interest for it had a 150cc ohv inclined engine with fully enclosed valve gear, gear primary drive and crossover, three-speed gearbox. In this form it failed to go into production but a revised design came in 1932 which continued with unit construction but had helical gear primary drive. Ignition was by coil with the points

Above
A 1931 model 7 New Imperial of 499cc with side-valve engine

Below
The Blue Prince 344cc model F10 New Imperial of 1931 with ohv and partly-exposed clutch

in the end of the dynamo, which was mounted above the gearbox and gear driven from the clutch. From this layout came the triangular chaincase shape that was to characterise the model series from then on.

The move to unit construction in both rigid and pivoted-fork frames continued for 1933 with few models in the old style. Both lines extended for 1934, some using the new gear primary drive while others kept to chains, the result of this being a wide range of conventional and radical models for the customers. New and exciting were two Grand Prix models of 245 and 344cc which were replicas of the works racers and built for fast road work or road racing. Engines were tuned and the specification adjusted to suit, while both had the oil tank combined with the petrol in a pistol-grip style which was distinctive and attractive.

The range continued extensive for 1935 with more new models in the radical form, but was thinned

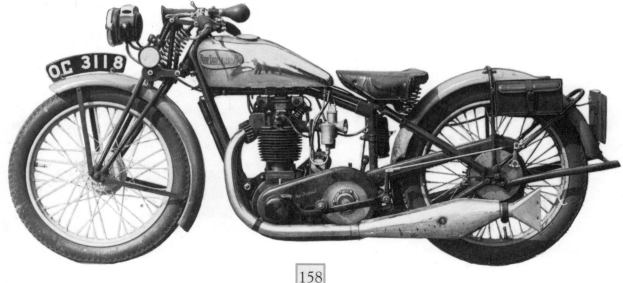

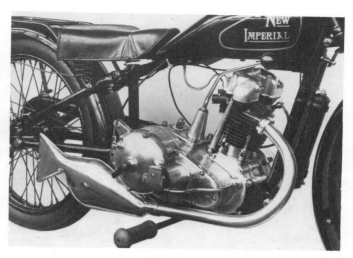

Above
A unit construction New Imperial of
1933 with oil bath chaincase and pivoted
fork rear suspension

Below
1933 New Imperial model 30 of 247cc

Above
The prototype 150cc New Imperial of
1932 with valve gear behind the cylinder

Bottom
The 1933 TT New Imperial which led to the models 50 and 60 the following year

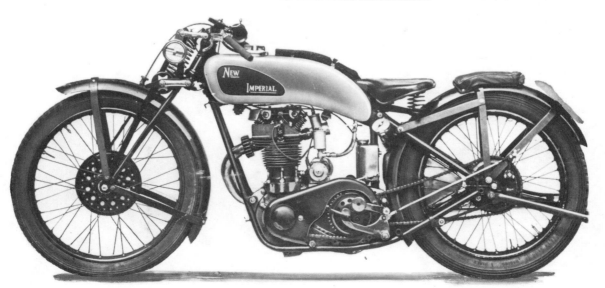

Right
*The 344cc 1935 model 49
was supplied
complete with Watsonian
sidecar*

Centre
*Engine unit of the 1935
New Imperial 496cc model
80 with full train of gears
on the timing side running
up to the magneto*

Bottom
*New Imperial model 60 of
1939, a 346cc ohv listed as
the Grand Prix*

a little for the next year although unit and non-unit models ran on side by side. All but one had ohv, the exception of 554cc, while the Grand Prix models became pure racing machines fitted out accordingly as regards equipment, magneto and carburettor.

The spring frame had fallen from favour but was back for 1937 for all but the smallest 148cc model and all kept they gear drive and had ohv. Most were available with the choice of three forms of electrics, hand or footchange, standard or de luxe finish and other options including tuned engines. This took the firm up to 1939 but by then they were in some degree of financial trouble and were sold to Jack Sangster who planned to move the New Imperials to the Triumph works in Coventry, where there was some empty space. This happened in August but the range shrank to four basic unit construction machines for 1940 and then just faded away. Like many others it was not revived after the war.

*Far right, top
The 1939 Norman Motobyk with 98cc
Villiers engine*

NEWMOUNT

This was not really an English machine at all but a German Zundapp with new tank badges. It was the model S200 with a 198cc two-stroke engine driving a three-speed gearbox. The frame was built up in the German style of the time and in 1931 was joined by a further model with a 300cc engine having pump lubrication. As well as the two-strokes the firm added four strokes using 348 and 499cc ohv Rudge engines. All these models continued to be offered for 1932 and 1933, after which the make was no longer available.

Below
A 198cc Newmount from 1931, really a German Zundapp in disguise

NORMAN

This bicycle company was sited in Ashford, Kent, and came into the motorcycle field with two models for 1939. One was an autocycle called a Motobyke and the other the Lightweight 122cc. The autocycle was much as others with a 98cc Villiers Junior engine fitted in an open frame with rigid forks. The motorcycle had a 9D 122cc Villiers engine housed in a simple loop frame with blade girder forks, a cylindrical toolbox under the saddle and a rear stand. It came with legshields as standard.

The Lightweight was listed for 1940 along with three versions of the Motobyke, one as before, one with

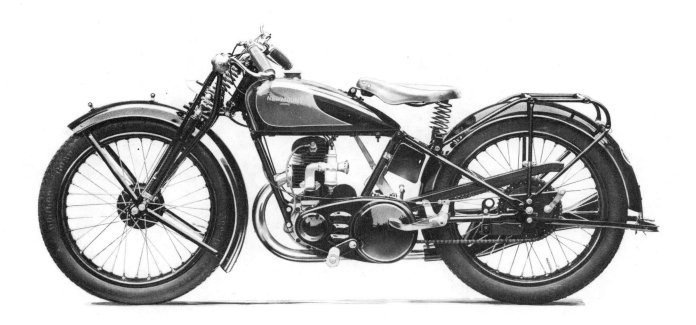

Webb girder forks and the third the carrier which was lower geared. All changed to the JDL engine with the detachable cylinder head. One final model was created by fitting a 98cc engine into the motorcycle frame, and on this note production ceased until 1946 when they picked up their prewar models more or less where they had left off as the Autocycle and Motorcycle.

These two models comprised the Norman range until late 1948, when they were replaced by more modern machines. The Autocycle changed to the 99cc 2F engine in a suitable frame with girder forks and the finish was in maroon. The other models used the 122cc 10D and 197cc 6E engines in a rigid frame with tele-

scopic forks and built in standard and de luxe forms.. They were joined by another for 1950, this using the 99cc 1F engine in the same cycle parts except for girder forks which were changed for telescopics for 1951.

There were no changes until 1953 when the 122cc models were replaced by economy versions but were joined by both that size and the 197cc in a pivoted-fork frame. This differed from most in that the spring units were positioned as upper chainstays, so were laid well down, while the rear subframe was formed to run around them. They were joined by a 197cc competition model which was altered for trials work with changes to wheels and tyres, the result work-

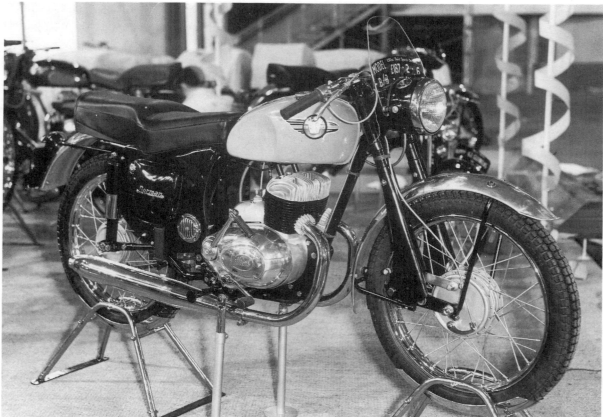

Far left, top
Norman model C autocycle with 2F Villiers
99cc engine enclosed by rather bulbous shields

Far left, bottom
Norman B1S with 122cc 10D engine unit and
their laid-down rear units, as still used on this

1954 example

Top
Showtime late in 1955 at Earls Court for the
Norman model TS fitted with the 242cc
British Anzani twin engine

Above
The B3 Sports Norman with
2T engine, leading-link forks,
low bars and small screen

163

ing well.

For 1954 the autocycle stayed as it was but the smallest motorcycle changed to the 4F engine. The 197cc models all changed to the 8E engine, the competition one to the 7E while the economy model and the rigid ones were dropped during the year and the spring frames were given normal suspension units. More changed for 1955 when the 122cc engines were changed for the 147cc 30C type and a twin was added using the 242cc British Anzani engine, both this and the 197cc singles being fitted with Armstrong leading-link forks.

New for 1956 was a moped named the Nippy, which was based on a Continental design and powered by a 47.6cc Sachs engine with two-speed gearbox. This unit went into a rigid pressed-steel beam frame with leading-link forks. It was a smart machine, and the firm intended to gradually increase their own production of parts in place of buying them in. The autocycle entered its last year in 1957, when the two 147cc models were joined by another de luxe one, fitted with the 148cc 31C engine unit. The three 197cc machines ran on, two with 8E engines and one with the 9E, as did the twin and competition machines. Most had a degree of rear enclosure, which had been developed from prototype designs seen two years earlier and this incorporated toolboxes and mountings for the electrical equip-ment, so tidied the machine up nicely. The Nippy continued, but in a plunger frame.

The moped took over the duties of the autocycle for 1958 and the range ran on with the twin fitted with the 249cc Villiers 2T engine in place of the Anzani. A Sports version was added for 1959 and this had dropped bars, alloy mudguards, plastic flyscreen and knee recesses in the fuel tank, the same parts also going onto a 9E-powered version while the 8E units were no longer used. Two more Nippy mopeds were added, one using a 49.9cc Villiers 3K engine and the other, the Lido, in a pivoted-fork frame and with styled enclosure for the engine unit which extended back to the rear wheel.

In this way the firm reached the end of the decade with eight models, three of them mopeds. These used Sachs, Mi-Val and Villiers engines in a variety of frames both with and without suspension. The motorcycles were the road models with 197cc single 9E or 249cc twin 2T engines, while the competition one with the 9E engine was joined by two more, one still with the 9E and the other with a 246cc 32A engine.

The next year, the firm was taken over by Raleigh, so the motorcycles were soon dropped, while the mopeds went no further. Thus, another firm disappeared after some good years and nice, well finished machines.

Left
Norman Lido moped of 1959 fitted with the Villiers 3K engine unit with styled enclosure

NORTON

At the end of the 1920s the range of Norton road models was looking very vintage in appearance, having altered little during the decade. The machines had a frame that was long and tall, a crude gearchange, vague lubrication and the magneto stuck out in front of the engine, albeit under a large polished cover for 1930. The format was truly much as had been laid down by the firm's founder with solid engineering and upright cylinders. Never was a Norton to incline its barrel even at the height of such fashion, for that was just not Bracebridge Street style.

While the road models were dated, the competition side had brightened up no end in the 1920s with TT wins and successes in Europe and at Brooklands. Thus 1930 saw Norton poised for a decade of success even though the range was in need of an update. It still used the familiar model numbers which would continue on for many more years regardless of format and there were 14 in all. The more basic had a diamond frame, three speeds and front-mounted magneto and were the 490cc sv 16H, a variant with footboards as the model 2, the 634cc Big 4 and model 14 with four speeds, the 490cc ohv model 18, its twin-port version as the 20, and the 588cc ohv 19. There was also the 24, a 19 with four speeds, and the 21, an 18 with different oiling system.

The other five models had a cradle frame and their magneto sited behind the engine and driven from the crankshaft. With ohv were the 348cc JE, the 490cc ES2 and its twin-port variant as the 22. Finally came two camshaft models, the 490cc CS1 and the 348cc CJ, both with the early Moore design of engine with the blister on the right of the crankcase for the camshaft drive and a rear magneto. Outside the road range there was one short-lived special model for dirt-track use, as speedway racing was then called, which used the twin-port model 20 engine in an abbreviated frame with a Webb speedway fork.

1930 was a year in the doldrums for Norton, both on the race circuits and in the showrooms, but 1931 changed all that. Moore had left the firm and taken his camshaft design with him, but in his place came Arthur Carroll, who redesigned the engine into the form that was to run to 1963. At first it had teething problems, but by late 1930 it was winning races and ready for the decade.

1931 brought a radical change to the side- and overhead-valve models, which assumed what was in effect their final form for the next three decades. The engine changes were straightforward and simple. The magneto went behind the engine, where it was chain driven from the inlet camshaft and had the dynamo strapped to its back. The lubrication became dry sump with a simple gear pump in the timing chest.

The model numbers and engine dimensions remained the same, so the 500s still used the famous 79x100mm sizes. The models remained the 348cc JE and CJ, the 490cc 16H, 2, 18, 20, 22, ES2 and CS1, the 588cc 19 and the 634 Big 4. They continued in the diamond and cradle frames as before and the camshaft engines were the Carroll type with its bottom bevel box, outboard magneto drive and new look that was to become very familiar.

From then on the singles continued through the decade with gradual development as the years passed, most changes appearing first on the camshaft models and then moving to the ohv the next year. There were two additions to the range for 1932, these being the International models listed as the 348cc 40 and 490cc 30 and these were based on the existing camshaft machines but with racing magneto, tuned engine and four-speed gearbox, but no lights. They were intended for racing while the CS1 and CJ were for road use but fast road men went for the Inter as they wanted its four speeds and seductive petrol tank, while the tourers preferred the ES2 which was simpler and cheaper.

The JE and 22 faded from the range for 1932, when quickly-detachable wheels were first seen, and 1933 brought Norton forks with check springs for the Inters and a four-speed gearbox for the camshaft and ohv models. At the same time the capacity of the 19 was amended to 597cc and two smaller ohv models of 348cc were added as the 50 and twin-port 55. The forks with check springs went on all models for 1934 when a Norton clutch and an oil bath primary chaincase was adopted. The famous Norton four-speed, footchange gearbox went on to all models for 1935 and in 1936 the ohv models lost the spindly look about the engines as the pushrod tubes were made fatter while 1937 brought a change to the two-brush dynamo and separate regulator box for all models.

1938 brought noticeable changes to most models with the option of plunger rear suspension for the Inters. For the ohv machines the valve gear was fully enclosed, as it was on the sv ones, and all were fitted with a strange silencer with twin rear outlets that found favour with no one. The odd fitment was even used on the trials Norton. This format dated from 1935 and had taken over from the old Colonial specification for competition-oriented riders. In theory at least it could apply

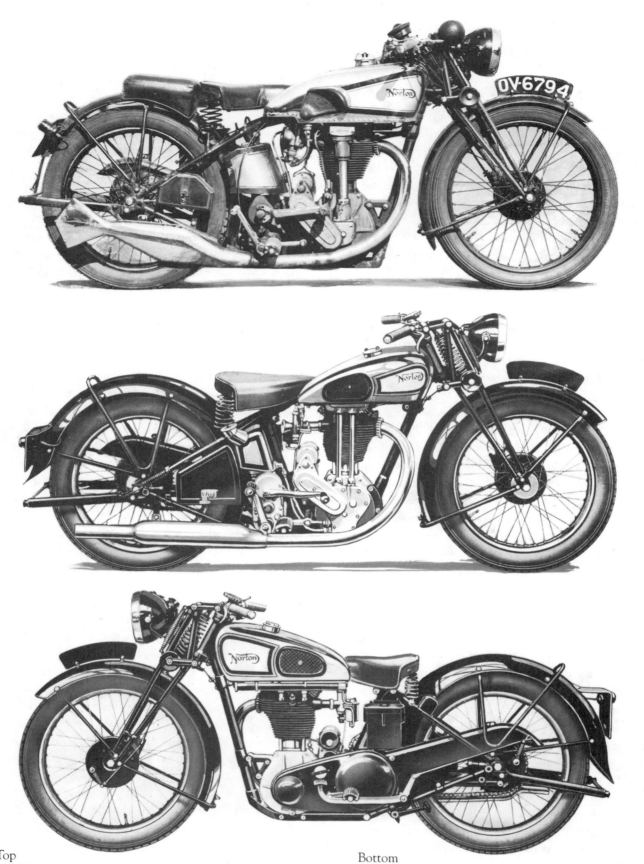

Top
A 1932 Norton International with famous Carroll camshaft design

Centre
Typical ohv model 50 Norton of 348cc from 1935

Bottom
This 1937 348cc Norton CJ has the same transmission as the ohv models

Above
*Norton 490cc CS1 fitted with the
strange silencer common to all models
in 1938 including the trials one*

Bottom
*The side-valve 16H built by Norton
for many years and seen here in 1939
form with enclosed valve gear*

to any model in the range and really was a factory kit of
options fitted on the assembly line. Items used included
special gear ratios, raised exhaust system, high-clear-
ance frame, narrow front fork and hub, folding kickstarter and chrome-plated mudguards, chaincase and
chain-guard.

Also rather special but not in the catalogues was
the big banger camshaft model. This first appeared
around 1936/37 and was of 597cc capacity, based on
the CS1, but was only intended for sidecar use and
then for road racing or ISDT work. To get the tall
engine into the frame the top tube had to be kinked
and there were not many of them, but they dominated
sidecar racing in the early post-war years.

The last year of the decade saw a return to a
tubular silencer and two options for the ES2. The first
was the plunger frame and the second the International
type of petrol tank which transformed the appearance.

The CS1 and CJ were also given the option of the
plunger frame and the Inters were listed in two forms.
The first was a road machine much as the C models,
but with bigger petrol and oil tanks plus more highly
tuned engine. To supplement the road machines there
were a pair of Racing International models, referred to
also as the Manx Grand Prix and the forerunners of the
post-war Manx model. These machines were built for
racing with bench-tested alloy engines, racing magneto
and carburettor, close-ratio gearbox, megaphone
exhaust, plunger frame and conical hubs.

It was a fine model on which to finish off, for
ahead lay the war, many thousands of 16H models and
then peacetime austerity, but a full range was listed for
1940 and should have included revised engines and
frames for many models. These never came, for post-
war the need was for immediate production rather than
innovation. During the war Norton concentrated on

Left
*Nice 'Garden Gate'
Norton with the ohc
engine and all the racing
goodies of the late 1940s*

producing their 16H model in its 1937 form, some 100,000 being built with few alterations. They also built the Big 4 as a sidecar outfit which had the third wheel driven via a dog clutch so that it could be disengaged for road use. Several thousand were built using the 1938-type engine as the basis.

On the face of it, all Norton had to do to produce civilian machines after the war was to change the paint colour in their spray guns from khaki to black. In practice, they did rather more by changing to a cradle frame for both the 16H and the ohv 18. Both were based on the 1939 engines and the machines kept the prewar girder forks but lacked the tank-top instrument panel.

The two models were announced in August 1945 and continued as they were through most of the following year. During 1946 a few road racing machines were built and supplied in full racing trim for the Manx Grand Prix. They were the first to carry the simple Manx Norton name and were listed as the 348cc model 40M and 498cc model 30M. Both were fitted with the famous Norton Roadholder telescopic front forks which had hydraulic damping, so were an improvement on the prewar works type. The frame, with the plunger rear suspension, became known as the 'garden gate' type.

The range was expanded for 1947 when the 16H and 18 were fitted with the Roadholder front forks and joined by the 634cc Big 4 and the ES2, which had plunger rear suspension. The two International models were also back, with the single overhead camshaft engine in 348 and 490cc sizes. The cams were designed to run best on an open pipe, which was to be allowed in the 1947 Clubman TT, and the cycle parts were as the ES2 with the plunger frame and Roadholder telescopic forks, but the tanks were larger with wing-nut filler caps. To complete the range, there were 350 and 500 Trials models, based on the wartime 16H frame fitted with the ohv engines and telescopic forks but these were far too large and heavy for their task. The 490cc side- and overhead-valve engines were modified for 1948, with a new timing case and direct-action tappets in place of the followers, while the Big 4 had the bore and stroke revised and the capacity reduced to 597cc.

The major news from Nortons for 1949 was the launch of their model 7 Dominator twin, the 497cc engine of which was a conventional vertical twin with

Right
*One of the nicest trials
models of the period was
the Norton 500T intro-
duced in 1949 and built
for just five years*

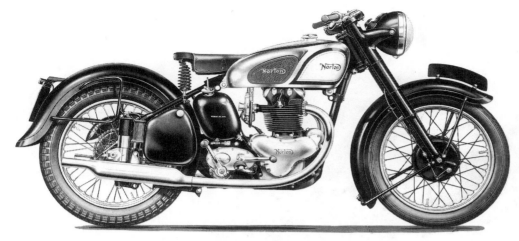

Left
*First of the many Norton
twins was this 1949
model 7, which had a
plunger frame and new
laid-down gearbox*

overhead valves and both head and barrel in iron. The camshaft ran across the front of the crankcase, where it was driven by chain and gear, with a further gear drive on to the dynamo. The magneto went behind the crankcase and was chain driven with auto-advance. This engine went into the ES2 cycle parts with plunger frame and telescopic forks, but the gearbox had to be modified to suit the shape of the engine and the new box became known as the laid-down type. Also new was the 500T built purely for trials use with an all-alloy 490cc engine fitted into a short diamond frame. The result worked well for many private owners.

The rest of the range ran on with little alteration that year, except that the Manx models supplied to riders in the TT had twin overhead camshafts and alloy tanks and wheel rims. For 1950 all the side- and overhead-valve road models changed to the laid-down gearbox, but not the 500T, as the short frame could not accommodate it. Norton fortunes had taken a real upturn in 1950, thanks to the advent of the famous Featherbed frame for the works racers, coupled with the skills of Geoff Duke and Artie Bell. The frame was the result of eight years of work by Rex McCandless and was deceptively simple, with its duplex tubular loops welded to the headstock with a cross-over arrangement

and bolted-on subframe. The petrol tank sat on the top rails with a strap to retain it and the design remained in use for many years.

For 1951 the Manx went into the Featherbed frame with the laid-down gearbox and 19in. wheels and was an immediate success. The other singles and the twin stayed as they were that year and for 1952, when the twin was joined by the machine many riders had been asking for since the Featherbed frame had first appeared. It was a marriage of the new frame and the twin engine, and for 1952 it became available, but for export only, as the model 88 Dominator. It had its usual gearbox and short Roadholder forks and was finished in grey, the result a very smart, fast and well handling motorcycle.

Another new frame appeared for 1953 and, like the Featherbed, this had a pivoted rear fork, but was based on the cradle frame and used by both the model 7 Dominator and the ES2, both models also adopting a pear-shaped silencer. The model 88 ran on with little change, while the two side-valve machines and the 18 were given a dualseat, despite remaining in rigid frames. There were, in fact, some side-valve models built with the plunger frame, but these were made in small numbers only.

Right
*A rather special Manx
Norton with Featherbed
frame, for this is Geoff
Duke's 1951 Junior TT
winner*

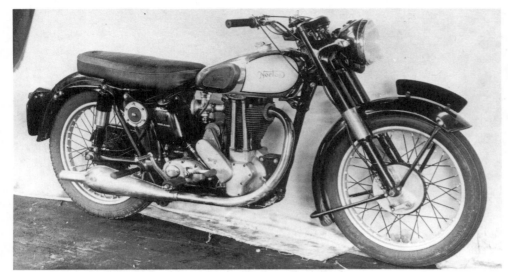

Top left
The ES2 Norton in its new pivoted-fork frame for 1953. Note the pear-shaped silencer

Centre left
The Norton model 88 Featherbed twin, as it was in 1957 and one of the best machines of the decade

Bottom left
The 1958 Norton Nomad 99, which used the larger twin engine in off-road parts to make an export model

Above
*Norton 99 de luxe for 1960 with slimline frame and rear
enclosure, but little change to engine or gearbox*

The Manx was unaltered for 1953, but the
Internationals received their last real changes. The
engines became all-alloy and went into the Featherbed
frame with the laid-down gearbox and pear-shaped
silencer. They had become, in effect, a model 88 with
an ohc engine, but with a larger front brake which
went onto the rest of the range, other than the 500T,
for 1954, a year when the Manx changed to short-
stroke engines and a welded subframe.

At the end of the year, the two side-valve
machines, the model 18 and the 500T were dropped
but in their place appeared two new singles with a
597cc ohv engine in either rigid or pivoted-fork frames
so really they were simply enlarged versions of the 18
and ES2. There were detail improvements which
included a chance to Monobloc carburettors and alloy
head for both singles and twins, while the Featherbed
frame had the subframe welded in place and full-width
hubs.

The model 7 went at the end of the year, along
with the rigid-frame 19R, but the ES2 and the 19S ran
on for 1956 with another similar single. This was the
348cc model 50, which was as the others, except in
capacity, so was stuck with the weight penalty all such
machines have to suffer. Meanwhile the International
ran on in small numbers and to special order while the
Manx had numerous minor changes, but was really very
close to the limit of its development and proving the
point of diminishing returns.

The 88 was joined by a larger 596cc version for
1956 listed as the 99, and this used the same cycle
parts. The same engine was used for a further 1957
model, this being the 77, which was intended for sidecar work and had the frame from the later model 7. All
the road machines, changed to a revised gearbox in
May 1956, the new type being known as the AMC. It
was much as before and was also used on AJS and
Matchless machines, and continued in service for over
20 years.

There were few changes for 1957 but 1958
brought alternator electrics for the 88 and 99 which
had twin carburettors listed for them during the year
and were joined by the 99 Nomad. This was an export
enduro model, which used the 596cc engine, model 77
frame, an alternator, magneto and off-road cycle parts.
Its finish was bright red and chrome, and it had twin
carburettors for performance.

The singles were little altered for 1958, and at
the end of the year, the International models and the
19S were dropped. For 1959 the ES2 and 50 were con-
siderably revised, with alternator electrics and the
Featherbed frame. This was to prove a great blessing to
Triton builders, as in later years, more often than not,
the donor frame was to come from the underpowered
model 50. The Manx engines took their final form in
1959 when they lost the lower bevel housing, the 77
was dropped but the other three twins ran on much as
they were and were joined by a new model, which was

to sire a further small group.

The new twin was the 249cc Jubilee, which differed in concept from the Dominator series in most areas. Again, the engine was designed by Bert Hopwood and was a conventional, parallel twin engine, built in unit with its four-speed gearbox. It had a short stroke, nodular iron crankshaft, separate iron barrels and alloy heads. Two gear driven camshafts were employed, with the points on the end of the inlet, and the oil pump went into the timing cover.

Complete with gearbox, it made a compact unit and was installed in a frame built up from tubes and pressings with a pivoted rear fork and telescopics from the AMC lightweight range. Both wheels had full-width hubs and the front wheel was shielded by a deeply valanced mudguard. There was more extensive enclosure at the rear, with a deep tail unit, which combined with massive side panels that ran forward to conceal the single Monobloc carburettor.

The Jubilee style of rear enclosure was adopted by the larger twins for 1960, and in this form they became the 88 and 99 de luxe models. To suit the panels, the frame was modified by pulling in the top rails, which

also enabled riders to tuck in their knees more easily. In its new form, the frame soon became known as the slimline, so, inevitably, the earlier type became the wideline.

The new frame was also used by the twins without rear enclosure, and these became the standard 88 and 99. The Jubilee ran on as it was, while the 99 Nomad was joined by a 497cc version. For the singles, the new decade brought numerous detail changes for the Manx racers, but little alteration to the road models.

On this note, the firm continued into the 1960s with much more to happen to it. There was to be a move from the traditional Bracebridge Street to London, the end of the Manx, bigger twins and finally the Commando range. Then, with the late 1980s, came a revival of the marque with a rotary engine.

NUT

Newcastle upon Tyne was the home-town of this marque, hence the initials for the name. It was founded in 1911, and in 1913 a NUT won the Junior TT but there were financial problems so production was not continuous. There was none for 1930 but later in the year a range became available.

The power units were JAP V-twins specially prepared for NUT in 500cc ohv, 700cc ohv and 750cc side-valve forms plus sv and ohv 350cc singles. The cycle parts were conventional and the machines were fully equipped to a high standard. The same range was offered for 1932 and for 1933 the range was extended to add several models but it is unlikely that any of these were built, for production was by then minimal and during the year came to a final halt.

Top
1931 OEC Flying Squad model with 980cc ohv JAP engine in the duplex frame with rear suspension and duplex front end

Below
148cc OEC model 34/1 of 1934 with rear suspension, an unusual feature for a small machine at that time

OEC

The Osborn Engineering Company was far removed from the centre of the motorcycle industry, for their works was at Gosport in Hampshire. In spite of, or maybe because of, this they produced some unusual machines, with the design work going into the steering and suspension systems, while the power units remained the same as those used by many other small companies.

They were involved with record breaking in the 1920s and in 1930 Joe Wright broke the world record twice, but the second record, when the figure went over 150mph for the first time, became the subject of a scandal. An OEC went on show as the record breaker, but then someone realised that it was not the correct machine and that Wright had used his own Zenith for the run that counted. The difference was important, for the OEC had their duplex steering system with the inference that it had played its part, whereas the Zenith had a normal frame and girder forks.

The duplex steering system dated from 1927 and went on the firm's duplex cradle frame which was first

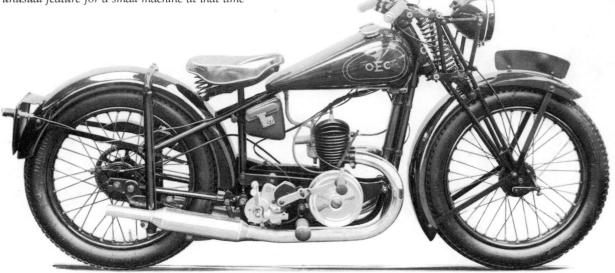

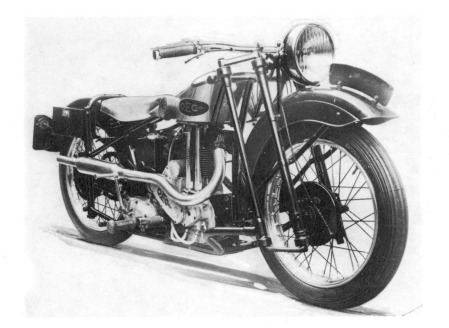

Left
A view of the front end of an OEC model 36/2 with 497cc Matchless engine and odd rear suspension. A 1936 model

Below, centre
The very strange OEC Atlanta Duo of 1936 with feet forward riding stance and the usual duplex steering

Above
OEC Atlanta Duo viewed from the saddle to show the odd steering linkage and instrument panel detail

used late in 1924. It used a system of links and pivots which gave the steering a high degree of self-centring and motorcyclists a headache in working out its mechanism. A couple of years later OEC added rear suspension as an option for their machines. This was more conventional but combined a pivoted fork with plunger units, the two linked as was common in Europe in the late 1930s but not in England.

In 1930 when you bought an OEC you received the duplex steering, but the rear suspension was still an option. A range of engines were offered from Blackburne, JAP or Sturmey-Archer in 350 and 500cc sizes and with sv or ohv. This variety was to continue for some years with engine and suppliers changing from year to year, but not the basic concept. As well as the singles, there were also V-twins ranging from 498 to 1000cc with either valve position and all manner of options were available for both engines and the rest of the machine. By 1934 Villiers engines were listed and Matchless engines were the norm for the four-strokes, even including the ohc V-four.

In July 1934 the Press carried details of a novel

Top
1939 OEC Commodore with short rear suspension arms, megaphone exhaust and
Girling wedge action brakes. The engine is
an AJS of 497cc

Above
Press test OEC model ST2 with 6E Villiers
engine leaving watering hole for rider in
1953

OEC which was enclosed to form a two-wheeled car and in production became the Whitwood. Only four-strokes with Matchless engines were listed for 1935 and all except the V-twin had ohv, but all continued to have rear suspension and the duplex steering option. Aside from the Whitwood, OEC themselves introduced an innovative design on rather similar lines for 1936. They called the result the Atlanta Duo and its major features were a low seat height allied to footboards that positioned the rider's feet well forward. It retained the usual OEC suspension at front and rear while the listed engines were installed to suit the layout. A windscreen was available as an extra and the machines were fully equipped.

There were few conventional models that year but the range for 1937 was announced as using three ohv singles and three sv V-twins, all from Matchless. Then, early in the year this was changed to three singles and one twin, but all from AJS. All had a revised rear suspension system which used short pivot arms and plunger spring units. At the front went Druid girder forks or the OEC duplex steering.

There were five models for 1938, all with names and still using AJS ohv engines. These were the 245cc Ensign, the 348cc Cadet and the 497cc Commander, the last two of which added Duplex to their names it supplied with the special steering system. The range was smaller for 1939 with the Cadet, Commander and similar Commodore which had a tuned engine, and on all models Girling brakes were adopted and these were cable operated with a wedge action.

In March 1939 the firm added two lightweights to its list with 98 or 122cc Villiers engines in a simple rigid frame with blade girders. It is likely that few were built, as they were not in the 1940 list, which just had the three basic ohv models. Then production stopped

and did not restart until 1949, when OEC machines were totally conventional.

The new models were lightweights, much like other manufacturers, for they used 10D and 6E Villiers engines in rigid frames with telescopic forks. The two machines listed were both called Atlanta, and this name was to continue to apply to all the firm's two-strokes. In 1950 they were joined by competition models but these differed little from the road ones other than for tyres and exhaust.

Pivoted-fork rear suspension appeared for 1951 to increase the range so that with the options of direct or battery lighting the range seemed extensive. It increased by one for 1952 when it was joined by the Apollo which used the 248cc, side-valve Brockhouse engine unit. For that first year, it went into the rigid frame, but for 1953 it was also available in a pivoted-fork one.

All the other road models ran on, but the competition pair was replaced by a single 197cc machine which had a pivoted-fork frame and an unusual two-stage final drive. For this, there was a sleeve, which ran on the rear fork pivot centre, with a sprocket at each end. That on the left was driven by a short chain from the gearbox, while the right-hand one drove the rear wheel.

For 1954 there were two 122cc models, one each with the 8E and 7E engines, and the Apollo and in this manner, the range ran to late 1954, when motorcycle production ceased.

Above
The OEC Apollo with Brockhouse 248cc side-valve engine in rigid frame form in 1953

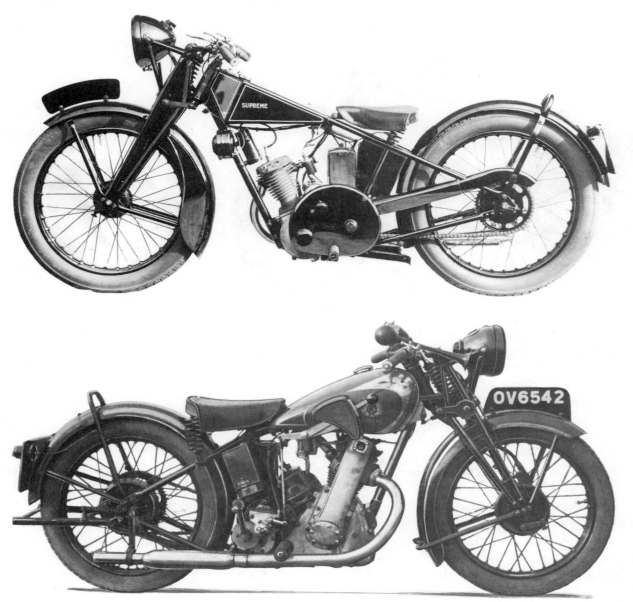

Very basic 1932 model P/32 OK Supreme fitted with a 148cc side-valve JAP engine and built to fall into the 150cc tax bracket

The famous Lighthouse model OK Supreme with 248cc ohc engine that had the cams at the top of the vertical shaft and window to inspect them by. A 1932 model

OK SUPREME

1928 was the year that OK won their solitary TT but they dated from the turn of the century and up to 192 were simply the OK. The partners then split and Ernie Humphries added the Supreme part of the title and went on to produce some interesting but hardly profitable models.

Through the 1930s they only built models using four-stroke engines and most of these were bought in from JAP or Matchless. Like others of those times, the result was a large range which was aimed to give any buyer just what was wanted by using options for engines, gearboxes, frames, electrics and all the cycle parts. The result was models ranging from a 148cc sv to a 75-cc V-twin with many sizes in between.

The 1930 range was prosaic and based on JAP engines alone but in May that year it was joined by their own 248cc model whose engine was known as the Lighthouse. It had an inclined cylinder on top of a very substantial crankcase and the camshaft drive went on the right with a vertical shaft driven by bevel gears. It ran in a tunnel and carried bronze cams at the top end which moved short tappets to move rockers to open the valves. The top of the shaft tunnel had a small glass window in it for checking the oil supply and it was from this that the model gained its nickname.

It was much the same for 1932 with eight models, one a 148cc sv to fit into the tax bracket just for that year. In 1933 model names appeared for the 245cc Flying Cloud and 346cc Coeur de Lion, but the others retained codes. All had names for 1934 with the first two joined by the Britannia, Phantom and Hood plus further Flying Clouds.

There was a new ohc design for 1935 built in 248 and 346cc sizes and called the Silver Cloud. Each came in standard or racing forms and the same engines were also used for a pair of trials models. The engines were more conventional than the Lighthouse with a straight-forward vertical shaft and bevels layout for the single-camshaft design. The remainder was conventional and as expected to suit sports or racing use. A low-cost model named Dauntless was added along with a 600cc sv called the Road Knight and only sold complete with a Hughes sidecar.

The Silver Clouds continued for 1936, as did the 490cc side-valve Hood. The rest of the range was new with 346, two of 498cc and no fewer than five 245cc models. All had ohv and the largest a camshaft mount-ed high in the timing chest, where it was chain driven. They were listed as Flying Clouds and Sports. The range was thinned out a little for 1937 with only four ohc models listed, two of each size for road or track use.

The 248cc road model took the name Pilot, but the 346cc remained a Silver Cloud as did three machines of 245cc which were joined by the 490cc ohv Phantom with JAP engine

The policy of something for everyone continued for 1938 with 14 models mainly from the previous year's range and included the four camshaft machines The high-camshaft and ohc models could be obtained in trials trim as an option, but the last model in the list was a pure competition one with a 344cc JAP engine set up to run on alcohol fuel. It was the GT Special/38 and built for grass-track racing.

For 1939 the high-camshaft JAP engines were dropped and six models with Matchless single power unit appeared, although a few machines from the past remained, still with the Flying Cloud name. Two sizes of Matchless ohv engine were used but in various forms. The 348cc models were the Snowden Ranger, Utility, and Gladiator, while the 497cc models were

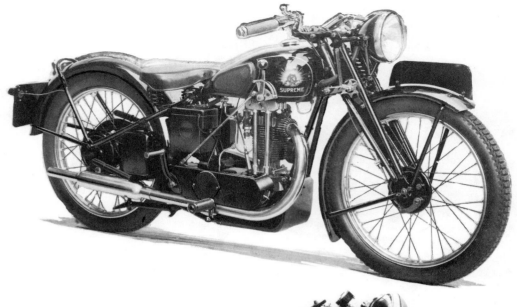

another Gladiator and Dominion. In April 1939 a further special 348cc model was added to the list in the form of a road-racing version of the grass model, but supplied with full road equipment.

The whole range less the racer and the camshaft models was listed for 1940 and in November 1939 a big V-twin was added to it. This had a 750cc side-valve JAP engine and was first shown in a matt service finish. In a later listing it no longer appeared, but by then the firm was engaged on more vital work.

Post-war they were rumoured to have assembled a small batch of models, but then turned to making accessories.

OMC

This 1930 make was marketed by C. G. Vale-Onslow, brother of Len Vale-Onslow, who manufactured the SOS, and indeed the OMC was built at the SOS works. It was a typical lightweight and powered by a 172cc Villiers super sports engine which had auto-lube and a flywheel magneto for ignition and direct lighting. This was installed in a pin-jointed frame with conventional fittings and the petrol tank was finished in French grey

with a red panel and lining. Few of these machines seem to have been built and the make was not listed for 1931.

OSCAR

This all-British scooter was sprung on an unsuspecting motorcycle world late in 1953, with full descriptions and exhibits at shows. Not a lot more happened, but the prototypes did exist, and one, at least, continued running for several years doing development work for the Siba importers based in Surrey.

The scooter presented bulbous lines with its two-section bodywork, which was fabricated in fibreglass, so the manufacturers in Blackburn were in the vanguard of the use of this material. Underneath the skin went a conventional scooter design although the suspension was by bonded-rubber units. The power units were hardly exciting, being either the 122 or 197cc Villiers with fan cooling and a three-speed gearbox but they were rubber-mounted to reduce vibration.

The machine was finished off with a dualseat and could have a spare wheel, but following the first announcement all went quiet. Aside from acknowledging its use by Siba five years later no more was heard.

P&P

Packmann & Poppe machines were built at the Montgomery works in the early 1920s when their best-known model was the Silent Three which used a Barr and Stroud sleeve-valve engine.

Their machines ceased to be listed from around the mid-1920s due to a fire at the Montgomery works and a little later P&P linked up with the Wooler concern. The make was then revived and for 1930 was listed with four rather different models, three with spring frames and four-speed gearboxes. Engines were a 199cc two-stroke, 245cc ohv JAP, 500cc ohv and 500cc ohc, but during 1930 production of these machines ceased and the marque withdrew from the market.

Top
Rare 1930 OMC fitted with 172cc Villiers engine

Bottom
The Oscar scooter launched late in 1953 with bonded-rubber suspension units and basic Villiers engine

Top right
Rare 1930 P&P model 90 with 500cc ohv engine

Bottom right
Panther 25 with 247cc Villiers engine as in 1931

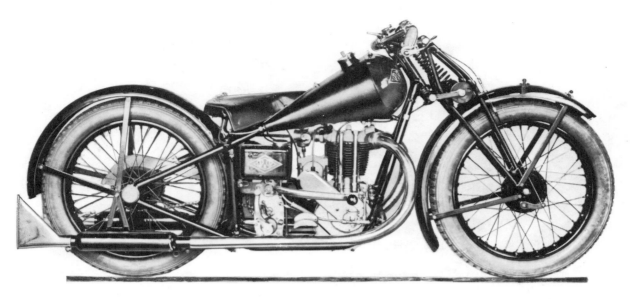

PANTHER

Mention of this make brings one of two images to mind for most people. Either it is of a massive sidecar outfit propelled by a machine with sloping engine in place of its downtube and turning over slowly but with great finality, or it is the incredibly cheap Red Panther in the line-up at Pride & Clarke's emporium in Stockwell Road, Brixton.

The firm's name was Phelon & Moore and it was founded in 1904, but Joah Phelon was involved with powered transport as early as 1895. In 1901 he took out a patent covering the use of the engine in place of the downtube and the idea of long bolts to hold the main bearings, cylinder and head as one unit to contain the stress.

The Panther name came in the 1920s and at first applied to one model, but in time became the range, although the company was still P&M at the end. There was also a Panthette, a 250cc transverse V-twin with

unit construction, but it did not sell well and led in time to a small range of Villiers-powered models.

These were still listed in 1930 and made use of the Panthette frame members to house 147,196 and 247cc Villiers engines. The machines were simple but inexpensive, so sold well. The other models in the range had the traditional inclined engine and were of 499cc and 594cc and listed as the Redwing. They were very easy to spot on the road with the engine laid in as the downtube and the timing cover at right angles to it and stretching far up to the dynamo. With a saddle tank they had nice lines and a style of the 1930s rather than of the decade before. As with all good Panthers they carried their oil in the crankcase for the dry sump system, had ohv and the pushrods enclosed in a single tube.

For 1931 the Redwing line was revised with a new 490cc engine and these machines had twin head-lamps, the left one of which swung down and left for the dipped position while the right went out, both con-

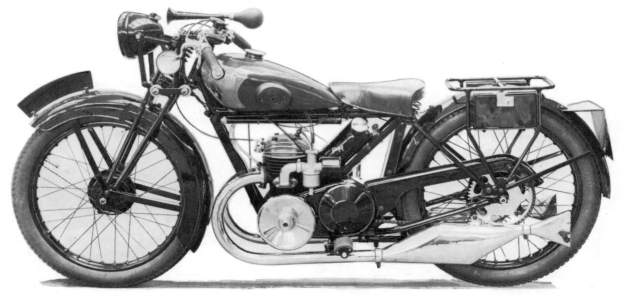

trolled by a twistgrip.

The most important model in the 1932 range was the new 249cc ohv single which had the engine inclined in the frame, the oil tank formed in the front section of the crankcase and magneto ignition. This drove a three-speed gearbox and went into conventional cycle parts. The larger models ran on, the 594cc one now known as the Redwing 100, and there were just two left with Villiers engines.

For 1933 Panther bored out the 249cc single to create a 348cc version which had a new and stronger frame, bigger brakes and more options. The big singles also had new frames and their engines were modified to use two long U-bolts to clamp crankcase, barrel, head, rocker box and steering head as one. New petrol tanks appeared, and the handchange lever worked in a slot in

Top
Famous Panther sloper, this being a 1932
Redwing 90 of 490cc

Below
Dipping system with the left shell moved by cable

the tank top which allowed large, soft knee-grips to be used. The two-strokes were no longer listed.

Early in 1933 Panther reached an agreement with Pride & Clarke of Stockwell Road, London, which helped both in those hard times. The outcome was the Red Panther, which was based on the 250 but with a red panelled tank instead of the normal green one and whose price was cut to the bone by bulk buying. There were two models with acetylene or electric lighting and the low price brought plenty of customers, which kept the factory very busy. The standard version remained, but there were few buyers, for the price difference was significant. The firm got round this for 1934 by upgrading their own models while the Red Panther's price was kept down with three speeds, one exhaust system, handchange and coil ignition. This applied to the basic 249cc model and a new 348cc model which joined it.

The four big singles were little changed and retained their coupled brakes and twin headlamp option. New were the Stroud trials models, which were based on the smaller singles but fully prepared for their specialised use with competition tyres, narrow mudguards, raised exhaust and crankcase shield.

Just how good the Red Panther could be was shown to all when the firm won the Maudes Trophy late in 1934 for tests carried out a year earlier. These had been at Brooklands and were to highlight economy, speed, safety and easy servicing.

1935 saw the Red Panthers with fully enclosed valves and listed in four forms, one 348 and three of 249cc, while the rest of the range continued with little change. It was much the same for 1936 with just two big singles left in the 490 and 594cc sizes and fewer models for 1937 and 1938 as the firm concentrated on the ones that sold well. Steady development continued on into 1939 with the Red Panther still leading the

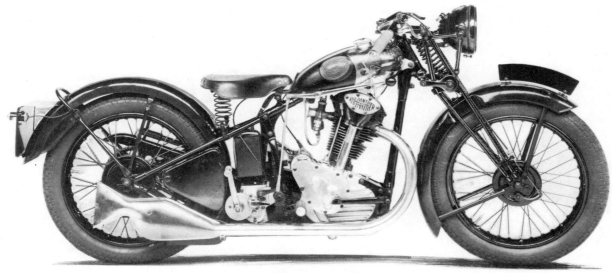

Above
The 1935 249cc model 20 Red Panther
sold by Pride & Clarke

Left
The 1940 Panther model 80 with
594cc side-valve engine mounted verti-
cally

way and the cheapest fully-equipped 250 on the market.

For 1940 there was to have been a spring frame using four leaf springs which worked well until one spring sheared on test, and then its cost and the advent of war removed it from the scene before it reached production. Aside from the frame Panther had other surprises for 1940 with a trio of Redwing models with vertical engines, 594cc sv and 498cc ohv singles plus a vertical twin but these were not to reach production.

The range was completed by the inclined engine models, which were the Redwings of 249, 348 and 594cc. There were no Red Panthers so the ultra-cheap 250 was no more and the larger singles were listed with the spring frame. Panther then turned to war contracts, although motorcycles continued to be built well into 1940 for export but only in the inclined-engine form.

During the war, they made aircraft parts, but late in 1945 came news of their simple postwar range. This ignored the excursions into upright engines and spring

Left
Prototype Panther 90 with
498cc engine and rear sus-
pension by leaf springs that
sheared on test

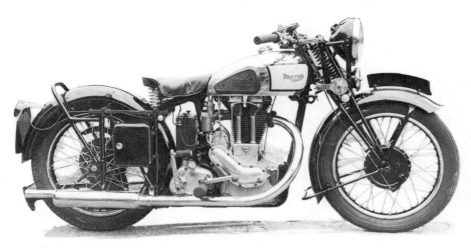

Top Left
Early postwar Panther single 60 or 70 from the 1947-8 period, when the inclined engine was used with the Dowty forks

Centre Left
This Panther 100 ran in the 1949 ISDT, but retired on the fifth day with side-car chassis trouble

frames that had been scheduled for 1940, and kept to their well tried, inclined engine formula. There were three models, listed as the 60, 70 and 100, all with ohv, but with capacities of 249, 348 and 594cc. They kept their proven oil system with the lubricant carried in a separate chamber cast within the sump. The two small-

er machines had coil ignition, the larger magneto, and the smallest had three speeds, the others four. All had rigid frames with girder forks.

It was a good, solid range for the times, so Panther stuck to it for a while, but with a change to telescopic front forks for 1947. These were Dowty

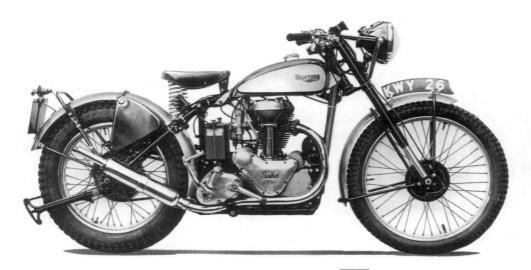

Left
Panther Stroud 348cc model from 1952 with vertical cylinder and odd exhaust-pipe run

Top
The 1958 model 75 Panther in pivoted-fork frame
Above
Panther twin model 45 from 1959 with 324cc 3T
engine and Earles leading-link forks

Oleomatic, which relied on air for suspension and oil for damping and lubrication. Dowty had extensive experience of such designs in the aircraft industry, and with its progressive rise in effective spring rate, it offered an improvement over conventional springs. Of course, it also offered disaster if the seals failed, and both Panther and Dowty were to find out that using aircraft-quality components, serviced to commercial standards, could give problems.

The range was continued for 1948, and during the year, the firm began to compete in trials, using one each of the smaller models. These differed from the road machines in that the cylinder was set vertically, but were otherwise little altered in their essentials. Naturally, there were alloy guards, a 21in. front wheel, competition tyres and a high-level exhaust to suit the use.

The road models adopted the vertical cylinder for 1949 to become the models 65 and 75, much as before, while the model 100 rolled on, usually hauling a sidecar along. The works competition models led to a further pair of machines which were based on them and listed as the Stroud in either capacity. They were much as the works machines, but came complete with full lighting

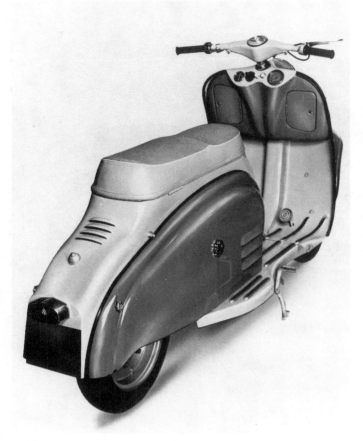

Above
The Panther Princess scooter of 1960 with 174cc Villiers 2L engine under the body panels it shared with Dayton and Sun

Far right, top
The Phoenix 150 model with 31C Villiers engine under a body shared with the whole range

Below
Phillips P39 Gadabout with Rex engine and two speeds in a rigid spine frame with telescopic forks

equipment and no great weight reduction.

The range then ran on with few changes from 1950 to 1952 but then the smaller models went over to pivoted-fork rear suspension and new telescopic forks with springs. The Dowtys stayed on the rigid versions and the Stroud models changed to a light alloy head and barrel. At the end of 1952 the Strouds were dropped but the others ran on to be joined by a model 100 in a pivoted-fork frame with the telescopic spring forks for 1954. All models had the option of a dualseat. In this way the singles continued on through the decade, gradually leaving the rigid frame except for the model 100 to suit the die-hard sidecar man.

For 1956 the ohv models were joined by two lightweights using 197cc Villiers engines, one fitting the three-speed 8E and the other the four-speed 9E. Both went into the same cycle parts comprising a loop frame, pivoted-fork rear suspension and Earles leading-link front forks disguised to appear as telescopics at a casual inspection. The range was extended for 1957 with further two-stroke models, one with the three-speed 9E engine, one with the 246cc 2H single and the third with the 249cc twin but the larger single was not a success and was soon dropped. The final addition to the Panther line-up was an imported 125cc Terrot scooter, which failed to match the Vespa or Lambretta in style or much else.

The rigid 100 was finally dropped at the end of the year, but the others continued for 1958 and were joined by a Sports model, which had a tuned 249cc twin engine and revised finish to distinguish it from the basic model. It retained the same cycle parts, and this policy ran on into 1959, when two more twins were added as the models 45 and 50 Sports, using the larger

324cc Villiers engine.

The four-strokes also had a new model for 1958 in the form of the 120, which was a 645cc version of the big single. It shared cycle parts with the de luxe 100, and both models still used the archaic twin-port head, unlike the standard 100. The Terrot scooter activity continued, but there was news, late in the year, of a Panther scooter, although it was not to reach the market until 1960.

This it did, along with the rest of the range, which continued much as before, although the light-weight twins were fitted with telescopic forks. The scooter was called the Princess and powered by the 174cc Villiers engine in kick or electric-start forms. Both had fan cooling and went into a conventional scooter frame with pivoted-arm suspension at front and rear. The bodywork had a better line than that of the Terrot and was produced in conjunction with Dayton and Sun to reduce costs.

On this note, Panther entered the 1960s, but times were soon to become harder for them, and few models survived more than three years. A couple did for a while longer, but with a receiver at the company's helm and built from the stock bins.

Many survivors still demonstrate how tough they built them in Yorkshire.

PHILLIPS

This famous cycle firm moved into powered two-wheelers in 1954, when they exhibited a clip-on model at the Earls Court show as a complete machine. The engine was an all-alloy 49.2cc two-stroke with a clutch which mounted above the bottom bracket and drove the rear wheel by chain.

For 1956 the machine gained telescopic front forks and was joined by the P39 Gadabout which was in the moped image with a 49.6cc Rex engine and two-speed gearbox. The result was much as any other mid-1950s moped and had an adequate performance. The original model continued until late 1957, and the P39 into 1959, when it was joined by the P40 Panda, which had a single-speed, 49.2cc Rex engine in a simple frame. Later came the P50 Gadabout de luxe, which had three speeds, and then the P45 Gadabout which was as the P50, but with a 49.9cc Villiers 3K engine with the two-speed gearbox.

For 1960 the P39 was dropped, but the other three models continued and were joined by the P49 Panda Plus. This was as the P40, but had telescopic forks and well valanced mudguards, although it retained the single-speed Rex engine. During 1960 the P40 went, but the other three mopeds ran on, and were joined by others, before the name was dropped.

PHOENIX

Ernie Barrett went racing in the 1950s by building a trio of frames and fitting various sizes of JAP engine into them, so when he turned to scooters, it was not surprising that he adopted the same principle. He used the name of the mythical bird that arose from its ashes for his products, which were built in Tottenham, London.

All models used Villiers engines, and the prototype of 1956 had a 147cc 30C. When the production model was launched later that year, it kept the same engine, which was fitted into a typical tubular scooter frame with pivoted-fork front and rear suspension. The

frame carried a scooter form of body, although this lacked any great style.

For 1958 the range was expanded with Standard and De Luxe versions and some improvements in the body style. Later came more models using 148 and 197cc singles and the 249cc twin engines. In 1959 these were joined by the 324cc twin and for 1960 the 174cc single. The range ran on up to 1964 when the declining market again took its toll.

Above
Phoenix T250 scooter with stowage compartment in rear of apron and fascia above

POUNCY

This marque came from Dorset and in March 1931 listed a single model called the Cob. It was a conventional machine powered by a 346cc Villiers engine coupled to a three-speed Albion gearbox and the finish was black with a red panel on the tank nose. For 1932 the range was expanded to three models, including the Cob for which footchange became standard along with other options. A second 346cc model was listed as the Triple S and built for competition while third was the 148cc Kid with Villiers engine and three-speed gearbox. 1933 saw the range down to three models with new names as the 148cc Pup and 346cc Mate, joined by the 249cc Pal.

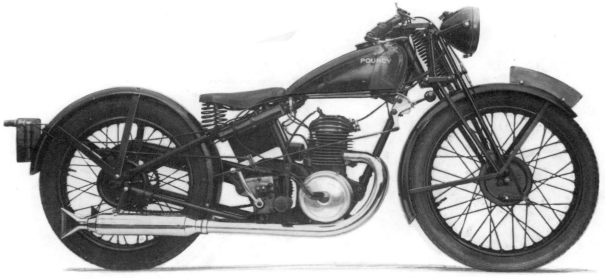

Above
Pouncy Cob of 1931 with a 346cc Villiers engine

Below
The Power Pak clip-on engine with inverted cylinder, which drove the rear tyre by friction-roller

During 1933 the firm moved to Hampshire and announced the two larger machines for 1934 but nothing was built until early 1935. Then a new 249cc Pal was announced alone using a later engine type in a duplex frame with the OEC form of rear suspension with a pivoted rear fork and plunger spring boxes, rare for a lightweight at that time. The single model went forward for 1936, but during that year production stopped.

POWER PAK

This was one of the many clip-on units on the market around 1950 which sat over a bicycle rear wheel to drive it by friction roller. The engine was a 49cc two-stroke with inverted cylinder and the petrol tank went above the crankcase. Control was by a single lever which worked both decompressor and throttle, and later a clutch as well.

The unit remained on the market until 1956 when the firm tried to use it to make a moped by fitting it under the bottom bracket while keeping the friction drive. However, nothing more was heard of this design which was never going to compete with the latest mopeds.

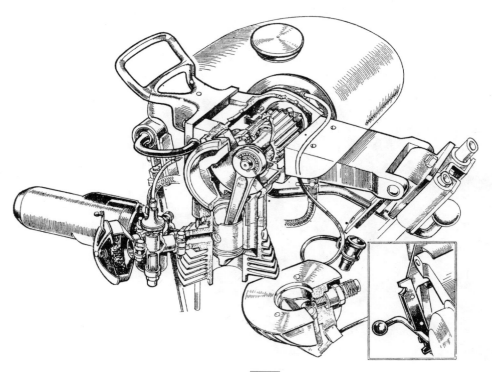

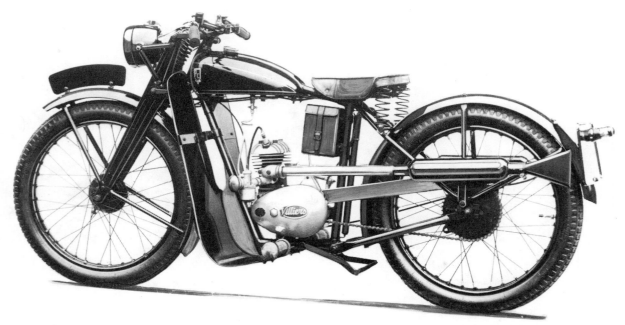

PRIDE & CLARKE

158 Stockwell Road, London SW9, was a very well-known motorcycle address and P&C had their premises along both sides for quite a length of the road. For years they were associated with Panther, but were always ready to do deals to fill their showrooms with machines at cut prices, a practice they were to continue for many postwar years as well.

In 1939 they ventured into making machines with a lightweight motorcycle sold as the Cub which used the 122cc Villiers engine in conventional cycle parts, all of which they would have been familiar with and no doubt stocked as spares. The model was only listed for that one short season and from then on Pride & Clarke kept to selling other firms' wares, which they did very successfully.

PROGRESS

This was the name of an imported German scooter that appeared in 1956, which was joined for 1957 by models with Villiers engines. There were three of these, all of which used the same chassis with fibreglass bodywork. The models were the 147cc Anglian and the 197cc Briton and Britannia which had a four-speed 9E engine. Sadly, the machines lacked the style and line of the Teutonic models, and by late 1958 had been discontinued. They were never seen again.

PULLIN

Cyril Pullin won the 1914 Senior TT and after World War I produced some interesting designs although few went into production for any length of time. The Ascot Pullin motorcycle appeared in 1928 and only reached the 1930 market as a job-lot sold off by the liquidator to Rennos, the London dealers.

Top
*Pride & Clarke 1939
model Cub with 122cc Villers
engine*

Left
*Progress scooter at the 1956
Earls Court show with its larger-
than-usual wheels*

Left
The Pullin scooter prototype shown and offered for manufacture in 1955, with monocoque body over its Villiers engine

Below left
The Ascot Pullin with its full enclosure and very advanced cycle features

Below
Ascot Pullin on show at Beaulieu about 1959. 496cc ohv engine but a model with problems and a short life

It was a machine with numerous new features and as such was a doubtful starter at the best of times. There were major development problems in 1929, so it could not have chosen a worse time to attempt to be 'The New Wonder Motor Cycle'. The design laid the 496cc ohv engine horizontal and had its three-speed gearbox built in unit in a section of the casting above the crankcase area and driven by double helical gears. The frame was part of the special nature of the machine, for it was built up from steel pressings into which the mechanics were fitted. Various covers then hid the works from view and provided access. The fork blades were made in the same way, as was a tank-top toolbox and a handlebar-mounted instrument panel.

The braking system was advanced, with hydraulic and interconnected brakes, but the original Ascot Pullin design was inclined to total failures so they quickly changed to Lockheed. Both standard and de luxe models

were listed and the latter was fitted out with legshields, mirror, screen and, best of all, a windscreen wiper. Finish was deep blue with the frame panels in cream. It was impressive but the word then went round that it did not steer and it was soon found that at speed it could throw its rider while the sedate performance did nothing to entice customers to it.

Late in 1951 Pullin's name appeared once more as the designer of the Powerwheel, which was to be made and marketed by Tube Investments. It was aimed at the clip-on market but, like the Cyclemaster and Winged Wheel, sought to build the motive power into a wheel.

What set the design apart was that it was a 40cc two-stroke, rotary engine in which the crankshaft stayed still and the rest of the works spun round it along with clutch, transmission and wheel hub. This made it a complex solution to a simple problem with

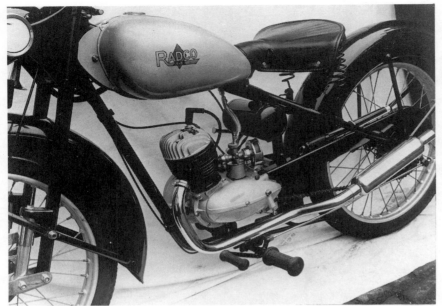

Left
The Radco Ace, which appeared in 1954 with its Villers 4F engine and short leading-link forks, but failed to reach production

many special features, ingenious but hardly warranted for the market so no more was heard of it.

After the Powerwheel exercise, Pullin turned his attentions to the scooter field, and in 1955 offered a design and prototype to any manufacturer willing to produce it. The machine was planned to need minimal and inexpensive tooling and used a 197cc Villiers engine under a monocoque shell formed in sheet alloy.

The result worked well and was well fitted out but, sadly, no-one took it up.

Below
1932 Raleigh MO32 with 297cc side-valve engine

RADCO

This firm dated from just before World War 1 and their range was powered by Villiers, JAP and their own engines.

By 1930 their machines were conventional, sturdy, well finished but perhaps rather old-fashioned in looks. The range ran to nine models and most were two-strokes. Smallest used the 147cc Villiers engine, then came the 196cc models and finally those using the 247cc Radco engine. There were three with JAP engines, using 245 ohv and 490 sv and ohv engines. Another 196cc model was added for 1931 while the JAP engines were dropped for 1932. There was no real change for 1933, but after that they kept to component manufacture for the next 20 years.

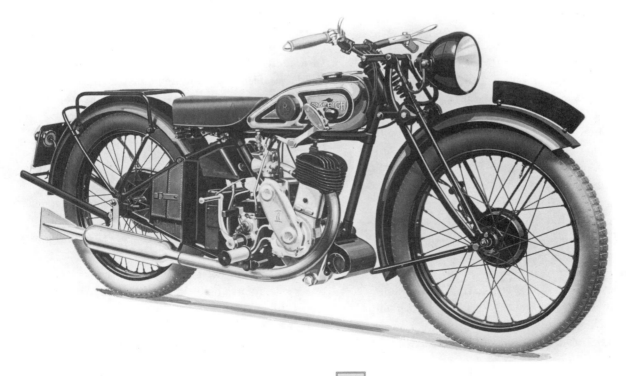

Right
*The Sturmey-Archer engine used by the
Raleigh moped when launched in 1958 as
the RM1*

Below
*98cc Villiers engined Raynal Auto in
1938 form*

In 1954 they returned to the fray with a single
model called the Ace which was much as others in
using a 99cc 4F engine in a simple loop frame. The one
feature on note was the leading-link front forks from
Metal Profiles. Otherwise it was basic with saddle, toolbox, centre stand and direct lights. As happened often,
there was an announcement, a prototype, and then
silence while the firm went back to making components.

RALEIGH

This name is best known for its bicycles, but they dab-
bled in power several times over the years

Their 1930 range was conventional with four
side-valve models using engines of 225, 248, 297 and
495cc. The ohv ones were of 348 and 495cc and all
went into a diamond frame with girder forks, the petrol
tank formed in two halves with a top strip to join
them. All continued for 1931 but with the engines
inclined instead of being vertical although the 225 and
248cc engines were dropped and a 348cc ohv one
added. For 1932 it was much the same with a 598cc sv
as well and they all ran on for 1933. By the end of that
year the company dropped motorcycles and just built
the three-wheeler cars and vans, which they had begun
in 1930. In 1935 these also ceased and the firm
returned to bicycles only.

In 1958 they returned to powered machines and
produced a moped late in the year as the RM1. It had a
49.5cc Sturmey-Archer two-stroke engine with V-belt

drive to a countershaft, and chain to the rear wheel.
The engine was made by BSA and clamped to the
downtubes of the frame which was basically a cycle
type with the pedal shaft running though the countershaft. Accessories such as screen and legshields were
offered, and during 1959 the original model was joined
by the RM1C, which had a clutch. Both were replaced
for 1960 by the RM2C, which had detail improvements, but at the end of the year it was dropped, for
Raleigh changed course to use imported engines and
designs for the rest of that decade.

RAYNAL

Raynal came on the motorcycle scene late in 1937 with
a production version of the prototype Jones autocycle,
powered by the usual 98cc Villiers engine. It was called
the Auto and its lines were much as others of the type.
with open frame, simple sprung fork and petroil tank
between the frame members. The lighting was direct

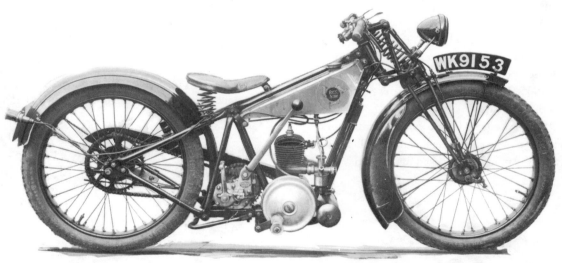

Top
A suffering Raynal autocycle struggling with too much of a load for its 98cc JDL engine in 1948 - actually a 1938 machine

Above
Early 147cc Rex-Acme from 1929

Far right
The Reynolds 1931 Scott special with its many extras built to provide a machine of the highest standard for any enthusiast of the marque

and the rear brake was rod operated by the pedals.

For 1939 the Auto with sprung front forks was renamed the De Luxe and joined by the Popular which had rigid forks but was otherwise the same. Both continued into 1940 until production ceased for the duration. Postwar, the JDL engine was used to produce the Popular, which was much as the prewar model, but with girder forks. After a season, it was renamed the De Luxe for 1947 with no real change, and in this form ran on until late 1950.

Above
*1932 Rex-Acme model R12 with 500cc
twin-port JAP engine*

REX-ACME

This company was formed in 1922 by the amalgamation of the two makes, the Rex which dated from 1900, and the Acme which appeared a little later in 1902. During the Edwardian era the Rex became well known and was quite successful in competition, but the Acme was a very minor make. Once joined, they soon had success in the TT and elsewhere but this was all during the twenties. By 1930 their best days were behind them and in the chill winds of the Depression they became one of many using bought-in parts to assemble their own machine.

For that year they gave the prospective customer plenty of choice from small two-strokes to a V-twin using Villiers, JAP, Blackburne and Sturmey-Archer engines. The two-strokes were of 147, 172, 247 and 343cc, all in diamond frames and one a super sports

with auto-lube. The others had cradle frames and there were three with Blackburne sv engines of 295, 348 and 596cc and two of 348 and 500cc with ohv. The JAP engines were sv of 346, 490 and 747 plus a single 346cc ohv. The final model had a 495cc Sturmey-Archer engine. In addition there was a speedway model available with a JAP or Blackburne engine, this machine having been first listed in 1928.

The 1931 range was smaller with just one 147cc Villiers model and two using the 348cc ohv Blackburne. Three had JAP engines, one new with a 300cc sv, the others of 346cc ohv and 490cc sv. The Sturmey remained and was joined by a model with a 499cc ohv Rudge engine, this also an option for the speedway machine.

Although a range was listed, production came to a halt soon after and that seemed to be the end of the company. However, the name was taken over by the Mills-Fulford sidecar company and reappeared in May 1932 with just two models, both with ohv JAP engines, and of 346 and 500cc. The machines had stainless-steel tank sides, a rain gutter on the tank top and waist-level

Top
1930 Royal Enfield model C of 346cc with out-side oil pump, oil tank formed with petrol one and rear magneto

Above
A 1933 export model K built with the 1140cc engine for the President of a South American republic

Far right
The 1934 LF four-valve Royal Enfield 488cc engine with crankcase oil tank

exhausts. Both models continued for 1933, and were joined by two more, one with a 250cc ohv JAP engine, the other with a 249cc Villiers.

During 1933 the new company ceased making Rex-Acme motorcycles and another well-known name fell victim to the difficult times.

REYNOLDS

Albert F. Reynolds was a Scott dealer based in Liverpool and a fan of the marque who specialised in it and marketed his own accessories and parts for it. In 1931 the firm agreed to supply him with machines to his own specification and these were known as Aero Specials due to his AER initials.

They used the TT engine, Brampton forks, Velocette style footchange and twin headlamps, and were built to a high standard with full equipment. Expensive, they were promoted as a Scott for connoisseurs.

In 1932 they were offered with the option of plunger rear suspension while for 1933 a model using a 249cc Villiers water-cooled engine was added. There was an attempt to market a model using the 747cc Scott triple but this plan was thwarted by the lack of engines. Later still Reynolds moved to other makes but did build another machine as the AER.

ROYAL ENFIELD

The Redditch firm never quite managed to acquire the charisma of some others, but for all that they remained in business for a long time. In the main they kept to basic machines that customers would buy and this policy must have served them well in the Depression years. Their slogan 'made like a gun' could perhaps have lost the suggestion of weight if it had changed to 'precise as a rifle', but at least customers knew it and used it.

For all that the firm kept clear of exotic designs that would not sell, and they were often at the forefront of improvements that did. Thus in 1928 they adopted saddle tanks and centre-spring girders, while in post-war years they were one of the first to adopt pivoted-fork rear suspension.

From 1930 on the models were given type letters and for that year these ran from A to K and in time were to stretch to Z, with a few omissions. The A was a 225cc two-stroke with a mechanical oil pump, an advanced feature for the time, which drove a three-speed, handchange gearbox and went into a rigid frame with girder forks. The model B had a 225cc side-valve engine, while the C had an inclined 346cc unit, also with side valves. Model D was a 488cc sv and E its ohv counterpart and again three-speed gearboxes were fitted, although four speeds were available as options.

The next batch of models were new and all had inclined engines and dry sump lubrication, the oil carried within a compartment cast into the front of the crankcase, a system the firm used for many years. The models were the 346cc sv F and ohv G, plus the 488cc sv H and ohv J. The range was completed by the 976cc model K, a V-twin, sv model and an old stager meant for sidecar use. While old-fashioned in some respects it did have the new-type forks, easy access to the rear wheel and good-sized brakes.

Early in the year there were additions to the range but these were created by varying the details of the existing models to attract every possible customer into the showroom. All were available in standard or de luxe forms to do this. This set the Royal Enfield range for much of the 1930s for many of these models were to run on for year after year with minimal change but with constant development. Some reflected new ideas such as four-valve heads, others styling trends, but all were to keep the range spread as wide as possible in those hard times.

The advent of the 15s. tax for up to 150cc machines saw many new models to take advantage of it, but few were as radical as the Enfield Cycar model Z. This was announced in March 1932 and was a machine with the works fully enclosed and equipped with legshields for the rider. The frame acted as the enclosure and was formed from sheet steel as an inverted U to run from the steering head to the rear wheel spindle. Depressions and flanges stiffened the structure, as did the forward part of the rear mudguard. The left side was

Top
The Royal Enfield 148cc Cycar model Z on
show late in 1934 at Olympia

taken in to form one side of the primary chaincase and a cover completed that aspect. A similar technique was used to enclose the flywheel magneto on the right and the legshields bolted into place.

The petrol tank went up into the channel section of the frame, where it was held by a ring nut round the filler cap and a single bolt. The left side of the chassis was smooth except for the chaincase, while on the right only the end of the gearbox with the kickstarter was exposed. The hand gear lever protruded through a slot on this side. The entire rear mudguard was quickly detachable in typical Enfield style.

Within this remarkable frame went a neat 148cc two-stroke engine with inclined cylinder, petroil lubrication and flywheel-magneto ignition to drive a three-speed gearbox. The front forks were girders with pressed steel blades and small drum brakes were used. A most enterprising effort to build a cheap ride-to-work model but not one with any pretence to styling.

It was minor changes for 1933 but with three new ohv models called Bullets for the sporting rider. All had four speeds, footchange, upswept exhaust and a high-compression piston, and they came in 248, 346 and 488cc sizes. In January 1933 the V-twin became available with a larger 1140cc engine for export only. For this it was fitted with the gearbox handchange lever on the left side of the petrol tank, footboards, pan saddle, American-style handlebars and hand or foot clutch operation. Three months later the model X was added to the range and fitted the 148cc two-stroke engine

into a light tubular frame. In other respects the X and Z were mechanically similar.

There were more revisions and changes for 1934 but most of the range continued but was joined by the model T, an ohv 148cc single with a four-speed gearbox. In May 1934 it was joined by a very similar 248cc ohv, which copied its engine features, duplex frame and blade girders. This was the model S and for 1935 the 248cc Bullet became a tuned version of it as the S2 and the bulk of the range remained as it was as the models Z, T, A, B, S, C, L, K and export KX, but the 488cc Bullet was fitted with a three-valve cylinder head just for that year.

1936 brought the first machines in a new style with vertical cylinders. The general construction followed the usual Enfield lines with a gear train to drive the camshafts and rear-mounted dynamo or mag-dyno, dry sump lubrication, the oil carried in a forward extension of the crankcase, and fully enclosed valve gear. There were two standard models, the 346cc G and 499cc J, with coil ignition and four-speed, footchange gearboxes. which went into rigid frames with girder forks. The third model in the new style was the Bullet, which represented a return to the four-valve head in the manner of the older model. The rest of the range continued as it was with its inclined engines and side or overhead valves plus the two-stroke Z and A models.

April 1936 brought competition versions of the G and J but these were not really that much altered from standard but did have the silencer tilted up, more ground clearance, competition tyres and narrow, chrome-plated mudguards. In July 1936 the trend to vertical engines continued with the appearance of the 248cc ohv S2 and the 346cc sv C.

When the range for 1937 was announced it proved to be a lengthy one, a sign of the firm's coverage of the market and its willingness to build a model if there seemed to be buyers for it. It also highlighted the move to vertical cylinders, for only the A and T retained inclined ones. Of the upright singles there were the sv B and ohv S and S2 of 248cc, the sv C and ohv G plus a tuned de luxe G2 version of 346cc, and the ohv J, de luxe J2 and four-valve JF Bullet of 499cc. There was also the H, which was a 499cc version of the 570cc sv L and the two competition machines. Finally came the 1140cc V-twin listed as the K and the KX de luxe. In April 1937 it was announced that the 248 and 346cc Bullets were back as modified versions of the S2 and G2. The range of options was large and the machines could be prepared for road racing, trials, scrambles or grass-track.

For 1938 the range stretched to 20 models with no fewer than six of 499cc with ohv, all built to the same basic pattern, and essentially all as for the previous year, but with the 346cc ohv CO as an addition. There was more rearrangement for 1939 and some new model letters in addition to the continued confusing Enfield practice of using the same letter for totally different models from one year to another. The model A was still a 225cc two-stroke, but was revised while the T was dropped and the 248cc sv became the D with a separate oil tank tucked in between the rear engine plates. In essence, the rest of the range for road and competition ran on in their various forms which included an all-alloy engine for the 346cc Bullet. At least all the models had a nice new green finish for the petrol tank, which helped to keep track of them.

Top
The three-valve 488cc model LO of 1935

Bottom
1936 Royal Enfield 346cc model C

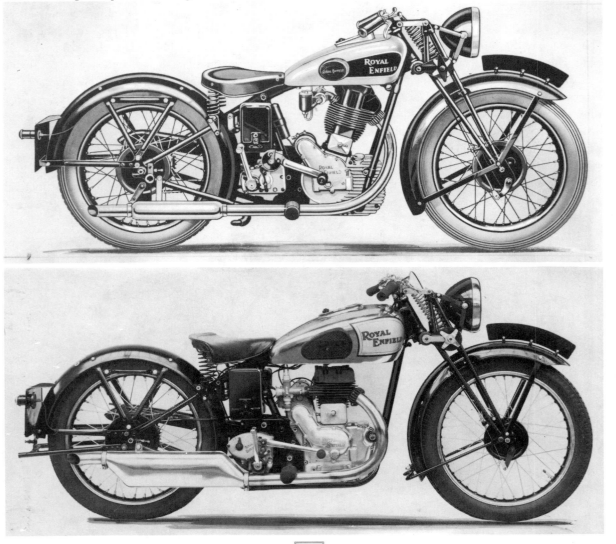

Top
*Similar, but heavier model J of
499cc seen from the drive side*

Bottom
*Competition Royal Enfield
from 1937 with 499cc engine
and tyres, mudguards and
silencer to suit*

This took the firm up to the war, but like most they announced a 1940 range. Included in this was one newcomer in the form of the 126cc RE two-stroke, which came in response to a request from Holland. This was from a firm in Rotterdam that had been handling the 98cc DKW and who had the concession removed in 1938 because it was Jewish owned. Their answer was to ask Enfield to make a copy but to enlarge it to 125cc. By April 1939 prototypes were in Holland and production began about the time that the war did.

The result was that England had a fully developed lightweight which served the paratroops during the conflict as the Flying Flea and the civilians after it for a good few years. The RE was a straightforward design with unit construction of engine and three-speed, handchange gearbox housed in a simple tubular loop frame with blade girders controlled by rubber bands for the front suspension. The rest of the range was based on the 1939 one and totalled seven machines ranging from 248 to 570cc with side valves and 248 to 499cc

with ohv.

And so Enfield went to war and in addition to the Flying Flea, the bulk of the Enfield wartime production was of the 346cc C and CO singles in sv and ohv forms. These were essentially as the civilian models in khaki and they also built a batch of the 570cc sv models and about 1,000 of the 248cc sv model D for training.

After the war their 1946 range was announced with just three models, the RE two-stroke and the ohv 346cc model G and 499cc model J, based largely on the prewar machines but with telescopic forks for the four-strokes. In addition, the firm carried out factory rebuilds of its wartime 346cc models, which retained the girder forks, to meet the intense demand for transport in the immediate postwar years.

With production so important, there were no real changes for two years, and for 1948 it was the RE that had a small amendment in the form of a distinct bulge in its exhaust pipe. This continued for 1949, when the

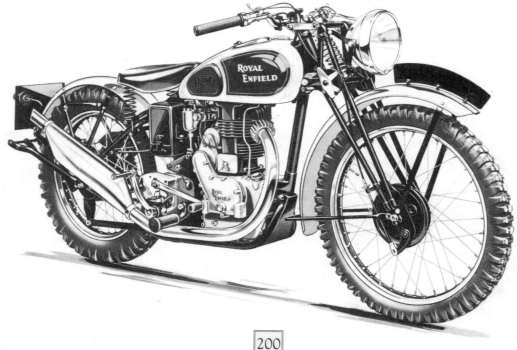

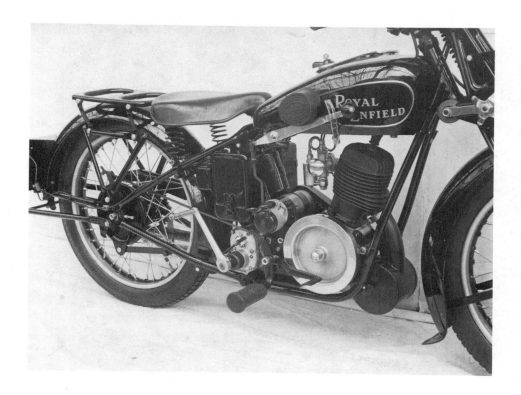

Top
Long-running 225cc model A Royal Enfield in its 1938 form with large expansion box, outside flywheel and rear dynamo with points on the end

Centre
1939 Royal Enfield 248cc model SF with separate oil tank tucked between the crankcase and gearbox

Bottom
The 126cc model RE of 1940 which became the wartime Flying Flea based on a 98cc German DKW

500 single became the J2 model, thanks to a change to
a twin-port head and the addition of a second exhaust
system for the left side of the machine. The real Enfield
news for 1949 was the introduction of two new models,
one reviving a prewar single name and the other a vertical twin. The single was the Bullet, and during 1948
the postwar prototype had been seen in trials and had
already raised eyebrows by using rear suspension.

The model was released in three forms for road,
trials or scrambles use, but the essentials were the same
for all. The engine followed Enfield principles, but

amended to suit, so the oil compartment was moved to
the rear of the crankcase to move the engine's weight
forward. The gearbox then bolted to the rear of the
crankcase so the resulting assembly was much as unit
construction. The engine itself followed Enfield practice but had a much taller crankcase and an alloy head.
The engine and gearbox assembly went into an open
frame with pivoted-fork rear suspension and telescopics
at the front. The wheel and brake sizes were as for the
tourers, but blade mudguards were used, along with
generally more modern features, except for the saddle.

The result was a smart motorcycle that stood out during a drab period, its silver-grey finish being topped off by a chrome-plated tank with frosted silver panels.

For trials, the machine was fitted with a Lucas racing magneto, wide gear ratios, raised exhaust and more suitable wheels and tyres. Both lights and a mag-dyno were available, for it was an era when most competitors rode their machines to and from events, as well as in them. The scrambler received a similar treatment, but without the options, and had close gears and an open exhaust.

The second new model was the 500 Twin, which had a brand-new, 495cc ohv vertical twin engine with separate heads and barrels in alloy and iron respective-ly. The crankshaft was a single alloy-iron casting with plain big-ends and ball and roller mains. There were two camshafts, which were driven by chain, with a further chain from the inlet camshaft to the dynamo. This ran at engine speed with a skew-gear-driven points housing and distributor for the coil ignition system built into it. Lubrication was by the normal Enfield pumps, and the oil was kept in a crankcase sump, as on the Bullet. Like that model, the gearbox was bolted to the rear of the case, and from then on, the Twin followed the lines of the road Bullet. Only the sprung front mudguard spoilt the machine's fine lines.

Enfield kept at it, and for 1950 the RE was fitted with telescopic front forks, and had a major redesign for

the 693cc Meteor. This was much as the smaller model, but it had dual front brakes, and a larger fuel tank. Despite the fact that the machine was their new top model, a dualseat remained an option.

More new models and variants were introduced for 1954, the Bullets and both twins being fitted with a styling cowl at the top of the forks. This carried a small pilot lamp at each top corner plus the headlamp, enclosed the top of the forks, and provided a mounting for the instruments and switches. Enfield called it a casquette, and it was to be a styling feature for many years. The new models were for the 250 class, one a 248cc version of the model G engine in a rigid frame but only built for the one year. The other was the Clipper which used the same engine and gearbox but in a pivoted-fork frame, so was a cross between the Bullet and G models.

The Clipper was fitted with a casquette without pilot lights for 1955, while the road Bullets were given a dualseat and dual front brakes. These items appeared on the Twin, and all the larger models had the gearbox amended so that the pedals were on concentric spindles. The Ensign continued with covers to hide its rear springs.

The range of Bullets was modified for 1956, and the two road versions changed to an alternator for charging, although they kept the magneto for ignition. All the competition machines were dropped, to be replaced by a Moto-Cross Bullet in each size for that

1951, when its engine unit became more streamlined and went into a new frame. The new frame remained rigid but had a full loop to carry the engine while the telescopic forks were revised to suit it and the details cleaned up. However, the cycle parts remained much as before so the RE2, as it was called, stayed true to its roots as a light, handy machine. The other models ran on with little change for 1951 and 1952, the G and J to both be dropped after 1955.

There were more additions for 1953, with new models at both ends of the range. Smallest newcomer was the Ensign, which had a 148cc version of the RE2 engine installed in a frame that appeared to have plunger rear suspension with exposed springs, although it was, in fact, a pivoted fork. Otherwise, the Ensign was very much as the RE2, which continued unchanged to the end of the year and was then dropped.

The 346cc Bullet was joined by a 499cc version which duplicated the smaller model on most points, but whose front forks were available with extended wheel lugs to give sidecar trail. The Twin had some new parts, but more important was the appearance of a larger version as

Top
A 1956 Royal Enfield 693cc Super Meteor on test, where its power and low-speed pulling came in for praise

Right
The Royal Enfield Dreamliner on the Isle of Man in 1957 where it drew the crowds as always, despite its basic Bullet engine

year only. The utility 250 Clipper was joined by a similar 350 model, which retained the same separate engine and gearbox format. It kept to a saddle, so was cheaper than the Bullet, and appeared to follow the typical Enfield trick of clearing the stores of excess stocks by building a model to use them. At the bottom of the scale, the two-stroke became the Ensign II with some detail changes and a dualseat. For the twins, the smaller stayed as it was and the larger was renamed the Super Meteor. In this form, it produced more power and had an alternator for charging, while retaining the magneto. The engine unit went into a new frame and the result was a fast, beefy motorcycle.

A new model was introduced for 1957 as the 248cc Crusader, which was to lead to many versions and be a mainstay of the firm well into the next decade. It featured unit construction, but otherwise followed Enfield methods in most respects, if not all. Both head and barrel were in iron, as was the one-piece crankshaft which had a plain big-end and alloy rod. The chain-driven camshaft went on the left and drove the oil pump, from which the drive to the contact breaker was by a cross-shaft. The oil for the dry-sump

system went in a chamber in the crankcase, as usual. The complete unit went into an open frame with telescopic front and pivoted-fork rear suspension. The wheels were 17in. with full-width hubs and 6in. brakes, and the final drive was by a fully-enclosed chain. There was a dualseat and a centre section with a lid on each side to carry the electrics and tools.

Alongside the new Crusader, the two Clippers continued for 1957 only, as did the two road Bullets, Ensign II and both twins. A Clipper II appeared for 1958 as a low-cost version of the Crusader, and an Ensign III ran alongside the II with a higher specification level. The two Bullets continued and were joined by another 346cc Clipper, which was based on the Bullet engine with iron top half, alternator electrics and Crusader-type cycle parts, but with 19in. wheels.

The Crusader itself was little altered, but became available with a factory fairing during the year. Earlier, in 1956, the firm had co-operated with The Motor

Top
The later small twin was the Meteor Minor, shown here in 1958 standard guise with saddle rather than dualseat

Right
The final development of the RE was the 148cc Prince, as seen in this 1960 version

Left
The Royal Enfield Crusader design gave rise to a whole series of models, including this 1960 Sports with low bars

Bottom
A 1933 Royal Ruby 346cc Super Sports powered by a Villiers engine. Oil tank for auto-lube under saddle and battery hung out in front of engine

Cycle to build a full fairing for a Bullet, so had learnt much from this project, which was known as the Dreamliner. That had been a complete front and rear enclosure with dual headlights, but the 1958 design was simpler, being a basic dolphin type plus a deeply valanced front mudguard. It was called the Airflow, and within two years was offered for all the road models as a factory fitment.

During 1958 the 500 Twin was replaced by a new model listed as the Meteor Minor in Standard and De Luxe forms. It followed the lines of the earlier machine, but had a short-stroke, 496cc, ohv engine and a number of detail amendments. The cycle parts were much as for the Crusader and, thus, in a style which had become a standard for the firm. An Airflow version of both models was offered from the start. In addition, the larger twin was joined by a high-performance version called the Constellation, which had more power, a TT carburettor, magneto and siamesed exhaust system. The cycle side was much as for the Super Meteor, but more sporting with chrome-plated mudguards.

Even the Ensign III was given an Airflow for 1959, when it was joined by the Prince model, which used the same engine in a pivoted-fork frame with extensive chaincase and side covers. An Airflow version was offered, as it was for the two road Bullets, which had other changes, including 17in. wheels for the 346cc model only. The Crusader was joined by a Sports version, while the two sizes of Clipper model continued, all with the Airflow option. All the twins ran on, with just a change to siamezed pipes for the Super Meteor, but the Standard Meteor Minor was dropped at the end of the year.

The one new machine for 1959 was the 346cc Works Replica Trials model, which was the final version of this long-running type. It had the all-alloy engine with heavy flywheels and a well-tucked-in exhaust system, but really came along too late, for the

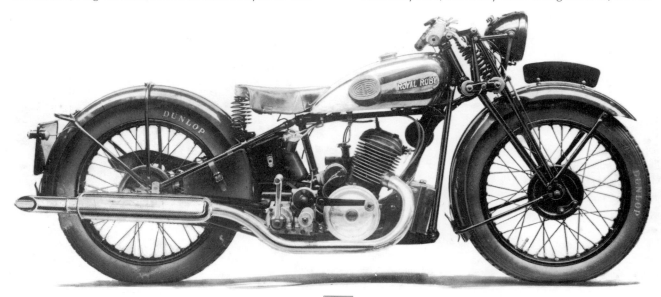

two-stroke engine was taking over in trials.

The range ran into 1960 and the new decade with limited changes. The Ensign was dropped, to leave the Prince, while the standard and Sports Crusaders continued, as did the Bullets, the trials model and the Clipper II. The larger Clipper was revised with an alloy head and 17in. wheels, so it became a cheap version of the Bullet. For the twins, there were changes for the Super Meteor and twin carburettors for the Constellation. The Meteor Minor ran on as one model only with a new silencer, but was joined by a Meteor Minor Sports with increased power and more sporting fittings.

It made a good range for the future, typical of the marque, and they carried it on for quite a while.

ROYAL RUBY

In this case the RR initials did not confer the prestige they did on four wheels. The company was sited in Bolton, Lancashire, and built motorcycles from late Edwardian days using their own engines. By 1930 they had turned to using Villiers units and for that year had two models, one of 247 and the other of 343cc. Both had a three-speed gearbox and conventional cycle parts.

For 1931 there was a single model with a 346cc long-stroke engine inclined in the frame listed as the Red Shadow and fitted with a three-speed gearbox while 1932 saw two 346cc models as the range, built as the Standard and the Club which was better equipped. They became the Sports models for 1933 and were joined by two similar 249cc machines available to various specifications but that was their final year.

Left
The radial four-valve Rudge engine with its many rockers as seen on a 1933 model of 348cc. The long lever is connected to the stand and raises the machine on to it

Bottom
1937 Rudge Sports Special with 493cc pent-roof four-valve head with rockers enclosed. Note gearbox enclosure also

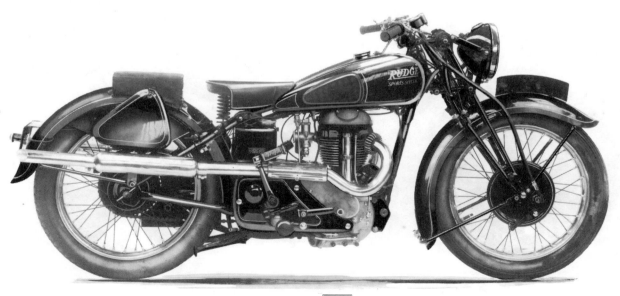

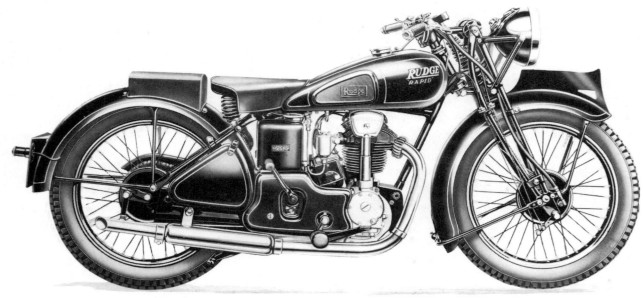

RUDGE

Rudge began with the earliest of bicycles and returned to them in the end, but from 1910 to 1939 also made motorcycles. They were innovative from the start with the one-piece fork link, the variable gear for belt drive and the four-valve engines of later times.

By the 1930s their reputation was well established as makers of fine machines and their name was in the list of TT winners and among the record books at Brooklands. In 1928 success in the Ulster Grand Prix led to the 499cc sports machine taking this name and in the same year they built their first dirt-track model. 1930 was a tremendous year for Rudge at the TT, when they won both Senior and Junior events.

The road range that year had three JAP-engined models with 248 and 300cc side-valve units and a 245cc ohv one, each driving a four-speed gearbox and

fitted with coupled brakes, a Rudge feature that dated from 1926. The other models all had four-valve, single-cylinder engines and three were of 499cc. The fourth was of 339cc, but all had dry sump lubrication and four speeds. The larger machines were the Special and the Ulster, the latter the more sporting machine. The other 499cc model was the Dirt Track, which had wet sump oiling, a countershaft in place of the gearbox, and upswept exhaust pipe to ensure adequate ground clearance.

Rudge aimed to cash in on their TT successes with the 1931 range but it was a time when the market was depressed and they were financially stretched due to the costs of developing both their racing and road engines. The 1931 line-up looked entrancing but was just too expensive for the time and sales dropped off.

Only Rudge engines were used with radial and pent-house layouts for the four valves, the first involving six rockers with their noise and wear potential. In addition to the engine costs, the gearbox was another expense as the firm made their own which had many needle roller bearings in it. The models were six in all with the 348cc TT and 350 plus the 499cc TT, Special, Ulster and Dirt Track. A 248cc model was added for 1931, but this too had a four-valve radial head so could hardly compete on price with others on the market.

For 1932 Rudge continued to work up to an ideal rather than down to a price and introduced a four-valve radial head for the Ulster and the TT Replica. The Special stayed with the pent-roof design and the road models had a new lever-operated centre stand. This lay along the chain case and made it easy for anyone to raise the machine. Footchange became an option for the Ulster, but the speedway model was no longer listed. The range continued in this form for 1933, the Ulster and 499cc TT adopting a semi-radial layout for the four valves, but for 1934 it was down to four models. These comprised two each of 248 and 499cc, the smaller with the radial head and the others pent-roof or semi-radial.

To help the cash flow they had begun to sell engine and gearbox units under the name Python in 1931. Although not as prolific as JAP, they went into a good number of the British marques and a number of European ones. This was not enough, so the firm withdrew their racing support for the 1933 season and then called in the receiver in March of that year.

The habit of road racing had died hard at Rudge, for despite the poor sales and financial problems they had in the early 1930s they could not stay away. Just to make it harder for them they were still successful with further TT wins and places in the years from 1931 to 1934. The racing had continued as a syndicate which borrowed the works machines with success before they began to fall behind the pace.

The firm continued with its reduced range, but the market for well-made but pricey machines was a limited one in those difficult times, so sales continued to be depressed. As would be expected there was little real change for 1935, other than to details, but the company was still unable to improve sales and at the end of the year went into liquidation. This could have been the end of the Rudge, but they were bought up by the giant EMI concern at Hayes and continued with the same programme.

For 1936 the 248cc Tourist became the Rapid with minimal alteration, but did get the coupled brakes, while the Sports was fitted with the big fuel tank as used by the larger models which continued as the Ulster and Special. The next year finally saw the 499cc models have their valve gear enclosed to move away from the vintage design with its minimal lubrication and heavy wear. The radial engine with its extra rockers and pivots had been very prone to this and the new arrangement was a great improvement. In addition to the two existing 499cc models there was also a Sports Special with the pent-roof engine, lighter mudguards, raised exhausts and other detail changes. There was only one of 248cc, the two-valve Rapid, as the four-valve model was no longer listed.

Sales of the range improved, but not to a level to justify the size of the Coventry factory, while control from Hayes proved awkward, so the decision to move was made and carried out. The 1938 range included one more model in the form of a Sports 250, which had a tuned engine and waist-level exhaust, but there were few other changes. The range stayed the same for 1939 and production continued to rise slowly, so, but for the war, the firm would have found its feet again. As it was, the main Hayes factory produced radar equipment and was desperate for space so motorcycle production ceased in December 1939 to make room.

With the move to Hayes it had been decided to investigate the autocycle market and a design was produced. This used the 98cc Villiers engine in a strengthened cycle-type frame and was similar to many others, being listed in Standard and De Luxe forms early in 1940, the latter fitted with engine shields, but both with rigid forks. The autocycle was made by the Norman firm in Kent using the Rudge name, and this continued for a while. In 1943 EMI decided they would not be returning to motorcycles and sold the name to Raleigh Industries.

Far left, top
Rudge Rapid with 245cc two-valve engine in 1938 form with the gearbox enclosure but exposed valves. Note coupled brakes

Left bottom
The 1940 Rudge Autocycle with 98cc Villiers engine, the machine built by the Norman firm in Kent

Top
1930 Scott Sprint Special, a beloved machine

Centre
Single-cylinder Scott of 299cc in 1931 form

Bottom
Flying Squirrel Scott of 1933 with water-cooled engine

Top right
Engine of the Scott three with one side panel lifted, this being the 1934 986cc version

Bottom right
1938 598cc Clubman's Special Scott with plunger rear suspension

SCOTT

The Scott motorcycle was a beloved anachronism by 1930, for the original light and rigid design had put on weight which stifled the performance from the Edwardian engine design. It was nearly two decades since the marque had won the Senior TT for two years in succession and since then there had been a war and in motorcycling a revolution.

In 1910 the Scott was an advanced design with a good engine and better frame and forks, but in two decades it had not really progressed at all. For the 1930s it deserved better than to remain in the mould of the past, but Alfred Angas Scott had been dead for seven years and had relinquished his connection with the company that bore his name in 1915. Sadly, those who came after lacked his vision and in the late 1920s were still building his original design when they should have been developing something newer.

The list of Scott models seemed lengthy, but was based on one basic engine and one basic frame, both in two forms, put together with a variety of parts to produce the range. All true Scotts had a twin-cylinder, water-cooled engine, but from 1929 they also built an air-cooled single.

This was a means of producing a model for the smaller end of the market, but unlike nearly all their competitors they chose to make the 299cc engine rather than buy from Villiers. The result was a crude design with iron barrel and alloy head sitting on a simple crankcase. It drove a three-speed gearbox and went into a rigid frame fitted with Scott telescopic front forks, but the whole machine was rather long and heavy for its job.

The rest of the range had the unusual Scott twin-cylinder engine with its central flywheel, inaccessible

primary chain, twin inboard mains, overhung crankpins and crankcase doors to allow big-end inspection or to take an oil pump drive. The mechanics went into a large alloy casting on which sat the block with non-detachable head. The alloy water jacket on top of the head could be removed to allow the water passages to be viewed. The engine was made in 499 and 597cc sizes for most models and known as Short Stroke units with a common stroke and change in bore. However, for one model the engines were built in Power Plus form with a longer stroke, and two more piston sizes to give 497 and 598cc.

The engines drove either a two- or three-speed gearbox and the mechanics went into the triangulated frame with triple chainstays as used from the earliest Scott. The older style was without top tube and had an oval fuel tank fitted to the seat tube. The later type had a petrol tank with integral top tube bolted at each end to the frame.

The models all came in either engine size and the two-speed ones were the Sports Squirrel and Super Squirrel fitted with Short Stroke motors. With three

long-stroke Power Plus engines were the TT Replicas, based on the model that had finished third in the 1928 Senior TT.

In addition to the road models with long-stroke engines there was the Sprint Special, which was listed for grass-track and hill climbs but could be used for any sporting occasions. Its options were numerous and each was hand-built in the competition department. Finally there was a dirt-track model built especially for that sport.

For 1931 the single changed to Webb forks, a shorter wheelbase and lost some weight but was soon

dropped. There were some changes for the twins but that year the company was in financial trouble and an Official Receiver was appointed.

Production continued at a low ebb and for 1932 the firm offered its two engine sizes in the Flying Squirrel Tourer, the de luxe of the same name, the TT

Replica and the new Sports Flying Squirrel, which was evolved from the Sprint Special. All except the first were fitted with Brampton bottom link forks in place of the Scott telescopics and the last had the Power Plus engine. This engine type was modified in 1933 with a detachable alloy head secured by 16 bolts. It also had a new oil pump whose output was linked to the throttle and was fitted into a body cast as part of the right crankcase door. The Tourer changed to Brampton girder forks. The range stayed much as it was for 1934 but with just the Tourer, de luxe and Replica in the two engine sizes. The Replica was also available with a four-speed gearbox.

There was a new machine being worked on and in February 1934 details were announced. The engine was an in-line triple of either 747 or 986cc and water-cooled as any self-respecting Scott always was. It had an Elektron crankcase, a built-up crankshaft inserted from one end and roller big-ends. One Amal supplied the mixture and a three-into-one exhaust went on the left. There were two oil pumps linked to the throttle and ignition was by coil. A four-speed gearbox went behind the engine and final drive was by chain. The cycle parts were conventional, with duplex frame and bottom link forks. The 747cc prototype had been built early in 1934 and was later road tested by The Motor Cycle but never reached production.

The 1935 range was reduced to a single model, the Flying Squirrel, with the choice of 497 or 598cc engines, both with a detachable cylinder head. There was also a change to the frame and detail alterations with an option of footchange for the gearbox. Then at the last minute Scott wheeled a new triple into the show at Olympia just before it opened. It was based on the earlier model but had a 986cc engine, a horizontally split crankcase, and the radiator blended into the front of the fuel tank. The whole machine had much more style and it caused quite a stir.

However, it was still not in production when the next show came round and Scott did not even have a stand at that one. They continued to just list the Flying Squirrel with either engine, while the three was said to be available to special order. The same statement and range held true for 1937 also, and at the end of that year the three was dropped with very few having been built. The two Flying Squirrels continued alone for 1938.

1939 saw a new model, the Clubman's Special, which had a tuned engine and a 90mph guarantee. Both it and the Flying Squirrel were only available with the 598cc engine, but plunger rear suspension that bolted on to the rigid frame was available. Less well advertised was the weight, which The Motor Cycle

quoted as 490lb in a 1939 test, and this made the brakes poor by any standards, for they just could not cope with the excess avoirdupois. The light, lithe Scott was now suffering badly from middle-age spread and had become a dull machine.

On that note the Scott stopped production for the duration, but they returned in 1946 with a Flying Squirrel, the one new post-war feature, a dual front brake in a full-width hub. The rear hub was also full-width, and the model was promised with a roll-on centre stand in place of the older rear one. Few machines were built with girder forks before these were replaced by Dowty telescopics, using air as the suspension medium and oil for damping and lubrication. These were similar to those also used by Panther and Velocette; all depended totally on the air seals to keep the model on an even keel.

In this form, the Scott continued until 1949, when a change was made to coil ignition with a distributor on the right. The changes and removal of the magneto drive chain allowed for a separate oil tank, which went on the right, below the saddle. The roll-on centre stand now made its appearance, and in this form the Flying Squirrel continued for 1950.

Unfortunately, the Scott had become a rather expensive anachronism, with a price tag well above most four-stroke twins and on a par with an Inter Norton. It also failed to offer a comparable performance, and the few sales to enthusiasts were not enough to prevent the firm going into voluntary liquidation.

The result of this was the sale of the old Saltaire works, while manufacture was transferred to the Aerco Jig and Tool Company in Birmingham, a firm owned by Matt Holder, who was a keen Scott enthusiast. They announced that the 1951 model would continue as before, but it was some time before new machines were made, and for a while only those which had been part of the purchase as stock were available.

It was 1956 before machines were available again. The new model was much as the old one in the engine department, but was available in 497 and 598cc sizes. Rigid and pivoted-fork frames were made available fitted with telescopic forks, and there was a Lycett dualseat for the rider. The fuel tank lost its traditional, sharp-edged style, which had always been so very distinctive, and the line seemed to suffer from this.

Thus, the Scott continued in small numbers and gained an alternator for 1958. During that year a new model, the Swift, was seen. This had a revised 493cc engine and six prototypes were built, but the model did not go into production. At the end of the year, the rigid models were dropped and the smaller-capacity

model was to special order only.

In this way, the Scott ran to the end of the decade and on for another. For those who understood the machine, there was no other way, and for the rest - well, they did not know what they were missing.

SEAL

The Seal was one of motorcycling's oddities, the three-wheeler Sociable in which the outfit was conceived as a motorcycle and sidecar but with the rider brought in from the cold and seated in the sidecar body which was widened to suit. The mechanics were left outside to get wet. The Seal dated from 1912 and sold for most of the 1920s using a large side-valve JAP engine and three-speed gearbox,. However, the frame that supported them was unusual and built up from four main tubes bolted or clamped together. These ran along the

machine and the mechanics could be slid along them to adjust the chains. The front suspension was also unusual as was the steering which was by a wheel located in the sidecar

If the passenger model was odd, the commercial one was stranger for the rider sat above the machine in a cabin so the whole of the sidecar could be devoted to goods carriage. Despite this, steering was still be wheel, while power was by a 343cc Villiers or 680 or 980cc JAP twin and the machine sold as the Progress.

For 1930 the passenger vehicle was extensively modified to three tracks and a central front wheel and the name was changed to New Progress and in July 1932 it was joined by a carrier version. This was even stranger, for it had front-wheel drive with the 680cc sv JAP engine carried above the wheel. Control was by handlebars which carried the gear lever and the whole front end could be quickly detached for service or repair.

Far left
A 1924 Seal pictured at a rally in 1959. Very unusual front suspension and frame built up from four long tubes. Driver travelled in the sidecar

Right
Strange front-wheel-drive New Progress Seal from 1932 in its prototype form

Bottom
1930 SGS with Villiers engine and auto-lube. Nice but short-lived

This strange design does not seem to have passed beyond the prototype stage and shortly afterwards the company ceased trading.

SGS

The initials stood for Sid Gleave Special who won the 1933 Lightweight TT riding an Excelsior. Before then he was in business in a small way as a manufacturer and for 1930 was offering five models with JAP or Villiers engines. The two-strokes were of 196 or 247cc while the JAP engines were 245cc sv and ohv units plus a 346 ohv, the first in loop frames and the last a diamond one to create a TT model.

Like many others Sid found the 1930s hard going for making motorcycles and left this to others while he got on with his racing.

SHARRATT

A 1920s firm that used proprietary engines but which by 1930 was only in limited production. For that year they listed just three models, all of which had 346cc JAP engines.

The model F had a side-valve unit, but the FS was ohv, as was the FSS. All drove three-speed gearboxes and went into a conventional set of cycle parts.

For 1931 only the FS and FSS ohv models were listed and that was the last year for them. After that the firm turned to car dealing, which in time became a substantial business.

SOS

At first Super Onslow Special and later So Obviously Superior, but through the 1930s the SOS was considered exclusive and superior to the usual run of Villiers-powered machines. They were produced at first at Hallow, near Worcester, by Len Vale-Onslow and as there was no gas supply laid on he had, perforce, to adopt electric welding. This led to a duplex frame with steel stampings for the fork ends in place of forged lugs. A platform was welded between the tubes under the mechanics to brace the frame and the result was a rigid structure. At the front went tubular girders and the wheels had good-sized brakes.

In 1930 SOS had two models fitted with JAP ohv engines, one 250 and the other 350cc. The rest of the range used Villiers power and came in 172, 196, 247 and 343cc capacities. They were nicely constructed and continued for 1931 alone, for the JAP engines were dropped from the line-up.

For 1932 manufacture was transferred to Birmingham and the two-stroke range continued, the largest model changing to the 346cc long-stroke engine. Early in the year a prototype model with a watercooled engine was seen and later came the news that engines of 148 and 172cc were to be built using Villiers bottom halves and SOS tops. The radiator was mounted beneath the petrol tank with enclosing cowls and the remainder of the machine stock SOS with three-speed Burman gearbox, flywheel magneto ignition and auto-lube for the larger model.

The 148 and 172cc models formed part of the 1933 range which was completed with a 172cc air-

Top
The 1931 SOS model CY fitted with the 343cc Villiers engine which was changed for the longer stroke 346cc one the next year

Bottom
1934 Magnetic model C SOS with 249cc water-cooled Villiers engine

cooled model which was fitted with the super sports engine with extensive head fins. Like the others it had twin exhaust systems. In July a 249cc water-cooled model was added to the range, and in October control of the firm passed to Tommy Meeten. Production remained in Birmingham, but at that time Meeten's shop was in Redhill, Surrey, where he sold Francis-Barnett and Villiers.

Meeten's 1934 range was retyped, given names and included air- and water-cooled engines. All had Albion gearboxes, mainly handchange but some with the option of footchange and two with four speeds.

The range comprised the 172cc Speed and Club models, the 249cc Club, the 249 and 346cc Magnetic models and the same sizes of Superb models. This mix of air-cooling, water-cooling. petroil, auto-lube, two to four speeds, and hand or footchange continued for 1935 and onwards. Tuned engines were also available and in 1936 Tommy Meeten opened new premises on the Kingston By-pass at Shannon Corner. He named them Meetens Motor Mecca and they became well known.

The SOS ran on in this manner right up to 1939 and the range did represent the quality end of the utility market. Several models were offered with all-weather equipment - legshields, under-shields plus well-valanced mudguards while there were cheaper versions with fewer fittings but as good a reputation.

When war came Meeten offered his facilities to the authorities but was turned down so he closed the Birmingham factory and turned to farming. His intention to restart production post-war was foiled by looting of his stock of engine units, so the Mecca became a shop specialising in Villiers-powered products.

STANLEY

This was a tricycle fitted with a 98cc Villiers engine in the manner of an autocycle but with three wheels. It appeared in 1932 and was intended to offer stability and a little power assistance to the elderly. The machine was based on a normal tricycle complete with pedalling gear and differential back axle. The fitments were bicycle with a stirrup front brake and external contracting one on each rear wheel, interconnected to a single handlebar lever.

It was a nice idea, but was launched at a difficult

time, and no more was heard of the little machine from Egham in Surrey.

STEVENS

When the old AJS firm was taken over by Matchless the Stevens brothers were left with the Wolverhampton factory and some old machine tools and engine jigs so in March 1934 they re-entered the motorcycle market.

Their machine was a straightforward ohv single of 249cc driving a four-speed gearbox, fitted into a duplex frame with Druid forks. It was well fitted out and ran on into 1935 when it was joined by a 348cc version. A third machine of 495cc was added in April 1935 and the two larger were given megaphone-shaped silencers for 1936. Competition versions were also listed that year and all continued for 1937 when the megaphone silencer went on the 249cc model.

The same range was listed for 1938, but during that year the brothers finally ceased making motorcycles and turned to other work.

SUN

Like many, this firm had its roots in the cycle industry and hailed from Birmingham. Motorcycles came prior to World War 1 and continued after it with JAP, Villiers and other engines, including a disc-valve two-stroke. By 1930 the range of models numbered six and they were much as others of that time. Two models had

Below
Stevens HP6 model of 1936 with 495cc engine. This was the competition version of the standard model and like it had a megaphone silencer

Top
Sun four-stroke with 490cc JAP engine in a 1931 model

Bottom
Sun two-stroke Tourist with 147cc Villiers engine

Far right
The 1953 Sun Challenger with 6E Villiers engine in rigid frame with telescopic forks

Villiers engines of 147 and 196cc and the other four were JAP powered. Two had side valves and were of 300 and 490cc capacity and the ohv were of 346 and 490cc. All had the engines set vertically and hand-change for the gears.

The only models to continue as they were for 1931 were the 196cc two-stroke and the two 500s with sv and ohv. New was a larger 343cc two-stroke with Villiers engine and a model with an inclined 245cc ohv JAP engine with rear magneto. In May 1931 the range was joined by a miniature which used a 98cc Villiers engine in the simple diamond frame where it drove a two-speed Albion gearbox with direct-acting hand-change. Lubrication was by petroil and ignition by fly-wheel magneto. Blade girders were used and the machine had direct lighting and with this was sold for 16 guineas.

In August 1931 it was joined by a similar model fitted with a 147cc Villiers engine to slot into the 150cc tax class, and for 1932 these two was called Tourist models. The large JAP-powered machines stayed on to use up stocks and the 196cc model as the Utility. A Sports machine was added using the 148cc

Villiers and the final models were two Tourists using either a 346cc ohv JAP or a similar size Villiers. In April 1932 a second version of the 148cc model with a fuller specification was added and ran on for 1933 along with the 98, 147 and 196cc machines plus the two 346cc ones. These six models ran on for that year, but then Sun gave up producing their own make for several years. They continued to make parts and even complete machines for other firms, but it was 1940 before another Sun was seen.

This was an autocycle powered by a 98cc Villiers engine and produced in three forms as standard, with Webb forks or with these and engine shields. The first had the stock engine but the others fitted the JDL.

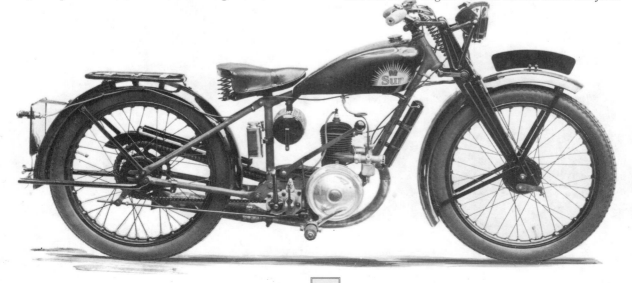

218

With the war production stopped again but the firm returned in 1946 with a single model with the JDL engine in the rigid frame with blade girders to provide the most basic motorised transport. The Autocycle was listed with the JDL engine up to 1948, but for the next year was revised to use the 2F unit. At the same time, it was joined by the Motor Cycle, which had the two-speed 1F engine in a rigid frame, also with girder forks, and was equally basic.

The two machines continued for 1950, at the end of which, the Autocycle was dropped and the Motor Cycle revised and joined by two more models. Its main change was to tubular girders, while it retained its saddle and rear carrier, but gained a nice maroon finish. The two new models shared cycle parts and had a loop frame with telescopic front and plunger rear suspension. The specification was intended to be better than standard, hence the rear springing, and included battery lighting and an electric horn. The power units were the 122cc 10D or 197cc 6E Villiers engines with three-speed gearbox, and the models were called the 122 de luxe and the Challenger de luxe. Both had 19in. wheels with 5in. brakes, adjustable footrests, and a good saddle.

The three models continued for 1952, and in March a 197cc Competition machine was announced, although it did not reach the market until 1953. It was listed as the Competition Challenger and was first seen with a plunger frame. However, it became rigid for production, but was a full loop type with the saddle raised on its own little subframe. The telescopic forks carried a 21in. front wheel, and there were alloy mudguards and wide-ratio gears with options of a tuned engine and close gears. The road models also had changes for 1953, smallest having the 4F engine unit, and the 122cc version the 12D. The largest model became available in a rigid frame, while a dualseat was offered as an option.

For 1954 the 122 and 197cc Challenger road

models went into a new pivoted-fork frame and kept their battery lighting. Despite the frame change, a saddle was still the standard fit, and the dualseat was the option. The engine of the larger machine became the 8E, which allowed the model to be offered in three- or four-speed forms. The competition model stayed in its rigid frame but was offered in three forms, all powered by the 8E engine. The range was completed by the 99cc model, which was unchanged, and extended by the addition of the Cyclone, which used the 224cc Villiers 1H engine unit. This went into a new pivoted-fork frame with telescopic forks. The machine also had battery lighting and a dualseat.

The Cyclone continued with little alteration for 1955, as did the 99cc model, which had a new tank and a new name - Hornet. The smaller Challenger had a change of engine to a 147cc 30C unit, becoming the Mk 1A, while the larger became the Mk IV. On the competition side, just two models were listed, one of which, the Trials, was much as before, but the other, the Scrambler, was new and had a pivoted-fork frame and Earles leading-link forks with a standard or tuned engine and three or four speeds.

The road range of Hornet, Challenger 1A and Cyclone continued as they were for 1956, while the larger Challenger became the Mk V. It was joined by the Wasp, which used the 9E engine in a pivoted-fork frame with Armstrong leading-link forks and a degree of rear enclosure. The same engine and forks were also used for the Wasp Competition model, which replaced the Trials and Scrambles machines.

There were more changes and additions for 1957, the Hornet becoming Saxe blue in colour and the smaller Challenger becoming the Mk IV with a 148cc 31C engine unit. The 197cc version stayed with its 8E engine, as did the Wasp with the 9E, but there was also a new machine of the same capacity. This was the

Left
The Wasp Twin which soon had its name changed to the Overlander, but kept its Villiers 249cc 2T engine and leading-link forks

Century, which used the 8E engine in a pivoted-fork frame with telescopic front forks and a degree of rear enclosure. The Wasp Competition continued, as did the Cyclone, and a second new model was the Wasp Twin with the 249cc 2T Villiers twin engine, whose name was soon changed to Overlander.

One further model was proposed for 1957, which was the Geni scooter with a 99cc 4F engine unit. It differed from most scooters in having a distinct tunnel behind the apron and 15in. wire-spoked wheels, which added to the stability. The frame had pivoted-fork rear and leading-link front suspension, and the rear was enclosed by a body that extended up to the dualseat.

When the Geni reached production, it was fitted with the 6F engine with foot-change and in this form, went forward for 1958 as part of a much reduced range. At the start of the year, this totalled four machines, including the Geni, but the Hornet was soon dropped, as were both Challengers, the Century, the Cyclone and the Wasp Competition. Left were just the Wasp and Overlander, which continued with the same cycle parts.

In June 1958 the Geni became the Mk II and went forward with the Wasp and Overlander for 1959. The last two had their rear enclosure improved to give a smoother line, but both were dropped during the year. This left the Geni, but during 1959 it was joined by another scooter called the Sunwasp. This shared its bodywork with Dayton and Panther, while under the skin went a tubular frame and a 174cc 2L fan-cooled Villiers engine with three-speed gearbox and Siba electric start. The suspension was by leading links at the front and pivoted fork at the rear, while the wheels were 10in. pressed steel with 6in. brakes.

The Geni and Sunwasp both continued for 1960, but there were no longer any Sun motorcycles. The smaller model went at the end of that year, while the other continued, but only for one more year. The family that had run the concern from Victorian times retired and sold out to Raleigh, who soon removed the name from the cycle and scooter market.

Left
The Sun Geni scooter, which was powered by a 99cc 6F Villiers engine and had a style similar to that of the DMW Bambi

SUNBEAM

Sunbeam were one of several companies whose best years lay in their early history. They built up a tremendous reputation for quality and finish, but to do this had to keep all the work in-house. They bought in castings and the usual proprietary items such as carburettor and magneto, but all machining, plating and painting was done on the premises to the very high standards first set by the founder, John Marston.

In 1928 Sunbeam became part of the ICI concern, but despite the benefits of improved conditions the workforce were not over-enamoured with the notion. Instinctively and correctly they could see that the future could bring unwelcome directives from afar and preferred the discipline of management on the spot.

Sunbeam won four Senior TTs in the 1920s, along with many other races, but from then on success was to elude them. As the 1930s progressed the works began to feel the hand of the ICI accountants on them and much of the tradition began to go. More parts were bought in and slowly some of the quality went,

although the standard of painting remained as high as ever.

The 1930 range reflected the 1920s Sunbeam line-up and although the company had changed to saddle tanks there was still the 599cc side-valve model 7 with flat tank made to special order. At the bottom of the list were the 346 and 491cc side-valve Touring and Sporting models which, along with the 7, were not to run on into 1931. With ohv there were the 346cc model 8 and 493cc model 9 and all had tall, vintage-style engines with rear magneto. The gearbox was of the crossover type, so the final drive one was on the right and could be fully enclosed.

Of more interest to the enthusiast were the ohv models 80 and 90, also of 346 and 493cc, but with hairpin valve springs and replicas of the TT winning machines. They had much racier lines, which were still vintage. There was one further competition model, which was the DTR for speedway use, but very few were made.

Top
1933 Sunbeam Little 90 racing machine of 246cc

Centre
1935 Model 16 with 248cc high-camshaft engine

Bottom
1933 model 8 Sunbeam of 346cc with the wonderful finish

Far right, top
The AMC-designed B28 Sunbeam of 598cc from 1939 with chain drive for the high camshaft and plunger rear suspension

Far right, bottom
The S7 Sunbeam twin with its fat tyres and in-line engine with shaft drive to the rear wheel

In June 1930 one more model was added to the list. This was the 6, also called the Lion, and had a 489cc side-valve engine. It heralded a new style of Sunbeam with Webb forks and chrome-plated tank, while the model list was shortened for 1931. The models 9 and 90 were still there and the model 6 Lion was trimmed down to cut the price. New was the 10 with 344cc ohv engine with wet sump, three-speed gearbox and no rear chain enclosure option.

The 1932 range was the same plus a 599cc sv version of the Lion, a tuned model 10 and a 596cc ohv model listed as the 9A. Most of this continued for 1933 but the 346cc ohv models 8 and 80 returned, much as they were in 1930, and were joined by a 246cc ohv model 14 plus the Little 90 which was a racing version built in small numbers. The 95 was in the same style, a 493cc ohv built to racing specification but for use on the road and 1934 brought the similar Little 95 but lost the 80 and 90 models.

The company was, however, in trouble with the ICI accountants, for they built too good a product. Hard though this must have sounded it was true at the time, for price was all in the early 1930s and customers had to be found by skimping quality and cutting prices

Above
A sectioned Sunbeam twin engine on display

Bottom
The lighter looking S8, as it was in 1951, with its cast alloy silencer

Far right
An S7 serving with the police in Wellington, New Zealand, in 1952. It had a white finish and was fitted with radio

to the bone. This was not the Sunbeam way, of course, and they found it near impossible to change their habits. Sadly there were few about who could afford the price of good work and those who could tended to be snapped up by George Brough.

The 1935 range had the stalwart 8, 9, 9A and Lion models and three more, two revisions and one new. The revisions were the 95L for the sports rider and

the 95R, which was without a kick-starter. Both models had four speeds, footchange and larger brakes. The new machine was the 248cc ohv model 16 with a high camshaft, hairpin valve springs and a bulbous silencer on its single exhaust pipe. It had a Burman gearbox, so the final drive chain went on the left, but proved to be a poor design and was not at all successful.

The larger Lion and 596cc ohv 9A remained as they were for 1936, but the other models went over to Burman gearboxes, so the final drive was moved to the left side of the machine. There were six in all, two each of 246, 346 and 493cc, and all had overhead valves. In each case one was the stock model and the other the sports while the largest had a new cradle frame and the others stayed with the diamond type. Little was altered for 1937 other than the addition of a 493cc Light Solo in standard and sports forms.

1937 saw the end of the road for Sunbeam as a part of ICI, for they were not producing the profit required of them. The result was a sale of the business to the AJS and Matchless combine in London, and late in 1937 the parts and data were moved south. The workforce in Wolverhampton was absorbed into other ICI activities on the same site and the London firm learnt a great deal about high-quality paint finishes, which went on to their machines from then on. The combination of the three firms became AMC.

For 1938 all ten models were listed with new designations but little other change. One item that had to go was the black painting of the gearbox end cover, as AMC production did not allow for this to happen to the Burman boxes. The two old Lion models of 489 and 599cc with side valves continued in 1939, but the rest of the range had new engines. These were of an AMC design with ohv moved by a chain-driven high camshaft. The chain also drove the mag-dyno and had a Weller tensioner, the whole enclosed by a large trian-

gular cover carrying the Sunbeam name in script. Four sizes of engine were produced in 245, 348, 497 and 598cc capacities. The three largest shared the same stroke, and dimensions were common with AMC engines. Hairpin valve springs were used and a duplex gear oil pump went in the base of the crankcase. In addition to the four standard models the three smaller were listed in Sports and Competition forms. The first of these had polished engine internals, upswept exhaust and a change of mudguard and tyres. The second was built for trials use with a smaller petrol tank, 4in. rear tyre and alloy mudguards, but were still heavy machines.

In June 1939 a rear suspension system was announced for the larger ohv singles. It looked like a plunger one but was not, although the springs were in plunger boxes at the rear of the frame. The wheel was, however, carried in a pivoted fork and this in turn linked to the plungers by a shackle. This went into the 1940 range, which comprised ten models in all including the three with rear suspension. The same three plus the 245cc model were listed in rigid frames and the 348 and 497cc ones in sports guise. Last but not least came the 599cc sv Lion. In practice very few spring-frame models were made and before long the AMC works was fully engaged in producing the Matchless G3 for the services. This brought the Sunbeams to a halt and in 1943 AMC sold the name to the BSA group. There were no more Sunbeams in the John Marston style. AMC continued to benefit from the paint know-how for many years and gained a high reputation for their finish, although few realised where this had come from.

Postwar the firm did produce one of the few really new British models, although the parent group failed to support it as well as they might have. The machine was first described in the press early in 1946 and offered a great deal that was new on the British market. Features of particular note were the in-line vertical twin engine, its overhead camshaft, unit construction, shaft drive, plunger rear suspension, fat 16in. tyres and a variety of interesting details.

The 489cc short-stroke engine was an all-alloy unit and the block and crankcase were cast as one down to the sump plate. Above went the alloy head, with the chain-driven camshaft, which had the distributor at its rear, and the valves in an angled row. The one-piece, cast-iron crankshaft carried a pancake dynamo on its nose, there were alloy connecting rods with shell big-end bearings and lubrication was wet-sump. The whole engine made a very neat unit, for there were no external pipes. On the left went the two sparking plugs, and on the right a single Amal carburettor, flanked by the two exhaust pipes. These swept down into one and then on to the silencer.

The engine drove back to the clutch and four-speed, all-indirect gearbox which stepped the drive out for the final drive. Despite the in-line nature of the layout, both gear and kickstart pedals were on the right and moved in the normally accepted planes. An open shaft took the power to the rear wheel and had a rubber-coupling universal joint at the front end and a Hardy-Spicer at the rear. The drive to the wheel was by an underslung worm, rather than the more usual bevels, and the rear brake was incorporated into the housing.

The engine unit was housed in a duplex frame with plunger rear suspension and telescopic, but undamped, front forks. The wheels were interchangeable and had 16in. rims carrying special 4.75in. Dunlop tyres. The brakes were 8in. offset drums, massive mudguards protected each wheel, while rider comfort was looked after by a pan saddle. This had rubber mountings and a long spring housed in the frame top tube to provide support. The machine was fully equipped and topped off with a handsome petrol tank.

Above
Sunbeam S7 pictured in 1973, but still much as it was when it left the factory
Bottom
The Sunbeam scooter built with single or twin engine and in these or Triumph colours, here with matching sidecar

That was 1946, and during the year there was also news of a sports model, which had a revised cylinder head. This gave a cross-flow layout, so the carburettor moved over to the left. The extra power pushed the maximum speed up. Unfortunately, all was not well, for

226

the machine suffered from bad vibration, a peaky power output, torque reaction and rapid wear of the worm wheel. The solutions chosen were to restrict the engine speed and power, which removed the torque and wear troubles, although it did leave the model underpowered. In this form, a batch was made with improved forks, as there had been dangerous breakages, and sent to South Africa, only to be returned as unrideable.

The original designer, Erling Poppe, had by now left the company, so BSA personnel had to deal with the problems and endeavour to tame what was meant to be a group flagship. They decided the answer was to mount the engine on rubber, which was done with two mountings and two sets of snubbers. As the engine no longer contributed to the frame's stiffness, a small cross-bar was added ahead of the engine.

Finally, in 1947, the model went into production as the S7, but the performance was hardly vivacious, for the weight was over 400lb, and the meagre power gave a top speed of only 75mph in contemporary road tests. Even allowing for the pool petrol of the time, this was not the expected performance of a 500cc twin, for the docile 3T Triumph was as fast. In addition, the ride induced by the combination of the fat tyres, long saddle spring and undamped suspension was lively and the machine snaked in fast bends. It was also an expensive machine to produce.

The result of these problems was a revision, plus a second model for 1949. The original became the S7 de luxe, and the new machine the S8 with narrower tyres and a lighter line. Both kept the same engine unit, rear drive and frame, but the forks became standard BSA for the S8 and stock legs in special yokes for the S7. The S8 also used a 7in. BSA brake at the front, where a 19in. rim with a 3.25in. section tyre was fitted. At the rear that model used a 4.00x18in. tyre.

The S8 had a different silencer and a conventional saddle. The mudguards were reduced to suit the tyres, and the handle-bars had stock controls, not the inverted ones with hidden cables used by the S7. A new air cleaner appeared, as did a prop-stand, while the S8 took the black finish previously used by the S7, which was painted mist green. There was also an option of silver grey for the S8.

As the 1950s rolled by, the two Sunbeams continued, year by year, the S8 being the more popular, but fewer and fewer buyers came forward. BSA made no real attempt to improve it, although a variant known as the S10 was built. This had the power-sapping worm replaced with bevels, while a crossflow head moved the performance up to a level comparable with its rivals. However, it was not proceeded with.

The models were announced for 1957, but pro-duction ceased before then, although new machines were stuck in showrooms for another year or two. It was not, however, the end of the name, because BSA found another use for it. To the horror of Sunbeam enthusi-asts, it appeared on a scooter.

When the group finally did get round to this fast-selling type of transport, they chose to produce both BSA and Triumph machines, by changes of colour and badges, and labelled the first a Sunbeam. For both mar-ques, there were two models, one with a 172cc two-stroke engine and the other with a 249cc ohv twin, offered with electric or kick starting. Both were launched in 1958 after a long development period, but it was 1959 before the twin reached the shops, and nearly 1960 before the single joined it.

The two engines differed totally, but otherwise the machines were nearly the same, with common transmission and chassis, except for minor details. The single was based on the D7 Bantam, although there were few common parts, and had a flywheel magneto with a fan to assist the cooling. The twin engine sat across the frame with a gear-driven camshaft to the rear. It was an all-alloy unit with one-piece forged crankshaft, generator on the right, points and oil-pump drive on opposite ends of the camshaft, and a Zenith carburettor to provide the mixture.

From then on, both twin and single drove back from the clutch by gears to a four-speed gearbox based on that used by the C15 and the Cub. The positive-stop change was controlled by a single rocking pedal, and final drive was by a duplex chain. This was enclosed in alloy castings, which also acted as the rear suspension pivoted arm to carry the 10in. pressed-steel wheel and its 5in. drum brake.

The chassis was in scooter style and the front fork was telescopic, but with a single leg on the left, which had two tubes, one each for the spring and damper. The front wheel and brake were as for the rear. The body-work was built up from pressings, but access to the mechanics was limited by the small panels provided. The dualseat was hinged to allow refuelling, and the one or two batteries were carried in boxes on the back of the apron.

All Sunbeam models were given a polychromatic green finish and there was a long list of accessories in typical scooter style, which were essential for the deal-er, who could do good business with them. The machines continued with little change until the mid-1960s, but were never able to challenge the chic Italian models in the mass market, or the sophisticated German ones at the top end. As time moved on, the market shrank, so BSA went in other directions. Sunbeam motorcycles were no more.

SWALLOW

This company was best known for its sidecars, but in the early post-war years it also built an elementary scooter called the Gadabout. Details were first released late in 1946 and at first it had to make do with the pre-war 122cc Villiers 9D engine. In other respects the machine followed scooter design with small wheels, floor, apron and rear body but lacked any suspension.

In this form, the Gadabout went its rather slow way in 1947, but was able to keep up with the traffic of those days. It was available with a box sidecar for commercial use, and for this had its gearing lowered. For 1950 it became the Mk II with a 10D engine while comfort was improved with the addition of leading-link front forks

It continued in this style, but became upstaged by the Vespa and Lambretta, which had much sleeker lines. For 1951 it was joined by the Major version which had a 197cc 6E engine but at the end of the year, both were dropped. From then on, the firm concentrated on its sidecars.

TAILWIND

This enterprising clip-on design differed from the rest in having two speeds. It achieved this by fitting a two-diameter drive roller to its 49cc two-stroke engine and arranging for the complete unit to move from side to side to change gear. A conical section between the diameters ensured a smooth transition.

The design was built by a Mr Latta of Berkhamsted in 1952 but he found, as have others, that building a prototype may not be easy but production is much harder. As it was the moped was soon to take over and no more was heard of the Tailwind.

TANDON

This firm was set up by Indian-born Devdutt Tandon to build cheap lightweights for both home and export markets, and their first model appeared in 1948. Initially, it was known as the Special, but later as the Milemaster, and had a simple specification of 122cc 9D Villiers engine, rigid frame and telescopic forks. The pillar-mounted saddle and angular fuel tank which hung from the frame top tubes did nothing to update the elderly lines of the engine, but there was a rear carrier, prop stand and direct lighting. The tank top was also arranged to carry the tools

This simple model was joined for 1950 by another of the same capacity, but with a very different appearance. The new machine was called the Supaglide and powered by the 10D engine which went into a new frame, which had pivoted-fork rear suspension controlled by a rubber cartridge mounted beneath the engine. Telescopic forks went at the front, and the tank continued to have a recess in the top for the tools, but was of a much nicer shape with conventional rounded lines. There was rectified lighting with the battery mounted beneath the saddle, a centre stand and a blue paint finish.

For 1951 the two 122cc models were joined by the Supaglide Supreme, which had a 197cc 6E engine in place of the 10D, but was otherwise the same. During the year, a further 125 appeared as the competition Kangaroo, which differed from standard in gearing, a 21in. front wheel, tyres, and alloy mudguards. In addition, the saddle was raised and the headlight quickly

Left
The Swallow Gadabout with the box sidecar
available for commercial use

Far right, top
The two-speed Tailwind clip-on, which drove
the bicycle front wheel with one of two roller
diameters

Far right, bottom
The 1948 Tandon with its 9D engine and crude
tank, built more for export than
home use

detachable.

All four models continued for 1952, at the end of which the Milemaster was replaced by the Imp, which used the 10D engine in a rigid frame with telescopic forks. The two Supaglide models continued, but the Kangaroo had rather more alteration. It went into a new frame, the rear fork being controlled by conventional spring units and the saddle replaced by a trials seat, and was joined by the Kangaroo Supreme, which had the 6E engine. The same frame type was also used with road cycle parts to create the Imp Supreme.

This was one of only two models to continue for 1954, but with an engine change to an 8E. The other was the Imp, which had a similar alteration to a 12D.

To make the range up, there were four other models, the Imp Supreme De Luxe being much as the basic model, but with four speeds, a dualseat and extra equipment. It kept to the 8E engine, which was also used for the Scrambler. This had Earles-type leading-link front suspension, an open exhaust, no lights and a racing seat. The remaining models were larger in capacity and used the best of the Imp cycle parts with a choice of engines. For the Monarch it was the 224cc Villiers 1H unit, but the Twin Supreme had the 242cc British Anzani twin.

Both had the frame improved for 1955, when it was also used by a new model, listed as the Viscount and fitted with the 322cc British Anzani twin engine.

All three were given full-width hubs front and rear with much needed 6in. brakes and short leading-link forks, which also went on the Imp Supreme De Luxe. The other Imps continued, but the smaller one had an engine change to the 147cc 30C unit. They were joined by the Imp Supreme Special, which had the 8E engine, three speeds, short leading links, rear suspension and direct lighting to reduce costs. For competition, the Scrambler continued, but with a 7E engine, and was joined by a 250 Scrambler, which used the British Anzani twin unit fitted with stub pipes.

However, time and finance were running out for the Tandon, and late in 1955 there was an order to wind them up. They had always operated on a knife edge, so it did not take much to push them over. This

was not the end of the name, however, for they were back by the middle of 1956 with a simple two-model range. This comprised the Imp Supreme Special and the Monarch, the former fitted with the 8E engine with three speeds and the latter the 1H. Both had a pivoted-fork frame had the short leading-link forks. These models remained in the lists until 1959, when production finally ceased for good.

TEAGLE

This was a clip-on engine made in Cornwall and first seen late in 1952. Derived from one designed for garden power tools, it was light and simple and the 50cc two-stroke engine was largely a single alloy casting, which formed the cylinder and crankcase, the rest of the construction conventional. The engine sat over the rear wheel and had its fuel tank mounted above it. It was 1954 before there was any more news of the Teagle and it remained on the market for some two years before the moped overtook it and all its brothers.

Top
The competition Tandon Kangaroo with 10D engine and rubber-block rear suspension, as built for 1951-2
Left
Tandon Imp introduced for 1953, still with the 10D engine, but in a rigid frame

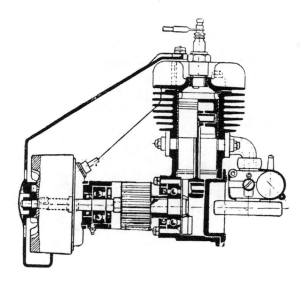

THREE SPIRES

This make was introduced for 1932 and made by
Coventry Bicycles using a 147cc Villiers engine,
two-speed gearbox and a diamond frame with girder forks. It was quite conventional for the type and,
like many others, failed to survive past the end of
the season so no more was heard of it.

TRIUMPH

In 1930 the range of Triumph motorcycles was made in
Coventry and at that time the same parent firm built
and sold bicycles and motor cars. The first of these was
sold off early in the decade, but it was 1936 before the
cars went their own way. They had run the company
into financial difficulties and the initial decision was to
stop all motorcycle production. This situation became
known to Jack Sangster, who already owned the Ariel
firm, and he completed a deal to take over the two-
wheeled side as the Triumph Engineering Company
early in 1936. It was to become very successful and
make a lot of money.

Back in 1930 the future was less clear and the
heady days of the 1920s were giving way to the dark
ones of the depressed early thirties. Like everyone else
Triumph had to trim their range to suit people's pockets
above all else. To do this they kept to six models to
begin the year, all with vertically mounted engines,
three-speed gearboxes and conventional construction.
From the 1920s came the WS with its 278cc side-valve
engine and mechanical oil pump supplemented by a
foot pump, aimed at the under 224lb market. Also from
older days was the 549cc side-valve NSD, which had
the same type of lubrication system. The remaining
models were from 1929 and the smallest was the 348cc
ohv CO. Next came the 498cc sv CN and ohv C, and
then the 549cc sv CSD.

Early in 1930, a unit-construction, 174cc two-

231

Top
1931 Triumph model NSD with 549cc side-valve inclined engine

Centre
Silent Scout model A Triumph of 1932 fitted with 549cc engine

Bottom
The 1933 model WA with partial enclosure of its 249cc engine

Right
Triumph 1934 model XO5/1 with three-speeds and 148cc engine

stroke was added to the range and this had a two-speed gearbox which had the input gears fitted to the crankshaft to drive the outputs, then clutch to drive the rear wheel. This unit went into a rigid frame with girder forks and the petroil tank fitted within the frame. Ignition and lighting were provided by a Lucas unit on the left end of the crankshaft and were included in the under £25 price. The machine was called the Junior. For the spring of 1930 the very old-fashioned NSD was replaced by a revised model whose engine was inclined forward and had dry sump lubrication, rear magneto and drove a three-speed gearbox

The WS was dropped for 1931 along with the CO and in their places came the ohv 249cc WO and 343cc NM with inclined engines and dry sump lubrication as on the NSD, which continued along with the CSD, CN and CTT with vertical cylinders, semi-dry sump oiling and cradle frames. New was the 348cc side-valve WL built on the lines of the WO, while the 174cc two-stroke continued as the model X. Later additions to the programme were the de luxe ND with 549cc side-valve engine and the NT with a 493cc ohv unit.

1932 brought further changes to the range as the firm sought to offer something for every possible buyer. At the bottom end of the scale the two-stroke had its

bore reduced to take the capacity down below the 150cc tax barrier and in this size was sold as the Z, while the X was still available. Most models were much as before and were joined by three newcomers. The WA, a single-port version of the twin-port 249cc WO and two competition models. For a little off-road use the exhausts were high level, a sump plate was fitted and both machines had ohv and were the 343cc CA and 493cc CD.

At the end of March 1932 two further models were announced as the Silent Scouts. They were simply the A with a 549cc sv engine and the B with a 493cc ohv one. Both followed the Triumph format of the year with inclined cylinder, dry sump cast into the front of the crankcase and rear-mounted mag-dyno. To reduce the noise level the pushrods were enclosed, while a concentration on quality in manufacture kept the noise down.

There were further changes for 1933, although most ran on. The two-strokes went, and new was the BS, which was a sports version of the Silent Scout. A second new model was the WP, which was a sports model based on the stock 249cc ohv machine with a four-speed gearbox and twin tubular silencers. The third new model was the XO, a 148cc ohv sports single with well-inclined cylinder and horizontal cooling fins.

It was designed to come within the capacity tax class and drove a three-speed gearbox. With a 47mph top speed it made a sprightly ride-to-work machine.

In July 1933 an important step in Triumph history took place with the announcement of a model fitted with a 647cc vertical twin engine. This was not the firm's first engine in that style for they had built one as early as 1913, but it was the start of a modern trend. The twin was designed by Val Page and its form was to reappear post-war in the BSA twin.

For Triumph, Page laid down an engine with overhead valves and a single gear-driven camshaft mounted to the rear of the crankcase. The mag-dyno was gear driven from the camshaft and lubrication was dry sump with the oil tank built into the crankcase. The primary drive was by double helical gears, an expensive design at any time, let alone in 1933 and this caused the engine to run backwards.

The four-speed gearbox was bolted to the back of the crankcase and the whole unit was housed in a massive duplex frame supported by heavy-duty girder forks at the front. This was done because the machine was

Top
De luxe model 5/4 Triumph with 493cc engine in 1934

Centre
The 647cc twin-cylinder Triumph model 6/1 with matching sidecar on show late in 1934

Bottom
When Triumph made a road-racing model. This is the 1935 5/10 with tuned 493cc engine and supplied with road silencer

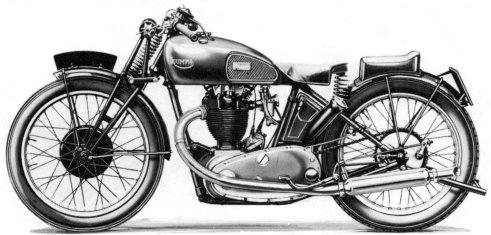

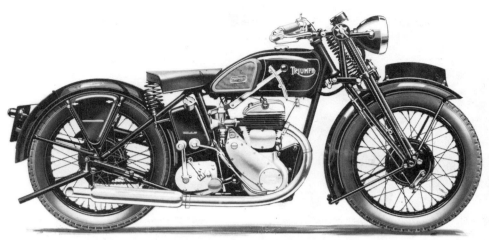

Left
Model 5/1 with 549cc side-valve engine in 1936 to make a sidecar single for the Triumph range

intended for sidecar use in the main so it was solid and rather lacking in ground clearance for solo use. To match the twin there was a special design of sidecar with a body that hid the chassis, and with this attached the firm ran the outfit through the ISDT and then round Brooklands for 500 miles at 60mph, for which they won the Maudes Trophy.

The twin was the largest model in the 1934 range, which was one of the most extensive in the industry. In addition most of it was new, although the B and BS Silent Scouts continued to be offered, as did the inclined-engine 150 with ohv and listed in a sports form as well as standard, these duplicated by a slightly

larger 175cc model using most of the same parts. These were also used to house a 148cc Villiers engine coupled to a three-speed gearbox.

Three models used the medium-weight frame and all had new engines with vertical cylinders designed by Val Page. As was usual with his work they were straightforward in layout, dependable in use but a trifle solid in appearance. They sold well to those who could see their worth, but at that point lacked any touch of glamour. The design could not have been more conventional and was much as the Ariel that Page had designed before. The magneto was gear driven rather than by chain as Triumph had the facilities for this, but for the rest it was a basic single with rear mag-dyno, dry sump lubrication and the expected cycle parts. The engines were 343 and 549cc side valves and 249, 343 and 493cc ohv installed in touring and sports models to provide a good range.

In April 1934 a further 493cc single appeared for

Left
The famous Speed Twin of 1938 with its 499cc twin engine that was to run on for so many years

Right
Triumph Tiger 80 from 1937 with 343cc engine and in competition form with tyres to suit

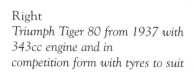

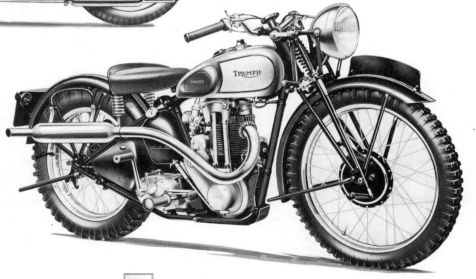

road-racing and was based on the road model but with a lowered frame and modified engine. Three of these machines were run in the TT by the factory, but all retired.

There was curtailment of the range for 1935 with the 148cc ohv and two-stroke models being available to special order only and the 175, B and BS going from the range. This left the same line of singles with vertical cylinders as listed for 1934 plus the 647cc twin and one new model. The addition was a 249cc ohv single with fully enclosed valve gear. It followed the lines of the other models in other respects and had a new light-weight four-speed gearbox and a frame with a single downtube. To advertise the range the entire line-up of

13 models was taken to Brooklands in September 1934 and each given a one-hour run round the track under ACU observation. All managed to complete the run with only three minor stops.

The range announced for 1936 seemed to have been reduced, but in effect they remained with their special fittings available as options. Others in the range had detail changes but none of any significance.

Early in 1936 the company changed hands and a statement was issued that the range would continue in production and that Edward Turner would be the General Manager. He set to work with his special skills to give real style to selected models and the result came in April. What Turner did was simple and effective. He took the 250, 350 and 500 models and fitted them with sports specification engines as a start. The alloy cases were polished and a high-level exhaust system fitted. He then added to the sparkle by fitting petrol tanks finished with chrome-plating and silver sheen panels lined in blue. The final and brilliant sales pitch was the names Turner gave the models, which were the Tiger

Top
Nice 1947 Triumph Tiger 100 on test with sprung hub to enliven the ride

Bottom
Smallest of the twins was the 3T, and this was the 1948 version

70, 80 and 90 in the three sizes.

There were further major changes for 1937 with new frames, forks and gearboxes with improved engines and revised model typing. Aside from the Tigers this used a number to indicate capacity and a letter to show valve position. The range was also reduced to remove an expensive ohv 250 and the 650 twin, which was about to be replaced by the Turner design. Each Tiger model was balanced by a de luxe version. For customers who preferred a side-valve engine the 343cc single was available and for sidecar use a 598cc one. It was a good compact range with plenty of appeal to buyers.

In January 1937 the range was extended by offering all three Tiger models in a competition form. These

Top
The Triumph Grand Prix, as introduced in 1948 with alloy top half and external oil filter in front of the gearbox

Bottom
The sporting TR5 Triumph Trophy with the die-cast head and barrel used from 1951 in the short-wheelbase, rigid frame

were intended for trials use, so the fittings were altered to suit, as were the gearbox ratios and the engine characteristics. The Turner touch worked like magic on the public. Sports riders turned to the Tigers in droves, while the more sedate owners bought the standard models whose lines had been improved with new tanks and some polish where it mattered.

The Tigers were chosen for another attempt on the Maudes Trophy in March. One of each size was selected at random from dealers' stock and subjected to three hours at speed at Donington followed by flying laps at Brooklands. This brought them the trophy once again and 1938 saw the range of singles continue with minor changes.

The very special event for Triumph was the advent of the Turner-designed 499cc Speed Twin. It had a simple ohv engine that was compact enough to fit the existing frame and in it were twin gear-driven camshafts, a built-up crankshaft and the twin-plunger oil pump. A mag-dyno was driven from the inlet cam gear and the iron block was held by six studs. The cycle

parts were as per the single and the finish amaranth red with the tank chromed before its panels were painted. The result was a very smart machine with tremendous appeal and a good turn of speed. It was immediately successful and started a trend to twins that was to affect all the major firms in postwar days.

Logically it had to have a Tiger version, and in 1939 this arrived as the T100 and replaced the T90 in the process. With its arrival came an eight-stud block fixing, chromed front number plate surround and a change to a silver sheen finish for the mudguards with a black stripe in reverse to the earlier Tigers. The machine was set-off by megaphone-style exhausts with rounded ends and tailpipes which could readily be detached. An optional bronze cylinder head was available to take advantage of the special pistons fitted.

The rest of the range stayed much as it was, but the 5T took the eight-stud block. All were fitted with the new style front number-plate surround and a new tank motif, cast and then coloured to match the machine finish. The T90 went, but a further side-valve model appeared with the 493cc engine on the lines of its larger and smaller brothers.

Triumph decided to have another try for the Maudes Trophy in 1939 and for this used a Speed Twin and Tiger 100 selected by the ACU at random from dealers' stocks. They were taken to Coventry for a delivery check and then ridden to Brooklands via John o'Groats and Land's End. The observer car was a

Triumph Dolomite, which was a nice touch. At
Brooklands they were subject to a six-hour run round
the track during which both averaged over 75mph. In
November the company learnt that they had won the
trophy despite competition, but by then everyone had
other problems to worry about.

No competition Tigers were in the 1940 model
list and neither was the ohv of 493cc, whose place had
been taken by the 5T. Also out were some coil ignition
models, but one stayed as an economy job. The other
models remained, so that although supply was limited
there was a choice for civilians. Not seen at all was the
new 350cc twin in its touring 3T guise or its Sports
Tiger 85 one. That lay six long years away and was to
be from another factory at Meriden.

During the early days of the war Triumph built
side-valve singles as the 343cc 3SW and 493cc 5SW,
these based on the prewar models. They also developed
a service model based on the 350cc twin that should
have been in their 1940 range and this was accepted by
the authorities to be the standard military machine.

Sadly for Triumph, the Coventry factory was then
blitzed which resulted in the move to Meriden and for
production to concentrate on the 343cc ohv 3HW single. This too was much as prewar and, although the
firm did build other twin-cylinder prototypes, none
went into production until after the war. What
emerged was essentially a side-valve version of the
Speed Twin and this was to be built using the contemporary cycle parts of the time. One wartime design to
have a postwar effect was a generator unit. This was
again based on the Speed Twin in outline, but had a
light-alloy block and head which were to become most

useful.

Triumph were the first firm to announce their
post-war range, in March 1945, well before the end of
the war. Not only were they first off the mark but,
unlike many others, their machines were not the
wartime ones with a new civilian finish.

There were five models in the range, as
announced, one single and four twins, the latter being
sports and touring versions in two sizes, but only three
models were to go into production. The two 499cc
twins were the Speed Twin and Tiger 100, and were
much as they had been in 1939. There were changes,
and the major one for the cycle parts was the adoption
of telescopic front forks of a neat, slim style. These
were based on a wartime design and had hydraulic
damping, while the front wheel diameter was reduced
to 19in. to match the rear. Otherwise, the post-war version had a separate dynamo clamped to the front of the
crankcase, where it was gear driven from the exhaust
camshaft.

These two models were to be matched by two
smaller ones with 349cc engines, to be known as the
3T and Tiger 85. On the face of it, they would have
been virtually the same models with revised engine
dimensions but, in fact, the engine differences went
deeper as they used a wartime crankshaft design and
there were other changes. In the event, only the 3T

Right:
Triumph Tiger Cub in its 1958 form, before it was given a rear skirt

Far right
First of the new breed of unit-construction twins was the 3TA, seen here in 1960 form, but still with bathtub

Below
A 1959 Triumph Tigress TW2 scooter enjoying cobbles in the rain, but better than queuing for a bus

went into production, in a black finish. The Tiger 85 would have mirrored the larger sports model in black and silver, but it made sense, at that time of acute shortages, for the firm to concentrate on the larger models.

With the Government screaming for production and exports, there were few changes over the next few years, but for 1947 there came the famous sprung hub. This was listed as an option, for it replaced the standard rear wheel and, at first sight, appeared to be a rather large, full-width hub, but it offered limited, if undamped, suspension movement.

Otherwise, the range ran on with its three models, but with the news that Triumph were to produce a real racing motorcycle in limited numbers. This was based on the machine used by Ernie Lyons to win the 1946 Manx Grand Prix and had a Tiger 100 engine with alloy head and block. It was called the Grand Prix. The alloy top half came from the wartime generator unit and, due to this origin, was of a square format to suit the enclosing cowl of the generator. The layout also dictated that both inlet and exhaust ports were parallel to each other, but despite this, twin Amal carburettors were crammed in and fed by a remotely-mounted float chamber.

Otherwise, the engine looked stock, but it had racing camshafts and magneto and a raised compression ratio. The standard gearbox was given close ratios while the cycle parts were essentially standard and included the sprung hub, but the front brake size was increased to 8in. There were alloy mudguards and wheel rims, a bigger oil tank and megaphone exhausts, but a saddle

240

and rear pad remained. On the circuits, the Grand Prix proved fast, but fragile for a year or two but time moved on and by the end of 1950 production ceased and the firm concentrated on what it did best, building good road motorcycles.

Prior to that, it was 1949 before there was any real change to these, and then it was mainly cosmetic with the appearance of the famous nacelle for the front forks. This enclosed the upper part and extended forward to carry the headlight unit, while its upper surface accommodated the instruments and switches. This removed the need for the tank-top instrument panel, so its place was taken by an optional parcel grid.

That same year saw another model join the range as the TR5 Trophy, which was aimed at the sporting off-road and trials rider. The design was based on the machines used by the firm for the ISDT, hence the model name, but both engine and cycle parts were special to some degree. The engine was mainly Speed Twin, but above the crankcase were the alloy head and block used by the Grand Prix, but with much lower-ratio pistons within. There were also softer cams, only a single carburettor and a lovely siamezed exhaust system, which curled round to a waist-level silencer on the left.

This unit went into a special frame with reduced wheelbase, so parts were a tight fit. The four-speed gearbox was used and the sprung hub was an option. The mudguards were short and sporting. A 20in. front wheel and 4in.-section rear tyre were fitted, along with quickly-detachable lights, so there was no nacelle. A saddle and pillion pad looked after the seating, and the finish was in chrome, silver and black to produce a very smart, dual-purpose machine.

The range had the tank styling revised for 1950 to four horizontal bars, and an additional, larger model appeared as the 649cc 6T Thunderbird. This took the Turner twin on to its next logical step, and the general

details were as for the 5T with the same gearbox, frame, forks and cycle parts.

Changes for 1951 were limited to the sports models for which there was a new die-cast head and barrel in light alloy with close-pitched fins. The T100 also had a dualseat fitted as standard, and all models had the parcel grid fitted as standard. The Grand Prix was not continued for 1951, but in its place was an official racing kit for the T100 which included high-ratio pistons and better camshafts, along with twin carburettors, all the associated pipes and controls, megaphones and a big oil tank.

The 3T was quietly dropped at the end of the year, and the other four models and the race kit continued for 1952, with an SU carburettor for the 6T and little other alteration. It was much the same for the twins in 1953, although the 5T was fitted with an alternator and the race kit was replaced by a complete model in the form of the T100c. This was effectively the same thing, but was supplied with silencers and full electrics, as well as the tuned internals.

There was a second new model for 1953 and it was to lead to many versions, including a whole range for BSA. The newcomer was the 149cc Terrier, which was aimed at the lightweight market, then the province of the Bantam, Enfield and a hoard of machines using the small Villiers engines. The Terrier had an ohv unit-construction engine with four-speed gearbox, inclined iron cylinder and an alloy head. The crankcase contained the gearbox, an alternator went on the left-hand end of the crankshaft in the primary chaincase, and the points for the coil ignition were in a housing behind the barrel. Their cam was skew-gear driven from the crankshaft, and the same shaft drove the twin-plunger pump for the dry sump oil system. An Amal supplied the mixture, and the exhaust system ran low down on the right. This engine unit went into a loop frame with

plunger rear and telescopic front suspension, neither of which had any damping. Construction was simple, but the front end looks mirrored those of the twins with a nacelle.

For 1954 the Terrier was joined by the larger 199cc Cub, which had an upswept exhaust system and dualseat as standard and a shell blue finish for the tank and mudguards in place of the overall Amaranth red of the Terrier. Other changes that year were to the 6T. which switched to alternator electrics, and to the T100 which was joined by a larger 649cc version, listed as the Tiger 110. Both went into a pivoted-fork frame with dualseat and an 8in. front brake to arrest progress. The other models stayed as they were but the T100c was dropped. In 1955 all the twins went into the pivoted-fork frame.

For 1956 the T110 was fitted with an alloy cylinder head and joined by the TR6, which used the same 649cc engine in the TR5 cycle parts. The singles also had changes, the most noticeable being to the Cub, which went to 16in. wheels. It continued alone for 1957, for the Terrier was dropped, but in a pivoted-fork frame with damped front forks and was joined by the T20C competition model, which used the same frame, but had an upswept exhaust and came with trials tyres and a crankcase shield, although it retained the lights and headlamp nacelle. There was also a new tank badge for the Cubs and twins. The 5T, 6T and TR5 had a full-width front hub, and the TR6 an 8in. front brake.

The range was joined by one new model, which was the first of the unit-construction twins listed as the model 21 or 3TA. The new machine had a twin-cylinder, 349cc engine, much as its predecessors, with twin gear-driven camshafts, plain big-ends and separate rocker boxes. Ignition was by coil, with the points and distributor in a housing behind the iron block and driven by skew gears from the inlet camshaft, which also drove

the oil pump. The crankcase extended rearwards to carry the four-speed gearbox, while an Amal supplied the mixture and an alternator went on the left-hand end of the crankshaft. This drove the clutch with a duplex chain within a polished alloy case, and much of the transmission was stock conventional Triumph.

The engine unit went into a simple loop frame with pivoted-fork rear and telescopic front suspension. The fixtures and fittings followed Triumph practice in the main, with a nacelle for the headlamp, but the real feature of the model was its rear enclosure. This was extensive and, thanks to its shape, quickly became known as the 'bathtub', a name it was to keep through the years. With this new model, the firm began to plan a new range, so there were few changes for the pre-unit models in 1958.

At the end of 1958 the 5T and TR5 were dropped, the former being replaced by a bored-out version of the 3TA, finished in the traditional Amaranth red, and it kept the Speed Twin name. Of the older models, the T100, T110, 6T and TR6 ran on much as before, but were joined by one of the most exciting Triumphs of all time, the T120 Bonneville. This was, in essence, a twin-carburettor T110 with the optional splayed-port head fitted as standard and was the final development of the original twin for Edward Turner. He maintained that 650cc and 6500rpm were as much as one could expect from the layout without excessive vibration problems. The Bonneville soon became a legend.

However, the Bonneville and the Speed Twin were not the only new models for 1959, as there were more, plus changes to the Cubs. Many of the latter were details only, but for the road model, there was some partial enclosure with rear skirts, which followed the lines of the unit twins, but not to the same extent. The final new models were scooters and replicas of those in the Sunbeam range, except for colour and badges. They were called Tigress with the Triumph badge, and all were in a shell blue colour.

For the new decade, Triumph kept nearly all their models from the previous year, but the T100 and T20C were both replaced. The first became the T100A and had a higher-powered version of the unit-construction engine with energy-transfer ignition. It used the same set of cycle parts including the bathtub, but in a black and ivory finish. The T20S also had energy-transfer ignition, as well as direct lighting, no battery and a small, off-road-style headlamp. The front forks were heavy-duty and based on those of the 3TA with gaiters, while there were other detail improvements.

The scooters continued as they were, as did the touring unit twins, while all the 649cc models had a new duplex frame and revised forks. The 6T and T110 were both fitted with the bathtub rear enclosure and its associated deep front mudguard, while the T120 lost its nacelle in favour of a separate headlamp shell. The T110, T120 and TR6 all retained their magnetos, but went over to an alternator to charge the battery.

Thus, Triumph entered the new decade with a strong range, which became fully unit-construction in 1963. Later came the trauma of the Meriden sit-in, the co-operative and the difficult times of the 1980s.

TURNER

This machine was one of the eccentricities of the motorcycle world and made its brief appearance in Brussels in April 1946. Its full name was the Turner Byvan, but there seems to be no record as to whether or not Turner was the builder, nor are there any details of his background.

The machine was an oddity because it had front-wheel-drive using a 125cc Royal Enfield Flying Flea engine unit mounted on the top of the pressed-steel forks. The whole of the remainder of the machine, from headstock to rear number plate, was fully enclosed to form a large parcel holder with a saddle on the top for the rider and a lid for access. The finish was in bright red and the machine was run on the day it was shown, performing well enough on steepish Belgium slopes and cobbles.

It was far too radical, even for Europe, which was to have its share of show oddities over the years, so no more was heard of it.

Far left
Flagship of the Triumph line was the T120 Bonneville, which lost the nacelle for 1960 when it gained a new frame and an alternator

Left
The strange front-wheel-drive Turner Byvan, of 1946, being tried out in a Brussels street

VELOCETTE

A family of motorcyclists built the Velocette and this showed through in the design and quality of manufacture. They were the Goodmans and three generations were to control the Hall Green firm over the years. Correct engineering solutions and nice machines resulted from this to enhance their reputation as builders of fine motorcycles.

By 1930 they had made their name in the TT with three Junior wins using their ohc engine. They had also reached the end of development for their first two-stroke engine and so had a new one to offer. This was the 249cc GTP and it moved away from the over-hung crankshaft of its predecessors to the more normal type, but it included an oil pump for lubrication and had coil ignition. The rest of the machine was conventional, although the three-speed gearbox did have the outboard final drive sprocket and the usual slim Velocette clutch.

The other machines all had the 348cc ohc engine with its slim, light lines and bevel-and-shaft drive on the right. The chain-driven magneto went to the rear, lubrication was dry sump and the dynamo, when fitted, went in front of the crankcase and was driven by a flat belt. There were three models, the KSS for sporting road work, the KTT for road racing and based on the 1928 works machines, and the KTP which had coil ignition and a twin-port head which did nothing for the performance.

Top
The well-known ohc Velocette KTS from 1932

Bottom
Drive side of 1934 KTS shows outboard gearbox sprocket

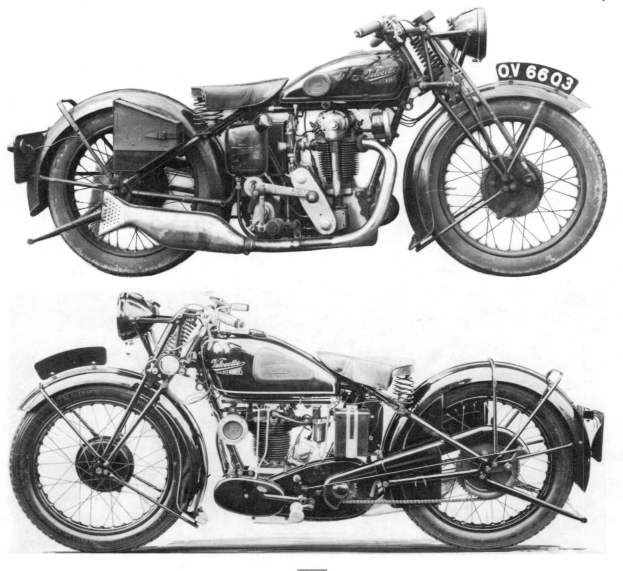

Left
*Velocette KTT Mk IV of
1934 on show and powered
by the famous 348cc ohc
engine*

Bottom
*The 248cc ohv model MOV
Velocette in 1934*

The four models ran on for 1931, the KTT in Mk II form. This practice of allocating mark numbers was introduced for stores identification purposes, but in time went into general rider use. For 1932 the KTP was replaced by the much nicer KTS, which was simply a KSS with touring mudguards and tyres, while the KTT moved on to Mk III. The GTP had a link fitted between the throttle and the oil pump to give the latter a variable output depending on the opening of the former. Novel at the time.

1933 brought four-speed gearboxes to the KSS and KTS models, while the KTT became the Mk IV with a new cylinder head and hairpin valve springs. The GTP continued as it was, but this did leave a big gap between the small two-stroke and the sports camshaft models. To fill this Velocette had experimented with a side-valve 350 in 1931 but this lacked power. They then came up with another classic, the 248cc MOV. This had ohv, a high gear-driven camshaft, enclosed valves and nearly square dimensions. It was obviously going to be able to rev and have a lively per-

formance and no one was disappointed, for early road models were good for 60mph and later tuned racers for 100mph. The basically simple engine with rear magneto, front dynamo and dry sump lubrication went into a cradle frame with a four-speed, handchange gearbox. None of the cycle parts came from the other models, but the result looked every inch a Velocette.

The MOV was announced in June 1933 and it and the other models made up the initial range for 1934. These models were then joined by a second ohv machine, the 349cc MAC, which came from extending the stroke of the MOV. In other respects it was a copy of the smaller model and was to have an even longer history. In April 1934 the GTP was given a face-lift with a four-speed, footchange gearbox and an oil bath primary chaincase.

The six models were all listed for 1935 without any real change, but in April a new version of the KTT was announced as the Mk V and while it followed the same lines as before it was extensively altered with a much-revised engine and new cradle frame. The equip-

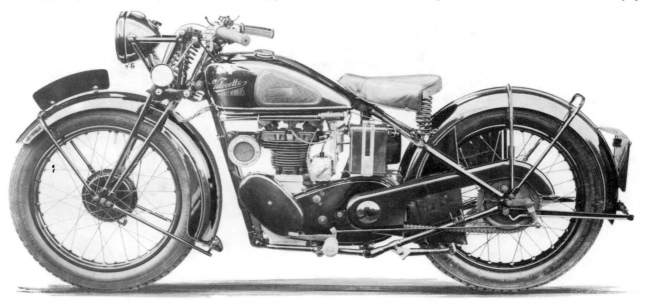

Top
Engine of a 1934 Velocette 249cc model GTP with throttle-controlled oil pump. Later in the year it was fitted with a four-speed footchange gearbox

Bottom
1939 Mk VIII KTT Velocette with rear suspension by air units with hydraulic damping

ment was pure racing with a suitable carburettor and magneto, open exhaust and, as before, a left-side filler for the oil tank to suit the TT pits. To complete a good year for Velocette enthusiasts a 495cc edition of the high-camshaft ohv design was launched in June 1935 and the new model was typed the MSS. The engine design was on the same lines as the others, but the frame was based on the new KTT one, and it was to run on in various forms for a long time.

There was little change to the ohv machines or the two-stroke for 1936, but the KSS and KTS were redesigned. The differences between them remained simply tyres and mudguards, but the engines now had an alloy, one-piece head and cam box casting with fully-enclosed valve gear. The gearbox was the usual four-speed Velocette and a full cradle frame was employed, while both machines were fully equipped.

The main change to the ohv engines for 1937 was the adoption of automatic ignition advance using a weight system in the magneto driving gear, very forward for a time when enthusiasts generally preferred to have a lever to play with. Otherwise it was detail changes to the range which was without the KTT pending major alterations.

The range continued on into 1938 and in May the KTT returned to the list as the Mk VII. The capacity was, as always, 348cc, but it now had an alloy head and barrel, both massively finned, and the head casting included the rocker box and large wells for the hairpin valve springs. The engine and four-speed gearbox went

Top
The Velocette MAC for 1951 when it gained mar-
que forks and changed to an alloy top half

Bottom
The MSS Velocette in 1954 with adjustable rear
suspension and odd dualseat

into a full cradle frame with new girder forks while the equipment continued to be pure racing although a prop stand was included.

There were no changes to the road models for 1939, but the KTT became the Mk VIII with pivoted-fork rear suspension. This was unusual in that it was controlled by units using air as the suspension medium and oil for damping. There were no springs at all, but the air was pumped up to a level based on the rider's weight and the circuit he was competing on.

The road range was listed for 1940, but before production could really get under way war broke out and the firm was switched to general service contracts.

These then were the production Velocettes, but

there were others built by the works as experiments, one-offs and for their own racing. With the easy inter-change of many parts or assemblies this was often no trouble to arrange and the practice spread to private owners as well. One such exercise was the KDT built for speedway use with a 407cc KTT engine in suitable frame and forks but few were made.

In 1930 there was the long-stroke KTT and the next year brought the supercharged KTT known as Whiffing Clara. 1931 also brought the 350 side-valve, whose poor power and high noise level led to the

MOV. Two years later the works raced KTT models with enclosed rockers which became known as the Dog Kennel engines due to the head casting shape. 1936 brought the Mk VI KTT, of which only eight were built, using what was to become the frame for the Mk VII.

The works had three twin-ohc machines for the 1937 TT, but the vertical shaft coupling on one failed early on and the design was put away for over a decade. There were also 500cc KTT machines for the works and one of these engines was enlarged to 596cc for use in the 1937 ISDT in a sidecar outfit and proved very good in this role.

During this period Velocette were working on a road MSS with pivoted-fork rear suspension. This machine was made more novel by the use of a stressed-skin construction for the rear frame section and slots which allowed the spring unit angle to be varied to alter their effect. This method of construction and suspension system went onto the model O twin-cylinder prototype built in 1939. Its 587cc engine differed greatly from other firms' twins, for the two crankshafts lay along the frame and were geared to contra-rotate. It had ohv, twin carburettors and low-level exhausts. The right crankshaft drove the transmission and the left the dynamo. Final drive was by shaft.

The road model was matched by a racing one known as the Roarer and built on the same lines using KTT-style heads. The right crankshaft drove a super-charger and the left the transmission to the shaft final drive. It ran in practice in the 1939 TT, but was never raced.

Velocette were mainly engaged on high-precision work during the war but did build some motorcycles for the services. All were based on the MAC with few changes other than to finish or to improve details for their use.

After the war, Velocette continued with their tradition of black and gold singles of high performance with ohv or ohc engines, and the range was little differ-

Far right, top
The 192cc LE Velocette on test early in 1955 when its water cooling was hardly needed

Far right, bottom
Velocette Venom, as tested in 1958, although the number plate appeared on another Venom test in 1956 - naughty

Above
Sporting S501 Steib sidecar hitched to a 1958 Venom during a road test

Below
The 1959 Velocette Valiant Veeline with air-cooled, flat-twin engine based on the LE unit

ent from 1939. Missing were the KTS and, at first, the racing KTT, while the GTP only appeared briefly as an export batch of machines. Present and correct were the three sizes of M-range, ohv models and the KSS. For 1947, the four models ran on, while the Mk VIII KTT reappeared, very much in its 1939 form.

The range continued for 1948 when the forks became Dowty Oleomatic telescopics, which used the same principles as the rear legs on the KTT which alone kept to the girders. At the end of the year, Velocette dropped the expensive KSS with its assembly problems, along with the MOV and MSS. The MAC continued as the most popular of the ohv singles, along with a limited number of KTT racers, but the sensation of the range for 1949 was the totally new LE.

This really broke with the firm's tradition, for it had a 149cc, side-valve, horizontally-opposed, twin-cylinder engine with water cooling among its many radical features. It also had a handchange three-speed gearbox, shaft drive, hand-lever starting, a monocoque frame and good weather protection. Telescopic front and pivoted-fork rear suspension were used, the rear having the unit tops in slots for load adjustment. It was

a very quiet-running machine.

The LE was aimed at the mass market and incorporated a host of ideas and ideals which, it was said, would ensure success in this fickle area of sales. Other firms had been along this path in the past and found that there were many obstacles. It was not until the scooter came along that there was much of a breakthrough, and it took the Honda Cub scooterette to reach a true world-wide market.

The Velocette came close, but was rather expensive, partly because the firm insisted on doing the job properly, as was their way. This led to looks without style, handling that the mass market would never appreciate, and too much of the mechanics on view. The social scene was no help either, for it was to be well into the 1950s before the scooter became accepted, and the LE was always too much of a motorcycle to fit the image. It really was an extraordinary achievement by the Goodman family, with their limited resources, and if they had had a BSA or Triumph purse they might have succeeded with it.

There were no changes for 1950, which was the last year for the KTT, so there were only the LE and

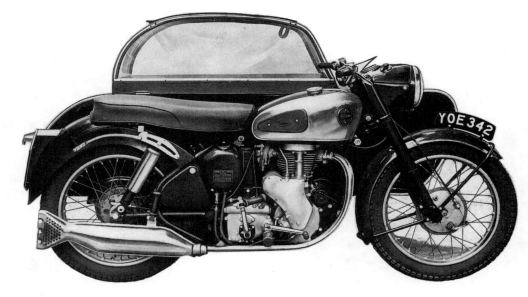

Right
The 1960 Velocette scrambler model was offered in both engine sizes, this one being the larger

MAC for 1951. Both had changes, the first becoming the Mk II with its capacity raised to 192cc, while the MAC went over to a front fork to a conventional design. In June 1951 the MAC was further modified with a new alloy cylinder and head to give full valve gear enclosure, both models ran on for 1952, but for 1953 the rigid MAC was joined by one fitted in a spring frame using the slotted adjustment feature as on the LE.

For 1954 the two MAC models and the LE were joined by a new version of the old MSS model. The newcomer was on the lines of the sprung MAC with alloy engine and a much sharper performer than in the past. With this revised MSS came the Scrambler, which used a tuned MSS engine with a TT carburettor and open exhaust pipe in cycle parts to suit.

There were more new models for 1956, but the LE carried on as it was for most of the year before its wheels were changed to 18in. rims and full-width hubs, while the carburettor became an Amal Monobloc. The rigid MAC was dropped, and the sprung one and the MSS ran on as they were, as did the Scrambler. An Endurance model appeared, which was based on the Scrambler, but fitted with lights and street legal.

However, the best news for Velocette single enthusiasts was the appearance of the 349cc Viper and 499cc Venom models. These were high-performance sports models based on the M-series with bigger front brake, full-width hubs, and a deep headlamp shell that carried the instruments in its top surface. Both sports models used the normal pivoted-fork frame and front forks. All the singles changed to a Monobloc carburettor and single-level dualseat, while the dynamo was driven by a V-belt in place of the older flat one. Early in 1956, a second Scrambler appeared with the Viper engine in the same cycle parts as the 500, and later in the year, the deep headlamp shell went on to the MAC and MSS.

The range continued for 1957 and was joined by

the 192cc Valiant. This had an engine based on the LE, but with air-cooling, overhead valves and twin carburettors. It was coupled to a four-speed gearbox with foot-change, and the whole unit was mounted in a duplex tubular loop frame. The forks and wheels came from the LE, and the engine unit was enclosed by a bonnet, which left the top halves out in the breeze. There was a dualseat for the rider and a good range of fitments, but the machine came to the market at a high price for a 200 and without the performance of a 250. Many felt that a revamp of the MOV would have been much better and more suited to the impending capacity restriction for learners.

The whole range stayed much as it was for 1958, with one addition. This was a Mk III version of the LE, which had the four-speed gearbox from the Valiant with foot-change and kickstart, so the Mk II was dropped at the end of the year.

For 1959 the Valiant was joined by the Veeline, which had a neat dolphin fairing with a good-sized screen as standard. The LE continued in Mk III form only, and the four single-cylinder road models were fitted with an enclosure around their lower engine half and gearbox. This was made in fibreglass and cleaned up the lines of the machine, while allowing the firm to omit the polishing of timing and gearbox covers.

For the new decade, there were two more models, listed as the Viper and Venom Clubman. Both came without the lower enclosure, but with a selection of extras from the options list to suit the needs of the sporting rider. The rest of the range ran on as it was and would do so for another decade, with even more variations on both the flat-twin and sporting singles.

The nadir was shared by the Viceroy and Vogue, but the zenith was the fabulous Thruxton.

VELOSOLEX

This was a French design of power-cycle, which sold in enormous numbers in its own country and, for a while, was built under licence in Britain. It always came as a complete machine, although the design was effectively a 45cc two-stroke clip-on, which drove the front tyre by roller.

It appeared in France in 1946 and was an immediate success. Two years later, a few reached Britain, and gradually British components were phased in, production being carried out by Solex in North London. This was well underway by 1949, and there were detail changes in 1951 and 1956. Otherwise, the model continued to be offered until 1957, when British produc-

tion ceased.

It never enjoyed the sheer volume of demand as in its home country, where it continued for many a year to carry people from all walks of life around the French countryside and towns.

VILLIERS

The Villiers engine was part of the British motorcycle scene from before World War I and served many marques at home and abroad from then to the late 1960s.

The firm produced an enormous range of engines for industrial and other uses, as well as the motorcycle ones. All were simple two-strokes and most singles although there were some twins. Prewar, they were usually just an engine unit, with flywheel-magneto ignition from around 1921, made in various capacities and with options of auto-lube, water-cooling or sports specification in many cases. Engines were normally given a mark number for type and a letter for capacity and comprised vertically-split crankcase, crankshaft with piston, and cylinder and head which were often made as one item.

Prewar, the smallest was the 98cc Midget built for 1931-40 and joined in 1934 by the Junior which was one of the few that differed in that it had the cylinder laid horizontal and the crankcase extended to included a clutch and countershaft to suit its intended autocycle use. It was built up to 1939 and then replaced by the similar Junior De Luxe or JDL which continued to 1948.

The next prewar size was one of the few true unit construction engines, being the 122cc 8D and 9D which were built complete with three-speed gearbox and continued on to 1948. The only other was the 197cc 3E of 1939 which had a postwar counterpart in the form of the 5E up to 1948 but was seldom used. Other prewar engines were the 147cc 8C, various

172cc's, the 196cc 1E and 2E, the 247cc 10A and 16A and the 343cc 9BA and 10B. There were also long-stroke versions of most of these which were the 148cc 12C and 15C, the 249cc 14A, 17A and 18A, and the 346cc 14B and 17B.

Postwar, the JDL, 9D and 5E were all replaced for 1949 by new designs which were to run on from then on. Smallest was the 99cc 2F with single speed and

Top
The two 99cc F-series engines, with one or two speeds, used for light motorcycles and autocycles

Below
The 1950 Villiers 10D of 122cc, which was built along with the very similar 197cc 6E; plug position indicates which is which

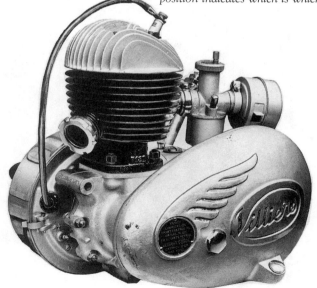

Top
A 1957 DKR Dove with 147cc Villiers 30C engine, which was based on the D-series

Bottom
The final development of the E-series was the 9E, used here by a 1956 Panther 10/4

Far right, top
Another Panther, but with a 324cc 3T Villiers twin engine, rather than the more usual 249cc 2T

Far right, bottom
1933 Vincent-HRD with 499cc Rudge engine

similar 1F with two speeds. Both had an inclined cylinder and the 1F was replaced by the better styled 4F in 1953, it and the 2F running on to 1958. In 1956 the 4F was joined by the 6F which had footchange to take the engine size into the 1960s.

The 122 and 197cc engines for 1949 were the first to use the style of unit construction while keeping the main assemblies separate. At first they did have a round cover for the flywheel-magneto and were built as the smaller 10D, 11D, 12D and 13D to 1954. They were then replaced by the 147cc 29C and 30C plus the

148cc 31C, the last having a streamlined single cover for the magneto and gearbox end to smooth that side of the engine.

The 197cc engine became the 6E in 1949 and later the 7E and 8E before the 9E arrived with the streamlined cover. It was followed by the 10E and 11E but the 9E was the one used by most firms. Slightly smaller were the 172cc 2L and 3L which came in 1957 and larger was the 224cc 1H of 1954, the first to have a streamlined style. It later became the 246cc 2H but this was soon replaced by the similar size A-series which ran from 31A to 37A over the years. Late in the decade there came a 50cc 3K moped engine and this was of true unit construction.

There were also twins in the same style and form of construction, the first the 249cc 2T of 1956 and this was joined by the 324cc 3T the following year. Both were available with the usual range of options which included electric start, fan-cooling and reverse-running to suit scooter and bubblecar use.

In addition to the stock Villiers engines there were square-barrel conversions from a number of other firms which were available for both 197 and 246cc engines. These enlarged the smaller engine and gave an improved performance, the new parts normally cast in alloy and of square format, hence the name.

VINCENT-HRD

Philip Vincent was a determined man who had some firm ideas on how a motorcycle should perform and how it should be built. He read Mechanical Science at

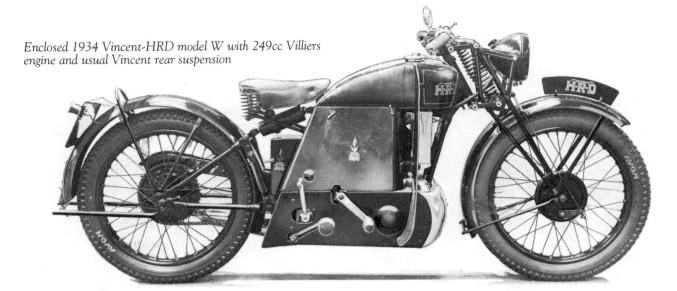

Enclosed 1934 Vincent-HRD model W with 249cc Villiers engine and usual Vincent rear suspension

Above
1935 Vincent-HRD 499cc single with Vincent engine

Far right, top
1935 Vincent-HRD with 490cc JAP engine list-ed as the model J

Far right, bottom
Vincent-HRD Rapide in 1939 with too much power from its 998cc for the clutch

Cambridge and had a poor opinion of many of the features of contemporary machines, so in the 1920s built his first motorcycle. Like all the others it had rear suspension with a triangulated pivoted fork and the springs mounted beneath the saddle to work against the upper frame. The engine was a Swiss MAG, the gearbox Moss, forks Webb and hubs Enfield.

In 1927, at the age of 19, he decided to go into the business of making motorcycles and after taking advice from Arthur Bourne, editor of The Motor Cycle, bought the established HRD name from the OK Supreme company. It might have only been three years old, but the name of Howard R. Davies was very well known for he had tied for second in the 1914 Senior TT, been reported killed in action in 1917 and had won the 1921 Senior with his 350 AJS. Having formed his firm he then was second in the Junior and won the Senior in 1925.

With this background the marque was in demand but was under-financed and was bought out before the name went on to Vincent. Davies was rather surprised

at the motorcycle that resulted, for the very fine rigid frame had gone, so the resulting machine was totally changed other than in the use of a proprietary engine.

By 1930 Vincent-HRD were known as makers of high-class, hand-built machines, produced in very small numbers and featuring rear suspension at a time when there was great prejudice against this. Thus, Vincent sales were minimal and all the 1930 models fitted a JAP engine with side valves for the tourers and overhead for the sports and a couple of competition machines

During 1931 they began to suggest Rudge engines as an option after some problems with the JAP ones. However, the odd appearance of the machines plus the sprung frame was a considerable handicap to sales, so it was decided to design a new diamond frame which would have a conventional appearance while retaining the rear suspension. It was late in 1931 that Phil Irving joined the firm and was immediately involved with the new frame. His practical knowledge was to complement the innovations that came from Vincent to produce good, working motorcycles. The new frame really set the format for the prewar Vincent and fulfilled the tasks it was set, the engine part of the structure, and either a 490cc JAP or a 499cc Rudge in standard or sports form.

For 1933 a lightweight model was added, powered by either a 247cc Villiers engine or a 245cc side-valve JAP, but it never actually went into production. The one prototype had the two-stroke power unit and was interesting as it was partially enclosed with panels round the crankcase and transmission. It retained the diamond sprung frame, as did the other models, which were all of 500cc with ohv.

The two-stroke was extensively modified for 1934 to become the model W with a water-cooled 249cc Villiers engine which was completely hidden by the extended enclosure. In addition to the W there was the JW, which used a 600cc side-valve, water-cooled JAP engine and was built as a combination. It had the same form of enclosure but only the show model was ever made. The three 500s had their stopping improved with Super-power Duo-brakes with two drums on each hub, and the rear assembly carried two sprockets for easy gearing changes.

Phil Vincent was badly let down by JAP engines in the 1934 TT and with Rudge units becoming hard to

get he decided the only answer was to make his own.
He had four months to do it in if he was to exhibit at
the next show. He succeeded with the usual show rush
and the design set the style for all his future engines.
The valve gear was what set the Vincent apart from
others and began with a camshaft placed very high up
with short push rods splayed out to run parallel to the
valve line. This allowed the rockers to run straight
across the head to the valves. The next unusual feature
was that each valve had two guides and the rocker
located on it between them. The hairpin valve springs
went above the rocker, and thus well away from the
heat, and were fully exposed. Two external pipes supplied oil to the rocker chambers and were the subject of
Press criticism, but, as Vincent pointed out, others just
relied on grease guns.

The timing gear was simple with a large idler
meshing with gears on the crankshaft, camshaft and
magneto, which went behind the cylinder. Both head
and barrel were iron and a dry sump lubrication system
was used. The crankcase was tall and very well ribbed
to provide a compact and rigid engine. It was built in
three stages of tune as the standard Meteor, sports
Comet and racing TT model and all had the sprung
frame and twin brakes on each wheel. Also in the list
was the J with a 490cc ohv JAP engine and the W
water-cooled two-stroke which was to special order.

For 1936 all models had the Vincent engine and
there were five models in all, three as before plus the
Comet Special and the TT road model. Four of the singles went forward for 1937 as Meteor, Comet, Comet
Special and racing TT Replica with little change.

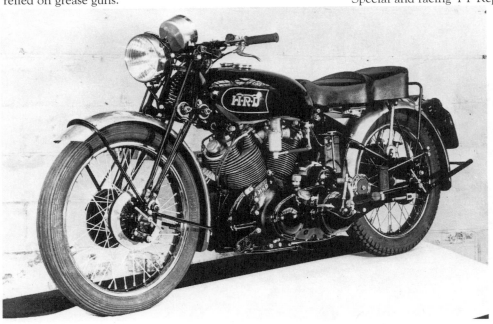

Right, top
*The Vincent-HRD was
also built as a 500 single,
and this is a 1949 Series
C Comet with the
Girdraulic forks*

Right
*Series C Black Shadow
with 120+mph potential
on pool petrol*

Bottom
*A modified 1950 Black
Shadow with many stain-
less-steel parts and other
detail improvements*

The news that made the headlines was the appearance of the Rapide with its V-twin 998cc engine and tremendous performance. This came from the combination of two Meteor cylinders and heads on a common crankcase which slotted into a lengthened version of the existing frame. It was little heavier than a 500 and it all tucked in well in a remarkably compact form. The result was a very fast machine, too fast, it was soon found, for the transmission, which could easily wilt under all that torque.

The Comet Special was dropped for 1938, but the other three models of 499cc continued along with the Rapide. For 1939 only three models were listed, the Meteor. Comet and Rapide, and while the first was the touring machine, to enthusiasts they were fast, faster and fastest; apart from the clutch slip, which had been commented on in road tests. The works had a racing 1000 by this time and its power proved an embarrassment with petrol starvation, wheelspin and lifting front wheels all making life hard for the rider.

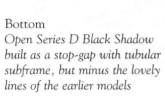

Right
The Vincent Firefly taken over from Millers and never discussed by the Owners' Club

Bottom
Open Series D Black Shadow built as a stop-gap with tubular subframe, but minus the lovely lines of the earlier models

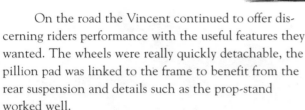

On the road the Vincent continued to offer discerning riders performance with the useful features they wanted. The wheels were really quickly detachable, the pillion pad was linked to the frame to benefit from the rear suspension and details such as the prop-stand worked well.

Production of motorcycles ceased late in 1939 and the company turned to war work, some special designs for the services and thoughts of a high-speed tourer for the years to come. During the war years, Phil Vincent worked with his chief engineer, Phil Irving, to design a better and lighter Rapide, which would do the same job as the prewar edition, but in an improved manner. The aim was to learn from the past and produce a very high-speed tourer with a host of rider features. They came pretty close to succeeding, too.

The pre-war model looked a mess, with pipes, plates, carbs, links and levers in a glorious disarray with no harmony at all. Post-war, all this was to change, with a shorter wheelbase, unit construction of engine and gearbox, the extensive use of light alloys, and a very clean appearance. All this and a host of detail improvements were promised in a March 1945 announcement, for both Vincent and Irving had been

hard at work on the new design, and in December the full details of the postwar Rapide were released.

The impact was tremendous, for the machine was as compact as a 500 single and incorporated many new features. The major part was the engine, which had the gearbox built in unit with it to provide a single, rigid structure. It was so rigid, in fact, that there was little frame at all, the rear fork being the major part, and even this was attached to the rear of the engine structure.

The rest of the frame comprised a beam over the engine, which had the headstock at its front end and also doubled as the oil tank. To its rear were fixed the rear spring and damper, which controlled the rear fork structure, while the beam itself was bolted to both cylinder heads. At the front were Brampton girders, as the two Phils considered telescopic forks to be inadequate for solo riding and totally unsuitable for sidecar work.

The 998cc engine was the heart of the machine and was a 50-degree V-twin with overhead valves and alloy heads and barrels. These were fitted to a massive crankcase casting, within which turned a large, built-up crankshaft with uncaged-roller big-ends. The timing

Right
*The Series D Vincent Black Prince
with Shadow engine under the full
enclosure*

side on the right used a train of gears which also drove the magneto and the valve gear was much as prewar but enclosed and with coil valve springs. Twin Amal carburettors were fitted, each with its own float chamber, and there were twin exhaust pipes which swept down to a single tubular silencer.

The primary transmission was by triplex chain which also drove the Miller dynamo, which sat above the gearbox section of the crankcase. The clutch was rather special to cope with the tremendous engine torque, which had proved too much for the Burman unit used pre-war. The new design was often thought to be operated by centrifugal force, but was, in fact, two clutches in one, with most of the power being transmitted via a drum and shoes, not unlike a brake. This clutch was engaged by a simple plate type and, thanks to its servo action, it was able to transmit all the power while remaining very light in action.

The gearbox was of a very compact, four-speed, cross-over design, so the rear chain went on the right. The kickstarter was also on the right, along with the gear pedal, and had a long, curved lever, which ran under the footrest to give the rider the best chance of a long swinging kick when starting.

The complete engine and gearbox unit, with its minimal frame, rode on spoked wheels, each with two single-leading-shoe brakes. The rear hub continued to have a sprocket on each side, and thanks to some good detail design, the wheel could be quickly taken out and turned round to provide an easy change to sidecar gearing.

Sporting alloy mudguards were used and there was a dualseat, rather than a saddle and pillion pad. The seat was supported at the rear by struts from the rear fork structure, so it rose and fell a little as the suspension worked. There was a rear stand, and at the front of the crankcase a prop-stand on each side. By

means of a minor adjustment, these could be used as one to become a front stand. The stands made it very easy to work on the machine, and it was a simple task to remove either the whole of the front end, plus the frame top beam, or the rear fork complete with wheel. In both cases, this left the engine unit ready and accessible for working on. This philosophy of making it easy for the owner to maintain the machine was continued throughout its design, while long-term appearance was enhanced by the use of stainless steel for many parts.

The result of all this work was a motorcycle with a shattering performance, despite the low-octane pool petrol the engine had to suffer in its early days. The weight came out at around 450lb, and the 45bhp produced by the relaxed and stress-free V-twin was sufficient to propel it quite fast enough for the road conditions of the times, when few were straight and most were excessively bumpy.

Inevitably, there were problems in getting the new design into production, and it was May 1946 before the very first machine was fired up and taken out on to the Great North Road by Phil Vincent, minus hat, gloves or goggles. Phil Irving was next and then Arthur Bourne of The Motor Cycle, with cap and goggles, followed by Graham Walker of Motor Cycling. The two editors were very impressed, while the factory personnel must have been thankful it had all worked out so well.

Thus was the post-war Vincent-HRD Rapide born, and it was soon, correctly, advertised as 'the world's fastest standard motorcycle - this is a fact, not a slogan'. It was September before the first production machine was built, and it went to Argentina. More followed, many for export, while the firm struggled with the shortages of materials and parts then so common.

Because the pre-war twin had been the model A, the post-war version became the Series B. It proved to

be a real grand tourer, with the maximum speed in top simply 'not obtained' during one 1947 road test. Another managed 112mph, and this with a low compression ratio, pool petrol, a riding coat and an engine with a docile tick-over for town use.

Early in 1948 the Rapide was joined by a faster version! This was the Black Shadow, which was tuned to produce a top speed beyond the 120mph mark with little loss of docility or easy town riding. To match the name, the engine was finished in black, and the result looked wonderful. In addition to the engine improvements, the brakes were given ribbed drums and, best of all, a large 5in. speedometer, reading up to 150mph, appeared and sat boldly at the top of the forks.

Never ones to rest on their laurels, the two Phils, Vincent and Irving, had more new offerings for 1949 to expand the range and provide even better motorcycles for the discerning rider. The two Series B models continued, but were joined by the Series C, which had totally new front forks, called Girdraulics. The series C Rapide and Black Shadow were listed in the same form as the Series B, except for the suspension, and were joined by two singles and a racing model called the Black Lightning.

The singles were the Series B Meteor and Series C Comet, which had the same suspension variation and a good deal in common with the V-twins. They reversed the events of pre-war days, when Phil Irving created the Rapide by mounting two single top halves on a common crankcase. For 1949 he simply replaced the rear cylinder with a cast alloy frame member and added some gearbox plates so that he could use a separate four-speed Burman gearbox. The crankcase was modified to suit the needs of the single and, thus, the general line remained. On the cycle side, the singles

followed the twins, the Meteor differing from the others in having a saddle and no pillion rests.

The Black Lightning was built for road racing, so its engine had TT carburettors, straight-through exhaust pipes, a rev-counter, but no kickstart, lighting equipment or stands. Both wheels had alloy rims and alloy brake backplates, there were short alloy mudguards and a racing seat, which used the standard mountings.

The new forks used for the Series C models were still of the girder type, and the design was based on a pair of forged alloy blades linked to the head stock by one-piece links which could not twist relative to one another. The bottom link pivot had a further ingenious arrangement, which enabled the fork trail to be adjusted to suit solo or sidecar riding and the change also altered the rate of the long, slim spring unit attached to it as needed.

For 1950 the range continued with one more single in the form of the racing Grey Flash. This was a Comet built on the lines of the Lightning, with tuned engine, no road equipment and the racing fitments. The Series B was dropped during 1950, so only the Series C continued for 1951, as the three V-twins, the Comet and the Grey Flash. The last was dropped for 1952, when the Lightning was built to special order only, but the two road twins and single continued to offer the same high-sped touring as always, that year and the next.

During 1953 the firm tried a totally different line with a clip-on engine unit which had been developed by the Miller company, who supplied Vincent with electrical parts. The 48cc two-stroke engine was designed to fit under a cycle's bottom bracket, to keep the weight low and to drive the rear tyre with its friction-roller. Thus, like the German Lohmann, it had to be made as narrow as possible. Otherwise it was conventional except for a gear drive to a countershaft which carried the friction roller and was called the Firefly. To the deep chagrin of members of the Vincent Owners' Club, the Firefly unit was listed alongside the three twins and the Comet for 1954. There were a number of minor changes to the motorcycles, which otherwise ran on as before.

To augment their range, Vincent did a deal with the German NSU company, and for a year imported the Quickly moped, which pointed the way to the future and killed off the clip-on engines. In addition to the moped, there was a range of small motorcycles listed as NSU-Vincent. These had German engine units, frames and forks, but British wheels, tyres, tank, carburettor and other equipment. This arrangement sidestepped the tariff rules applicable at the time.

Four models were to be available. All had unit construction of the engine and four-speed gearbox, a spine frame, leading-link front forks and pivoted rear fork. Smallest was the 98cc ohv Fox and next the 123cc two-stroke Fox but neither of these were made in any numbers to speak of. The larger models were the 199cc Lux two-stroke and 247cc Max, with overhead camshaft driven by eccentrics and connecting blades. This system worked well, and the German Max had a fine reputation, enhanced by the racing successes of the Rennmax model. For the venture with Vincent, both machines proved too expensive for the market, and neither went into production.

Vincent moved the Grand Touring machine on in 1955 when he launched the exciting, fully enclosed D-series models, a remarkable development for the time and to lead the firm into grave problems. However, the object, as always, was to provide the discerning rider with a high-speed tourer: a two-wheeled Bentley, as Phil Vincent put it. The enclosure was comprehensive with a deeply valanced front mudguard, a cowl to carry the headlamp and extended outwards to protect the

hands, a fascia for the instruments, and a windscreen to keep rain off the rider. The rear of the machine was enclosed by a single moulding mounted on a subframe and carrying the seat. It enclosed the rear wheel to below the spindle and was hinged to give access to the rear end. A normal petrol tank was used, but below it was a panel on each side. These ran forward to form legshields, each topped by a forward-facing beak.

Under the mouldings went the familiar engine, frame and forks, but with a number of alterations to suit the new layout and enclosure. Thus, there were Monobloc carburettors, coil ignition, a new home for the oil tank and a single unit to control the rear suspension. With their new clothes, the models were given new names; the Rapide became the Black Knight, the Shadow the Black Prince, and the Comet the Victor, but only one of these was built. The models created a sensation at the show that year, but production problems arose with the mouldings, which Phil Vincent insisted should be to his usual high standards.

As a stop-gap, he decided to build Series D models without enclosure to Rapide and Black Shadow specifications. The open Series D V-twins had a tubular subframe to support the dualseat, but retained all the other new features. The mudguards reverted to the usual Series C type, and a toolbox appeared on the left of the subframe. The machines kept the factory going, but the new seat and subframe lacked the lithe lines of the earlier models, and the company was, by now, once more in financial trouble. At the bottom end of the scale, the Firefly was offered as a complete machine, but in September 1955, at an Owners Club dinner in Cambridge, Phil Vincent announced that the motorcycles would no longer be produced. They had to build another hundred or so machines to fulfil outstanding orders, but in December the last official machine, a Black Prince, was completed. The Firefly continued for 1956 as a machine, and for two more years as a clip-on attachment, while the firm moved to other industrial uses for its engines.

Left
The NSU-Vincent Max with 247cc ohc engine seen at Earls Court, but never put into production

WABO

This was a Dutch make of scooter, but one which used Villiers power for the models imported into Britain. These were two in number and, except for the engine units and forks, they were identical. Engines were the 99cc 4F or the 147cc 30C and both went into a rigid frame with telescopic front forks. The wheels had 16in. rims, so were larger than usual, and the bodywork was on normal scooter lines. In continental style, it carried a saddle each for both rider and passenger. The models were fully equipped and had a certain style, but the enterprise was short-lived, for the make both came and went in 1957.

WATSONIAN

This sidecar firm built a prototype machine in 1950 to haul its products and, for a first attempt, it turned out rather well. For power. they chose a 996cc side-valve, V-twin, all-alloy JAP engine and coupled it to a four-speed Burman gearbox Both went into a duplex loop frame with plunger rear suspension and Dunlop telescopic forks while massive alloy hubs with 9in. brakes were used front and rear.

The engine had coil ignition and an alternator, the large battery fitted behind the rear cylinder and beneath the dualseat, and the oil tank went between the right-hand chainstays. A large petrol tank of over five gallons capacity was fitted, and the whole machine was finished in pale green.

It made an excellent sidecar machine, but by 1950 the market for a rather thirsty V-twin of modest performance was vanishing. To settle the matter, JAP proved less than interested in supplying engines for a project with limited appeal, so the idea came to a halt.

WHITWOOD

This was a machine built by the OEC concern but listed separately once it was past the prototype stage. It represented another attempt to produce a car on two wheels and like the rest sold to a very limited market.

The model was announced in July 1934 and from the side did resemble a small saloon car with a short bonnet. However, it was a true body on two wheels with two doors, two seats in tandem form, a windscreen, side screens and a folding hood.

The mechanics were fully enclosed and there was a stabilising wheel on each side to hold the machine up when at a standstill. Steering was by a wheel which was geared to the OEC duplex steering system used. A range of engines was to be offered and the equipment included twin headlamps. The engines went under the front seat and the gearbox under seat two. A long hand lever enabled the engine to be started without the rider leaving his seat.

Four models were listed as the 150cc Dart and 250cc Sterling with two-stroke Villiers engines and the 500cc Century and 1000cc Regent, both with side valve JAP engines, the latter a V-twin. If nothing else it was an enterprising design.

For 1936 the most significant change was to move the engine to a position to the left of the rear wheel from where it drove forward to a cross-shaft which connected to the gearbox. A self-starter was listed as an extra and in this case a dynamotor was fitted.

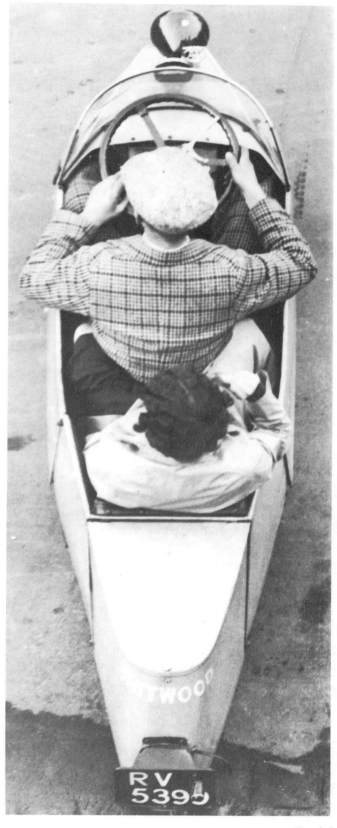

Top, left
The Dutch Wabo scooter with Villiers engine under the extensive bodywork, which came and went in 1957
Bottom, left
Watsonian prototype, as built in 1950 and seen here some 35 years later, with its distinctive engine, oil tank and forks
Above
Bird's eye view of the Whitwood showing its tandem seating, steering wheel and car type body

There were also body and chassis improvements so the revised machine was lower than before with cleaner body lines and once again twin headlamps were fitted. Only JAP engines were offered and the models were the 250cc ohv Devon, 500cc sv York and 750cc sv V-twin Rutland.

Early in 1936 the firm established with the Ministry of Transport that it was classed as a motorcycle despite its total of four wheels. As the outrigger ones did not normally revolve they did not count, so there was no question of car taxation applying. Not that this made much difference, for the make was no longer listed at the end of the year and sales were minuscule while it was available.

WOLF

This company really was on the fringe of the industry but managed to stay there for a long time. It always used proprietary parts and had fluctuating fortunes, being made by Wearwell Cycles in Wolverhampton. The machines were first built in 1901, but there was an occasional lapse and the marque was not listed for 1930.

Top
The Whitwood as seen from the side with its roof in place. The stabilising wheel can be seen under the body on the left

Far right, top
Wolf 122cc WA10 of 1937 with twin exhausts

Far right, bottom
Much earlier 1931 Wolf with 147cc Villers engine and listed as the minor

It returned in 1931 with two models using Villiers engines in a simple loop frame, the 147cc Minor and the 196cc Utility, these being joined in May by the 98cc Cub model. The 1932 range was extended by variations of these three plus a 148cc Vixen and 196cc Silver Wolf and little changed for 1933.

It was back down to three models for 1934, the 98cc Cub and two 148cc Vixens, and these carried on for 1935 and 1936 when they were joined by the returning 147cc Minor and two new models. One was the Super-Sports with a 249cc engine and the other had the new 122cc unit with twin exhausts feeding into an expansion box in front of the crankcase.

For 1937 this model, given the name Unit, was smartened up, the Cub was no longer listed and the others ran on. It was up to six models for 1938 thanks to variations and these continued on for 1939, but then reduced for 1940 to the 122cc machine and the two versions of the 148cc before production came to a halt.

WOOLER

The Wooler was one of the strange machines that make motorcycles so interesting. The industry is peppered with individuals who saw their way as being correct and often refused to deviate a fraction from their chosen path. They seldom built many machines, and those they did produce were frequently troublesome, but we all gained by the excitement they generated.

The Wooler was one such, and the first 1911 model had a horizontal two-stroke engine with double-ended piston to avoid the need for crankcase compression. It also had plunger front and rear suspension, while the fuel tank was extended round and in front of

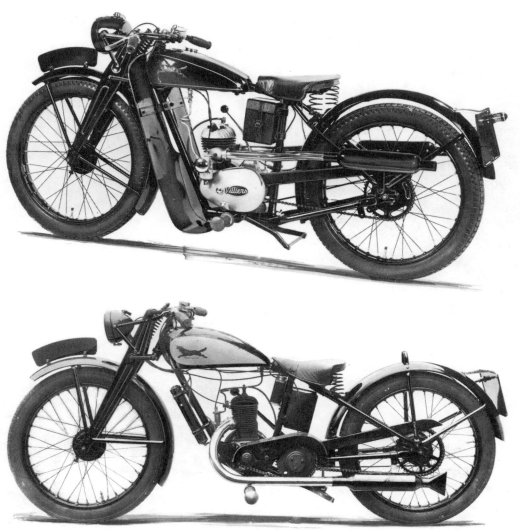

the headstock. In the 1920s came machines with flat-twin, four-stroke engines of rather more conventional form which were entered for a couple of TT races, for which they retained the tank form, but were painted in a bright yellow, so were quickly named 'flying bananas'. In 1926 there was a 500cc ohc engine but it was back to the flat-twin the next year after which all was quiet until 1945.

The postwar Wooler was announced in May that year and caused a sensation, being unique in engine, frame, suspension and details. The 500cc ohv engine created the most interest for it was a transverse four which had the cylinders placed one above the other on each side and connected to the crankshaft beneath them by a beam and master connecting rod. Thus, the block sat well above the crankcase while the camshaft was vertical and driven by bevel gears. There was a suggestion of a supercharger to replace the dynamo but normally there were twin carburettors. The exhaust pipes from each side swept down to join and then connect to the frame, which acted as the silencing system.

This unusual engine was then to drive either a four-speed gearbox or an infinitely-variable gear of mechanical operation with twistgrip operation. From

either a shaft drove the rear wheel. The frame was tubular and had twin plungers front and rear on both sides to provide the suspension which gave them an odd appearance. The petrol tank followed the style of the past, stretching out ahead of the forks and bars, with the headlamp set in its nose which certainly gave the machine an unusual line.

The Wooler created great interest and gained much publicity but it was some time before the prototype was complete and 1947 when it was shown to the trade. It was late in 1952 before there was further Wooler news which was that the engine had changed to a conventional 499cc ohv flat-four with alloy cylinders and heads. The four-speed gearbox and shaft drive were as before but there were only single plungers at the rear and the front ones looked more like telescopics.

All then went quiet for a while with some reports of being close to production but in 1956 the machine appeared with a revised frame having pivoted-fork rear suspension and a dualseat. However, this was the end of the line for the Wooler which never did make it into production, despite a decade of development.

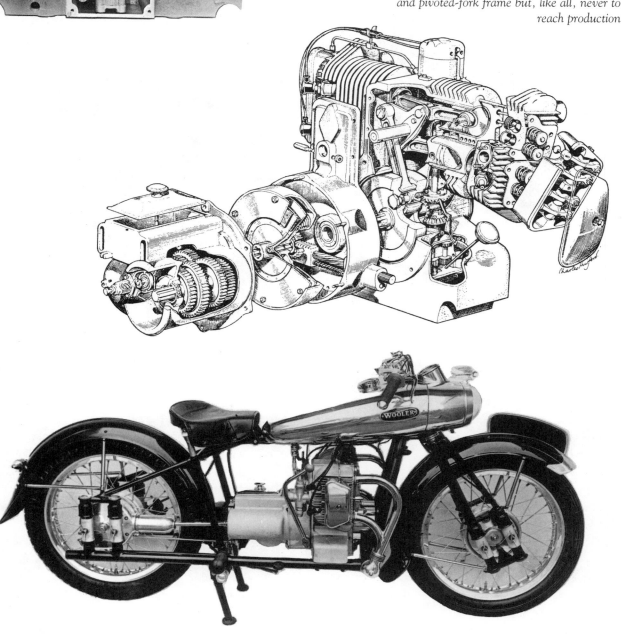

Left
Front aspect of Wooler beam engine, showing camshaft and drive down to oil pump in front of main crankcase and sump

Centre
The Wooler beam engine, plus clutch and gearbox, with primary kickstart via an optimistic quick-thread device

Bottom
The first of the post-war Wooler models with beam engine and curious duplex suspension units

Right, top
Final 1956 Wooler model with flat-four engine and pivoted-fork frame but, like all, never to reach production

ZENITH

This firm's best days were prior to World War 1 and in the twenties. In the first period they became very successful in the competitions of the day, which were mainly hill climbs and sprints, thanks to their variable-ratio belt drive known as the Gradua; so successful, in fact, that they were barred from some classes in 1911 and adopted a trademark which reflected this by showing their machine behind bars and the legend 'barred'. In the 1920s they had many successes at Brooklands, including the first 100mph lap, by Bert Le Vack in 1922, and they also built record breakers. With these they raised the absolute world record to over 124mph in 1928 and to over 150mph in 1930. The latter achievement was clouded by the OEC scandal, when the wrong machine was shown at Olympia, thus losing Zenith valuable publicity.

All this activity and success was heady stuff, but did not sell too many machines. For 1930 the range offered was all powered by JAP engines and comprised singles and twins. On offer were 300 and 490cc sv plus 346 and 490cc ohv singles and sv twins of 677, 747 and 980cc. Also available to special order were racing models of 350, 500 and 1000cc, all with ohv.

Not enough machines were sold in 1930 and production ceased, but in 1931 the firm of Writer's, a large dealer in South London, took them over and in July announced a smaller range, much as before but less of it. In essence this comprised the 346 and 490cc ohv singles, the 490cc sv and the 677 and 747cc sv twins which continued on for 1932 with new frames and listed in standard or de luxe forms. In May 1932 the range was expanded by adding models with 350, 500 and 600cc twin-port, ohv Blackburne engines, one in competition form with raised pipes, special tyres and other suitable fittings.

Below
1936 Zenith CP with 1100cc side-valve V-twin JAP engine

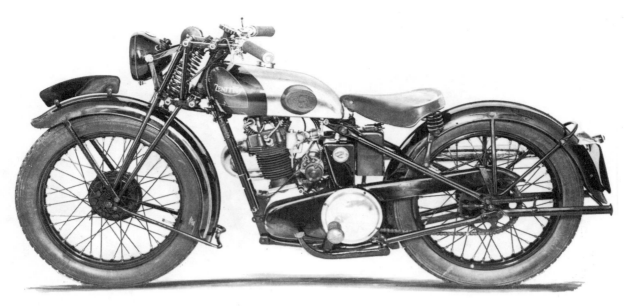

For 1933 Zenith listed no less than 20 models from a combination of JAP or Blackburne engines and standard or de luxe specifications. All had interconnected brakes and the model list was really as before. It shrunk to 14 models for 1934 but with two newcomers using 245 and 346cc ohv JAP engines inclined in a duplex cradle frame that was of bolted construction. Ignition was by coil with a dynamo mounted behind the cylinder and an upswept exhaust was fitted. The gearbox was a four-speed Burman with footchange and the petrol tank chrome-plated with the nose in black and purple.

There were no Blackburne engines listed for 1935, but otherwise the range was the same. There were 11 machines for 1936 and among them was the new Super with a 498cc TT Replica JAP engine with dry sump lubrication and Miller Dyno-mag. This sat upright in a duplex cradle frame with Druid tubular girder forks. The rest ran on with some alterations, and

for 1937 the same applied plus one new machine with a 500cc high-camshaft JAP engine. Two more similar engines in 250 and 350cc sizes were added for 1938 but were not listed for the next year.

The range was down to six for 1939, all using JAP engines and the smallest two with the 245cc ohv one. Others were the 490cc ohv, 600 sv and two side-valve V-twins of 747 and 1100cc. They were all listed for 1940, but with the war, production ceased at the Hampton Court works.

Postwar, a single model powered by a 747cc, side-valve JAP engine mounted in a rigid frame was listed from 1947 to 1950. Some 250 were said to have been built, but few were ever seen.

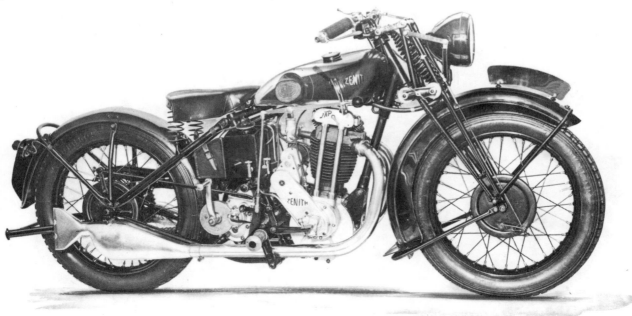

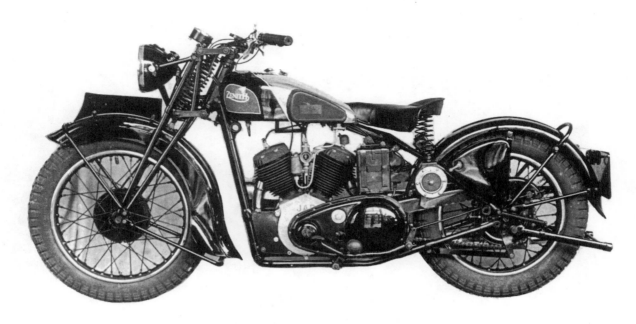

Far left, top
Single cylinder Zenith model LC1 with 245cc JAP power in 1934 and typical of the many machines in the range

Far left, bottom
Zenith B5 in 1932 with 490cc JAP engine and chrome-plated tank

Above
The 1947 Zenith 750 with JAP side-valve engine in pre-war-style cycle parts and mainly for export

Far left
*Typical lightweight used in town during the 1930s when you
just jumped on to the machine and rode to your meeting.
Machine is a Montgomery Terrier with 122cc Villiers engine*

Above
*1940 picture taken at a small show to promote the use of the
autocycle for basic transport in wartime*

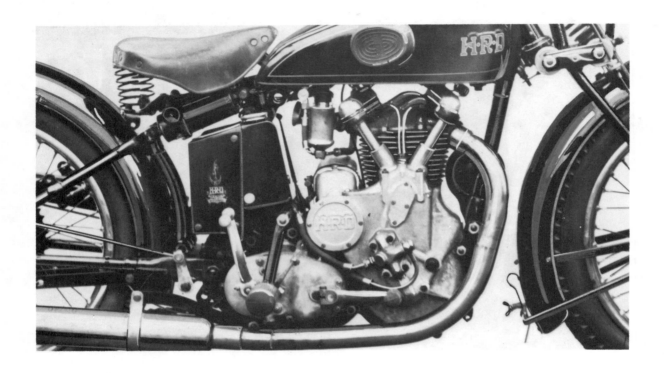

Above
The shape of things to come. The first of Phil Vincent's own engines appeared for the 1935 season. This is the 499cc Meteor

Above
*Another route was the scooterette, but the
BSA Dandy was not to be the best exam-
ple*

Above
*Typical mount for the enthusiast of the
1950s was this 1956 Triumph Tiger 110,
then one of the fastest available*

Above
The Cairn was built in 1950 by Mr Farrow of Reading in the Corgi mould but with full enclosure. It was based around a 99cc Villiers 2F engine, hung from a brazed, steel-tube frame

Above
The RCA was an engine rather than a machine and first appeared in 1957. Its name came from R. Christoforides and Associates, but the design was that of Peter Hogan. Here a Greeves with 349cc RCA twin engine on test in 1958

Above
Vic Willoughby tanking up a 1960 Norton
Dominator 99 de luxe during a road test

Above
The machine that changed the
motorcycle world and became the
two-wheeled Model T or VW
Beetle – the Honda 50, of which
many millions were sold worldwide.
This is a 1959 Super Cub

Above
*Scooters were an important part of the
scene in the late 1950s and 1960s, and
had a strong social aspect. This is the Isle
of Man rally, the competitors turning up
Summer Hill with Douglas seafront and
horse tram behind them*

Above
Trio of Matchless G50 road racers
lined up in 1959 for dispatch, and
typical of the type that was to revive
classic racing two decades later

Above
*Line of models outside Comerfords' show-
rooms at Thames Ditton late in 1959,
with a Super S Ambassador to the fore*

Above
Dayton Albatross in its original 1956
form with a 225cc engine

Above
Radco was a producer of motorcycles
until 1933 when it turned to component manufacture. During the 1950s a
machine was announced but it did not
reach production and it was not until
1966 that the Radcomuter was displayed at the Earls Court Show. It did
not enter production

Above
Sunwasp scooter on test late in 1959,
with Bob Currie doing the riding of this
174cc electric-start model

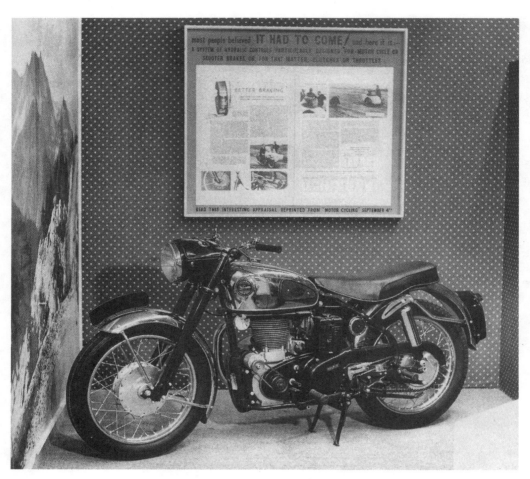

Above
Velocette single, on show in 1959,
minus its dynamo belt cover and left
side cowling